GUIDE IN JEANS
USA

D1104897

This edition first published 1980 by
Octopus Books Ltd,
59 Grosvenor Street, London W.1.

© 1980 Octopus Books Ltd
for the English translation
© 1977 Hachette et Editions de Cléry

Originally published by Hachette and Editions de Cléry
as *Guide des U.S.A. en jeans*,
compiled by Christian Girard.

ISBN 0 7064 1465 9

Set, printed and bound in Great Britain
by Cox & Wyman Ltd, Reading

Contents

Part I   An Introductory A – Z   5

Part II   Sixteen Towns   29

Atlanta   31
Boston   39
Chicago   59
Denver   75
Houston   83
Las Vegas   91
Los Angeles   95
Miami   111
New Orleans   117
New York   129
Philadelphia   153
Phoenix   161
San Francisco   167
Berkeley   187
Seattle   193
Washington   201

Part III The National Parks   215

Great Smoky Mountains National Park   216
Everglade National Park   216
Grand Canyon National Park   216
Monument Valley National Park   218
Mesa Verde National Park   218
Mount Rainier National Park   219
Olympic National Park   219
Shenandoah National Park   219
Yosemite National Park   220
Yellowstone National Park   220

Part I
An Introductory A to Z

Abbreviations

'AAA': American Automobile Association; 'COD': Cash on Delivery; 'CST': Central Standard Time; 'DC': District of Columbia (Washington DC); 'DST': Daylight Saving Time; 'EST': Eastern Standard Time; 'Fwy': Freeway; 'GPO': General Post Office; 'Hwy': Highway: 'L.A.': Los Angeles; 'PST': Pacific Standard Time; Y.M.C.A.: Young Men's Christian Association; Y.W.C.A. Young Women's Christian Association.

Activities

For each city, we list places and events of note, but if you plan to spend more than a week in a city, find out what's going on fast because you often have to book in advance to see plays or attend concerts. Tickets are sold in some record shops, but you can always try your luck at the door, where black-market tickets are usually on sale (but at a premium of course).

Alcohol

You can get anything and everything in the States; from a straight beer to the most elaborate of concoctions, there's something to suit every taste. There are the famous cocktails, unbelievable mixtures with exotic names and exotically delicious effects. The range of beers will satisfy the wildest of thirsts: from straight beers, like Budweiser (known as 'Bud') or Miller or Schlitz, to Mexican beers, it's all there! Watch out for 'Root-Beer' and don't be fooled by the name, there's not a drop of the stuff in it. It's a mixture of cola and aromatic roots, with a kind of caramel taste.

Watch out too for the very strict laws applied to the sale of alcohol in the States. Don't be surprised, for instance, if you are asked to show your passport or identity to prove your age when you order an alcoholic drink

As a rule, you have to be over 18 to buy alcohol, but the law varies from State to State and it's best to be clear about the law of the particular State you're in to avoid unpleasant hassles. So be warned, they take it really seriously over there.

Beer comes under the heading of alcohol and in the States it's illegal to walk down the street with a bottle or a can in your hand. Which explains the number of people who walk around with a paper bag from which they take the occasional swig. It's not strictly legal, but it's, shall we say, tolerated! No open bottles in cars either, you can only carry booze in the boot/trunk and unopened at that. The laws may seem outdated, but don't sneer at them for all that: it's best to stay on the safe side.

Architecture and urbanism

As far as architecture in the States is concerned, summaries and generalizations are impossible. What you find there is an open door to a fantasy world.

There is no predominant movement at the moment. The current trend focuses rather on the transformation and adaptation of existing methods to contemporary needs. American architects are too busy undertaking ever more remarkable technical feats to find a true architectural direction to their work.

Over the last 20 years, one of the strongest influences on architecture has been the work of Louis Kahn. You will find his creative 'mark' all over the States: in New Haven, with the Yale University Art Gallery and the magnificent Yale Center; in Fort Wayne with the Art School and the theatre; in St Louis with the Jefferson National Memorial; and in Philadelphia with the psychiatric hospital and the Samuel Roadbill Building.

When you arrive at Kennedy Airport in New York, have a look at its architecture. You may well feel that the very structure of the airport represents an invitation to travel. Its architect, Eero Saarineen, has made quite a name for himself. He is the creator of the famous Gateway Arch in St. Louis, famous as much for its elegance as for the technical prowess it embodies. American architecture is particularly remarkable for its diversity and its richness. New movements, linked to the rhythm of everyday life, are springing up. The 'bio' movement for instance: generally residential buildings of pure, unsophisticated line, using natural materials like earth, wood, ceramic and sometimes even canvas. Solar houses are also part of this movement, examples of which can be seen mainly in California and Florida.

Since there is no legislation governing the form or concept of a structure, anyone can, with a little imagination, create the home of his dreams. This has given rise to a movement known as 'architecture without architects': there are 'mole' houses, a network of underground passages and galleries; 'Tarzan' houses, elaborate cabins built in trees; even houses built out of junk-yard materials like scrap-iron and beer cans!

Another movement is called 'dead line' which is a collective re-evaluation of the architect's role. The architect acts only as advisor on projects and leaves the realization of building plans to those who will ultimately live in or use the buildings. By this means, architects become involved in collective projects, like the one in Paterson, to the South of New York, where a whole industrial town has been transformed into a residential city. There is also a touch of nostalgia in some American architects whose work is devoted to the restoration of old buildings or the application of traditional architectural principles to modern structures. For instance, it is interesting to note the evolution of European architecture transposed at the turn of the century to some of the first business and administrative buildings, like those built by Richardson and Sullivan in Chicago.

Some architects still turn to the layout and structure of the Plains Indian encampments, Cheyenne and Sioux, in their building. You can see the sources of their information in museums and Indian foundations, which are always fascinating to visit.

It's worth knowing, finally, that in the States, architects' offices and schools of Architecture are, so to speak, open to the public. If you are an architecture student or merely interested, don't hesitate to open the door and go in, you will usually get a friendly and helpful reception.

Bargaining

The idea of bargaining over prices in the States may seem surprising, but bargaining exists and what's more it often works! You can of course haggle over prices at the flea markets, but also in some little second-hand shops, where you can pick up any number of bargains, including electrical equipment and cameras, often in excellent condition and at very reasonable prices.

Bicycle

Cycling is still very popular in the States, even with the recent re-birth of the roller skate. You can hire bicycles by the day or by the week almost anywhere. For certain cities, you'll find the addresses of reasonably-priced hire firms in the second part of the book.

Budget

There are no prices quoted in this book, for two reasons. The first is that, as we are all only too well aware, costs for almost everything change so fast that indications of price, though correct at the time of writing, are almost invariably misleading by the time of reading. The second is that the hotels, restaurants etc. listed in the book are all of the most reasonable and will remain comparatively the best value for money, no matter what. So how does one work out a budget for a trip to the States?

Setting aside the cost of the return flight and transportation within the States (bus, car, plane), day-to-day expenses for sleeping, eating and entertainment are up to you, and quite impossible to generalize on. It's not a bad idea, at the outset, to set yourself a daily allowance and keep a note of everything you spend each day. If you are a few dollars over the top one day, spend a bit less the next by having a coke or a hamburger less, and vice-versa. This may seem an overly fastidious and rather simplistic system, but it's an easy way to keep a check on spending.

Of course, what a holiday in the States, or anywhere for that matter, actually costs once you're there, varies enormously with the individual. If you hitch from campus to campus and are prepared to 'rough it' a bit, your expenses will be less than half those of the guy who goes from Y.M.C.A. to Y.M.C.A., and a fraction of the cost of staying in even medium-priced hotels. It all depends on you and the kind of holiday you want.

One way to avoid 'eating up' too much money is to have breakfast! Breakfasts in the States are enormous, served until 11, sometimes even till midday, and are always terrific value. A late breakfast can double as lunch and see you through until the evening. It's a great means of not spending too much on food without suffering hunger pains!

Camping

For a camping holiday in the States, you must have a car. If you are mobile, camping sites are often very inexpensive, sometimes even free. As with everything in the States, hygienic conditions are rigorously observed. Sites are obviously a long way from the cities, often in or near a National Park. The

Visitor's Bureau of the nearest town will direct you to the closest site, or you can get a list of camping sites from Rand McNally map stores in the U.S.A.

Car

By far the best way of seeing the States, where everything is planned for the convenience of the motorist. A car also makes a camping holiday possible. But it's not cheap and petrol is an ever-more costly commodity.

You are strongly advised to respect the speed limits shown (55 to 70 miles per hour on highways depending on the State). Be particularly careful in California. Fines are on the American scale ... In towns, keep well away from 'Tow-away zones': your car will be towed away and impounded if you park in them. They are particularly strict in New York. Be careful also not to park in front of the numerous fire hydrants. If you are crossing the desert by motorway be sure to take plenty of water and petrol (petrol-stations are much rarer). Never have an opened bottle of alcoholic drink in the car: the law is the law. Petrol is still comparatively cheap. Most hire cars use unleaded petrol (Unleaded gas or No Lead) which is slightly more expensive. An average sized car does about 18 miles to the U.S. gallon. You can save petrol by not using the air-conditioning. The air-conditioning often has an 'Economy' position that can be turned to in order to reduce consumption. Turning to 'Vent' switches on the ventilator which is often enough on its own to keep you cool.

There are three ways of travelling by car: buying it, hiring it and 'drive-away' delivery. Find out before you leave home whether your driving licence is valid in the States. In any case, if you plan to hire a car or to do a lot of driving, get yourself an International Driving Licence.

Buying:

You buy a car on the East coast and sell it again on the West coast or vice versa. It's well worth it, especially if there are three or four of you. When you're buying and when you're selling, it's best to do so privately. Read the small-ads in the local paper, watch the notice board on the campus. Always ask for a receipt and for the relevant documents to prove that you are the legal owner of the car; the police may ask you to produce these. The car must be registered in the State in which you buy it. It's also worth getting it checked out at a garage. The really paranoid can find out if the car in question is being sold because of a manufacturing fault by phoning (202) 426.06.70 or 426.06.71, the Office of Consumer Services of the National Highway Traffic Safety Administration. Give them the make, model and year together with the Vehicle Identification

Number (V.I.N.: not the same as the number plate) and they will give you all the details on that particular car.

Without going to such extremes, here are a few basic tips: examine the underside of the car, press on the four corners by sitting on them to test the shock-absorbers. The car shouldn't be too springy. Examine the tyres, inner tubes as well. Try the air-conditioning if the car has it: it's one of the most delicate parts of the engine and you don't want to find out that it doesn't work when it's 104° in the shade in the middle of the Arizona desert!

When you come to re-sell the car, always allow a few days at the end of the trip! It's worth knowing that prices drop in September when the new models come on to the market. As for insurance (obligatory in the States of Massachusetts, New York and North Carolina), it'll be quite expensive if you're under 25. In any case, even if you avoid the three states mentioned, it's always important to have adequate insurance cover.

Hiring:

Can be economically viable if there are 4 or 5 of you travelling together. One of you must be at least 25 (or 21 depending on the company). The big companies, Avis, Budget, Hertz, National, have special 'Visit U.S.A.' rates. The smaller companies, Airways, Alexander's, Kinney etc., are often more competitive, and you'll find many more in the Yellow Pages. Make sure that you are quite clear on all the conditions of hire: daily rate, insurance, rate per mile etc.

If you are hiring the car for any length of time or to tour around, the 'Unlimited/Free mileage' system is often the best value. Otherwise the deposit paid on signature of contract is calculated on the average mileage for the number of days you have the car, and you pay the extra or get a refund when you return the car. Many companies also offer reductions for weekend hire. But don't forget that you take the car out with a full tank of petrol and that you must top up the tank again before returning it. There are several categories of car for hire from the two-door 'sub-compact' to the station-wagon. Avoid the Ford Pinto like the plague, the steering is hard, visibility mediocre and comfort pretty non-existent. On the other hand, in the same category, the Chevette is much better and very economical on fuel. A VW is often the ideal car for driving around a city, and one of the cheapest to run.

If you are going through one of the big international companies, it's worth getting in touch with your local branch before you leave home. You may be eligible for a visitor's reduction, especially for longer-term hiring. N.B. In the States, the major companies have a 'free' telephone number: you can ring up for information without paying for the call by dialling 800 before the number.

Budget Rent-a-Car: ☎ (800) 228.96.950

Dollar-a-Day: ☎ (800) 421.68.68

Econo-Car: ☎ (800) 874.50.50

National Rent-a-Car: ☎ (800) 328.45.67

For the third alternative, the 'Drive-Away' system, see later.

Charters

This is an area where it's really worth shopping around. The number of flights, fares and 'deals' available can be staggering!

Do remember first of all to check on the fares available on scheduled airlines. They have reacted to the inroads made into the market by the charter companies by offering a wide range of reductions and special fares. Compare these fares with those offered by the charter companies, which may appear cheaper but often carry hidden extras, such as cancellation insurance, overnight hotel charges en route etc. Read the small print!

Having said that, charter flights do offer good value, but, again, shop around for the best deal and do check the credentials of the company you are dealing with if you are coming to it cold. Make sure that they carry insurance from the appropriate bodies, that the dates and times of travel, particularly for the return journey, are clearly marked on your ticket and that you are issued with a receipt. Without wishing to sound alarmist, a little time and thought at the outset can save a lot of costly disappointment later on.

It's well worth getting hold of one of two cards when you are planning your trip. If you are a student, the **International Student Identity Card** (I.S.I.C.) is recognized almost everywhere and entitles you to reductions on transport, in museums, hotels, restaurants etc. If you are not a student, but under 26 years old, the **Federation of International Youth Travel Organisation** (F.I.Y.T.O.) card has the same advantages.

Last but not least, here's an address to remember in New York: **C.I.E.E. (Council of International Education Exchange)**, William Sloane House, 9th Ave/West 34th St in Manhattan. If you arrive in New York at night, jump into a taxi and go straight there, at least for the first night. You're sure not only to find a room (there are 1490 of them!) at a very reasonable rate (a rare thing in New York), but also a mine of information and advice for your holiday in the States.

Cinema

From the abundant commercial 'Movie Theaters' to the University film clubs, cinema buffs are well catered for. You can see the brand-new releases, some of which are not screened outside the States for almost a year. Or classics of the American cinema and foreign films at specialist cinemas or film clubs. Be warned though that screenings at university film-clubs are rarely free and often even quite expensive.

As the cities are often divided into different districts (Chinatown, Mexican district etc) you can often find local 'ethnic' films in Spanish, Chinese, Hungarian ... almost any language you can think of. They are usually sub-titled in English and can be interesting. In New York especially, with its myriad cultures, the variety of films covers an amazingly wide spectrum.

Coach

If you can't afford to hire or buy a car and you don't want to hitch, seeing America by coach is the next best thing.

Greyhound and Continental Trailways offer unlimited mileage travel within the States with the **Ameripass**, valid of 7, 15 or 30 days, and consisting of 15 coupons (extra coupons can be purchased in the States if need be). There are also special vouchers for travel between two predetermined points: You have fifteen days to reach your destination, but alas! you have to go in a straight line. Although the passes are available in the States, you would be well advised to buy them before you leave to avoid paying the American Sales Tax, which is applicable in situ. Passes can be obtained from American Express Travel or any major travel agent. The validity of the pass is calculated from the first day of use in the States, and the pass issued by one company is valid on coaches of the other company, if one serves a destination that the other one doesn't. Coupons can also be used in Canada.

The great advantage of this system is its complete flexibility: you get on a coach where you want, travel to where you want, when you want. You can stop for as long as you like in a town or city. The coaches cover a vast network and they certainly shift! They are air-conditioned and have toilets at the rear, and their only real fault is in their rather unsatisfactory suspension. Also worthy of note is the fact that the windows are tinted glass, so America will take on a sort of greenish tinge! In theory you can sleep in the reclining seats and so save booking into a hotel. It's always best to keep your luggage with you in the coach if you can, rather than have it put in the baggage compartment. It's also worth using the left-luggage facilities at the bus station when you arrive in a town, especially if you are only staying a few hours. If there are more than 45 people queuing up for a Greyhound, it's worth letting the first one go without you and waiting for the second coach which is bound to be put on the same run and will be much less crowded. Timetables are available in any bus station in the States or from the travel agent who supplies your Pass. Do take note, though, of the difference between 'local' bus services and 'rapid transit' express services.

Crash-pads

A crash-pad is floorspace in someone's apartment where you can spread your sleeping-bag for the night, a roof over your head if you are completely skint. You'll find crash-pads in most big towns, where you can spend the night for free or for a few cents, and especially in university towns, there are lots of them. To find them, buy the local underground paper. Or get hold of a copy of the Travellers' Directory, which lists crash-pads all over the world. The publication is only sent to people who agree to offer the same hospitality to others and to have their address listed as a crash-pad too. For more information, write to: Travellers' Directory, 5102 39th Ave, Woodside, NYC, NY 11377.

Customs and immigration

On arrival at Kennedy Airport, New York, you will probably be asked how long you intend to stay in the States, how much money you have with you and if you know anyone who is a U.S. resident. You should have enough money to live on during your stay.
At Canadian customs, you will also be asked how much money you have and permission to stay in the country depends on your being able to support yourself during your visit.

Drive-away

This is a particularly good way of travelling by car without paying hire fees. What happens is that you undertake to deliver a car to a given destination within an agreed number of days. You can cross the country this way from coast to coast and your only outlay will be on petrol and tolls.
You have to go through one of the Auto-Driveaway companies and they will give you a set route. You must be over 21 and pay a deposit (which will be returned to you in full when you deliver the car, undamaged, to its destination). The most important thing is to make a good impression and gain the confidence of the company that hires you. Look in the Yellow Pages of almost any big American city under 'Automobile and Truck Transporting' or 'Driveaway Companies'. Here are a few addresses:

In New York for example there are:

AAACON Auto Transport Inc: 230 West 41st St (between 7th and 8th Ave). ☎ 354.77.77.

American International Driveaway: 1133 Broadway. ☎ 255.30.70. See Quick Service Drivers, room 518.

Dependable Car Travel Service: 130 West 42nd St. ☎ 947.52.30.

Drivers Exchange Inc: 450 7th Ave. ☎ 868.99.25.

In Detroit:
Insured Driveaway Inc: 9970 Grand River Ave.

In Los Angeles:
Auto Driveaway Inc: 25 S. West Ave.
See later for each of the other cities.

Let's make it quite clear though, this is not a cheap way of touring the country. The time limit is short (5 or 6 days from coast to coast) and you are only entitled to an additional 10% of the mileage, by road, between the two points. If you exceed this additional 10%, your deposit may be forfeit when you arrive, so it is essential to check carefully your mileage allocation before you start. Your contract also forbids you to pick up passengers (hitch-hikers), but in fact, it's easy to stick an advertisement on a 'Ride Board' (see 'Hitch-Hiking') and take someone along to share fuel expenses without the company ever needing to know. It's common practice. Another tip is to pick up the car early afternoon when you plan to leave the next morning. That way you have the use of the car for an afternoon and an evening, very useful in Chicago, L.A. or any other big city where you still have things to see and do before you leave.

You don't always have to go through a specialised company. With a bit of luck, if you look through the small-ads for 'Help wanted' and 'travel' in the local newspaper, you might find someone who will use you to deliver his car somewhere.

Remember that the Driveaway system is much in demand by young people during the summer, and waiting lists can be long.

Drugs

As the laws on marijuana vary from State to State (lenient in California, very tough in Texas), it's best to ask around and find out just what risks you're taking if you buy. All the more so since young Americans, and not-so-young ones too, may offer you a smoke almost as soon as they say 'hi'. It's up to you then whether you accept or refuse, but on the whole attitudes towards the weed are far less emotive in North America than in a lot of other countries. Toxic products like amphetamines and hard drugs are quite a different matter and only a fool would play fast and loose with his health and the law where they are concerned. The specialist press, 'Heads' and 'High Time', will give you an idea of the extent of the drug scene in the States.

Eating

And it needn't cost a fortune! Needless to say, there are the ubiquitous hamburger joints, from the giants like McDonalds, Jack in the Box, Burger King to the little local burger bars: there's a hamburger on every street corner in America, from the West coast to the East, with, if anything, an even greater concentration on the West coast. Suffice it to say, that if one had to rate the various products available, first place would go to 'Jumbo Jack' from Jack in the Box, which seems to combine the best in mass catering with the best value for money.

Burger King's 'Whopper' would come second, with McDonald's 'Big Mac' trailing in third.

You don't have to eat hamburgers, of course. You can have a really good pizza at any one of the many pizzerias in every big town, you can go to a university cafeteria, you can tuck into an enormous breakfast at 11 in the morning in a luxury hotel (for the price of three Big Macs!) and for dinner try one of the many tasty and generous Mexican specialities.

Coffee houses:

If you think sandwiches are a bore, think again ... in the States they're something else! A Club-sandwich is a meal in itself and you should really try a 'submarine': known as 'subs', they owe their name to their elongated shape and they really fill you up too! In California and the student districts of big cities, coffee houses specialize in sandwiches and serve an amazing selection of weird and wonderful fillings on all kinds of bread, rye, wholewheat, buckwheat ... A glass of cider, a fruit juice or a coffee besides and you couldn't wish for anything more.

Steak houses:

As the name suggests, they serve ... you've got it! ... steaks. Prices are often very reasonable, as at 'Tad's Steak House' in San Francisco or New York.

Barbecue:

If you're travelling by car, it's fun to stop and cook yourself a barbecue. But don't take along your European camping stove, the gas cylinders sold in the States won't fit it.

Exotic food:

On the West coast, you'll find Mexican food everywhere. It's by far the cheapest way to eat, especially if you go to the little restaurants in the 'chicano' (American-Mexican) areas of San Francisco, Los

15

Angeles or San Diego. 'Tacos', 'Chilis' and other 'Encheladas' are not only tasty, but great value too. Chinese restaurants are usually quite expensive, except in New York or San Francisco.

American specialities:

There are a couple of things you really ought to try at least once during your stay. Ice cream comes in a mind-boggling range of flavours (peanut butter, bubble gum?), not to mention outrageously delicious concoctions like banana splits and giant sundaes. On a more serious level (for the wallet too), there are the sea-food specialities, 'rare-abalone' on the West coast for instance.

Drinks:

As a general rule, steer clear of canned beer. In the absence of anything else, stick to 'Black Label' rather than 'Budweiser' and to 'Bud' rather than 'Miller or 'Schlitz'. If you're not a beer-drinker, ice-tea is refreshing and good and so are all the Florida and California fruit juices. Contrary to popular belief, Californian wine can be excellent and not expensive either if you buy it on the West coast. But where the Americans really come into their own is with their cocktails! The list is endless, from 'Bloody Mary' (vodka and tomato), to 'Tequila Sunrise' to 'Whisky Sour' and many many more ingenious and delicious concoctions.

N.B.: If you're planning to spend more than a couple of weeks in one of the main cities of the States, it's well worth buying the book 'Underground Gourmet' for that particular city. This series of gastronomic guides lists the various restaurants in the city by price level.

Emergencies

Always keep a dime for the phone on you. If you are faced with any problem, large or small, that you really don't know how to cope with, dial 0 on any phone and the operator will put you in touch immediately with someone who can help you.

Entry requirements

You must have a valid passport and a valid tourist visa. To apply for a visa, contact your nearest American Embassy or Consulate, Visa Section. You will have to fill in a form, attach a photograph and send or take it with your passport and authorization from your parents if you are a minor, to the appropriate office. A tourist visa will then be stamped into your passport. Do remember though, especially if you don't live near enough to an Embassy or Consulate to go there in person, that the process can be a lengthy one, so make enquiries well in advance and allow plenty of time for the post as well. Insurance is optional but we strongly recommend that you take out adequate cover before you leave, as medical and hospital charges in the States are astronomically high. (see 'Health' below)

Health

If you are unlucky enough to get ill while in the States, it's worth knowing that some cities have 'Free Clinics', where advice and care is free. There are quite a few of these Free Clinics in L.A. and San Francisco and they are listed in the underground press. If there is no Free Clinic in the city or if you are more seriously ill, you should go to the nearest hospital (look in the phone book). Here again, we cannot emphasize how important it is to foresee the possibility, however unlikely it may seem, and to make sure that you are covered for medical expenses by the appropriate insurance policy. It is quite literally true that the most expensive thing you can do in the States is to get sick there. Your travel agent or charter company or the airline you are travelling with will recommend an insurance company or will issue you with their own insurance to cover the length of your stay.

Hitch-hiking

Hitching is still the best way of getting around, of meeting and getting to know different people and countries. In the States, as elsewhere, some people swear by it, others want it banned. So who do you listen to? We don't feel that we can plump for one side of the fence or the other, say you should or you shouldn't, because it's so much a question of individual outlook and character. Some kids will hitch the length and breadth of America without any problem at all, because they are optimistic and adaptable and only see the good side of everything. Whereas others, travelling only a few miles sometimes, will go from one jam to another if they don't know how to ward off the unwelcome attention of an over-sexed motorist. In the States you have to watch out for people who are only too eager to take advantage of your weakness and who pick up defenceless-looking kids (and not just physically defenceless either).

Although hitching is forbidden in quite a lot of States the laws and their enforcement vary so much that your best bet is to ask an American hitcher. Hitch-hiking is not allowed on the major motorways (Interstate Freeways). However, it is still one of the quickest ways of getting from coast to coast. In Texas hitchers are frowned upon. The only difference between the old-time cowboys and today's Texans is that you can't see the gun-belt, but the Colt is always there somewhere. In California, on the other

17

hand, hitching is common practice and not much of a problem. The advent of Gay Lib means that you will almost certainly meet people who will make all kinds of propositions. If this happens, just explain your position on the question clearly and you shouldn't have any hassles. Girls are (even in California) very strongly advised not to hitch-hike.

Always carry a minimum of cash dollars and your passport, as well as a very useful little sign giving your nationality.

A good way to find a lift is to read the notices on the university campuses. There is a special '**Ride Board**', a notice board with a map of the U.S. for appeals (ride wanted) and offers (riders wanted) for lifts. You'll find 'coast-to-coast' rides in the main East and West coast cities, usually with the passenger sharing the expenses. If you plan to put an announcement on a Ride-Board, we would advise girls not to mention their sex (so as not to attract freaks) and everyone to give their nationality.

There are also small organizations called '**Ride Lines**', which match up drivers and passengers by telephone. Most of them charge a few dollars for the service and you have to ring them several times a day to be sure of getting a ride.

Hotels and hostels

Hotels:

As a rule, hotels in the States are expensive, even when they give reductions for students (always show your student card and don't hesitate to ask for a reduction). In some towns (New Orleans, for instance) you can still find quite cheap little tourist hotels, but there are also some pretty awful dumps. As elsewhere, it will be cheaper if you can do without air-conditioning. If you don't mind being a little cramped, some hotels will let 4 people sleep in a room for two. It's worth a try anyhow! Always ask for a receipt when paying your hotel bill: if nothing else, it's irrefutable proof of your good faith.

Watch out for check-out times, usually 10 in the morning or midday. If you're not out of the room by then, you can be charged for an extra night.

The following abbreviations are worth knowing:

S.W.B. Single room with bath

T.W.B. Twin-bedded room with bath

A.P. American Plan = Full Board

C.P. Continental Plan = Bed and Breakfast

E.P. European Plan = Bed only

M.A.P. Modified American Plan = Half Board (breakfast and dinner)

Brunch: combination of breakfast and lunch (esp. Sunday)

The Hyatt Regency chain of hotels, and there's one in almost every large city in the States, are remarkable for their architecture. The same theme is followed throughout but each hotel is ingeniously adapted to reflect the character of the city around it. Going into one of these hotels for a drink is less expensive than you might think and the attractive and peaceful surroundings can make a welcome change, especially if you're travelling by Greyhound. You don't have to be an expert on architecture or interior design to enjoy it, but don't go in looking too scruffy.

Motels:

You can't drive very far along an American motorway without coming across a motel and they are certainly worth looking into if a few of you don't mind sharing a room. Steer clear of the big motel chains, Howard Johnsons, Holiday Inn, Ramada Inn etc., which are the most expensive. Some reasonably-priced motel chains are American Family Lodge, Days Inn, Econo Travel Motor Hotel, Motel 6. The small motels don't always display their prices, but it's worth stopping to go in and ask, even to bargain a bit, especially in the evening.

You can usually hire a camp-bed, or roller-bed, for a couple of dollars and by sharing rooms, make tremendous savings on hotel rates, while still enjoying all the conveniences and comforts of much higher-priced accommodation: bathroom, sometimes a kitchenette, colour TV, air-conditioning, swimming pool ...

Hostels:

American **Youth Hostels** are very cheap, but not easy to get to in certain towns, so a car is a must. You must have a Youth Hostels card, which you are well advised to buy before you leave home.

The **Y.M.C.A.** (Young Men's Christian Association) and **Y.W.C.A.** (Young Women's Christian Association) are hostels for boys and girls respectively. They are really more like hotels than hostels and are open to all. If, in practice the guests aren't all that young, these centres abound throughout the States and are a useful last resort if you can't find anything better or cheaper. Never start with the 'Y' when looking for a bed in a new town: their prices keep going up, and with luck and legwork, you'll find somewhere cheaper to sleep.

The main advantage of the 'Y's is that they are always in town, often right in the centre, that they always have rooms, even in summer, that there's one nearby wherever you are and that they're reasonably clean. Some have a cafeteria, a swimming pool or a gym on the premises. Their main drawback is that quality varies enormously from town to town and that they are often frequented by some pretty seedy characters.

That is why they will be listed for each town in the book under the heading 'Refuge' and that is how you should consider them. The 'Y' is an adequate solution to accommodation problems for a day or two, but more than a couple of nights is just too depressing ...

Ecom (Economy Accommodation)

This is a potentially interesting scheme operated by the **N.A.S.C.** North American Student Centers. You buy vouchers for 7 or 20 nights accommodation which you can use at any one of about 40 campuses. Vouchers can only be used by the holder and are not refundable. Unfortunately, a lot of the campuses in the scheme are difficult to get to and badly served by public transport. The best vouchers are those for California and for New York where the centre is right in the middle of Manhattan (but you have to pay a small supplement there). Voucher holders can use University cafeterias and restaurants. To find out more about this system, enquire at your local Student Travel organization or ask your charter company.

N.B. Be warned: the accommodation at Grand Canyon is primitive to say the least: open tarpaulin-covered shelters!

Literature

One of the best ways of getting to know a country and its people is to read their literature. Since America itself is a 'young' country, the 'classic' authors were only writing a hundred or so years ago: Nathaniel Hawthorne and Mark Twain who immortalised the South with his tales of Tom Sawyer and Huckleberry Finn.

To talk of 20th century American novels may well be preaching to the converted and in such a short space far more authors and works must be left out than are mentioned. But, with all due deference, here are some of the great, and some lesser, giants:

John Dos Passos ('*Manhattan Transfer*'): William Faulkener; Ernest Hemingway ('*A Farewell to Arms*', '*For Whom the Bell Tolls*'); Henry James ('*Portrait of a Lady*', '*What Maisie Knew*', '*Washington Square*' ...); Jack London; Norman Mailer ('*An American Dream*'); Henry Miller; Carson McCullers; Nabokov; J. D. Salinger; F. Scott Fitzgerald ('*The Great Gatsby*', '*Tender is the Night*', '*This Side of Paradise*'); John Steinbeck ('*The Grapes of Wrath*', '*Of Mice and Men*'). And the 'Beat Generation' of authors and poets:

William Burroughs ('*The Naked Lunch*', '*The Soft Machine*'); Jack Kerouac ('*On the Road*') and Corso, Ferlinghetti, Ginsberg, Kaufman and Orlovsky.

Local information

A touch of technological wizardry here: If you have arrived in an area you know nothing about, there is a number you can dial for information about the region: ☎ (800) 255.30.50, except in Kansas where the number is ☎ (800) 332.43.50. The call is free, as are all calls to numbers beginning with 800.

Mail

Post Offices in the States are not easy to find. But do buy a good supply of stamps at the first one you find, because if you run out and buy stamps from one of the automatic vending machines, they'll cost you more! You can use the 'poste restante' as your mailing address; letters should be addressed:

Your name,
General Delivery,
Main Post Office,
Town and Code
State

Find out the zip-code for the town in question, and always carry identification on you when you collect your mail.

Maps

The cheapest ones are free, given away at filling stations. Don't miss out, it may not last! A lot of garages only sell them, but they are worth having as they are very good maps, particularly the Exxon town maps. Some car-hire firms have a stack of city maps on the counter. Ask with your friendliest smile if you can have one without hiring the car to go with it! Failing freebies, there are plenty of good maps available from commercial outlets.

Money

It is absolutely vital to realize that unlike bank notes in most other countries, American notes are all the same size and colour regardless of denomination. It's all too easy to mistake a one dollar bill for a fifty dollar bill, or vice versa, so do be careful!
The International Barclaycard/Visa credit card is a terribly useful thing to have in the States. Some car-hire companies accept your card number as a deposit and that way you don't have to tie up a large sum in cash or leave a deposit in the form of counter-signed travellers' cheques. (Watch out for that, by the way: although you get them back, you may have a lot of trouble cashing them or settling bills with

21

them, as most banks and shops insist on seeing you
countersign a traveller's cheque in front of them.)
The Barclaycard/Visa also has all the usual credit-
card advantages in restaurants and shops. In the
States, you can buy almost anything with a little
piece of plastic. The only thing you won't be able to
do is withdraw cash from the automatic dispensers.
If you can buy American Express travellers' cheques, do: they are the only ones that are accepted all
over the States without any problems at all. Of
course you can use other travellers' cheques, but in
some little towns you may have to wait while they are
minutely examined, held up to the light, discussed
at length, and still have to show your passport
before they are accepted. But there's no problem if
you're not in a tearing hurry!

Motorbike

If you are a real motorbike fanatic and rich to boot,
you can fly your own machine out with you (Enquire
at your travel agent's). Otherwise, without going to
quite such lengths or expense, you can hire one over
there, particularly from companies that operate in
the areas of the National Parks. But that's by no
means cheap either. All in all, it's transport for rich
kids!

Motor home

A very practical, and much practised, idea for those
whose route takes them to the National Parks, the
wide open spaces or the vast States of the North-
West. You hire a sort of half-truck half-caravan,
known as a motor home; if you've got kids it's ideal.
If there are just two of you, it's more economical to
do without the toilet and the fridge and hire a station-
wagon. You can fold down the back seat and leave
plenty of room for a foam mattress on which to lay
your sleeping bags.
Motor home holidays are becoming very popular in
the States, so if the idea appeals to you, find out
more from your travel agent and book up well in
advance (and that means several months). Here are
a few addresses:

East Coast:
Com Coach Corporation: 103 Fort Salonga Rd,
Northport, NY.

Richmar Leisure Vehicles: 189–03 Northern Bld.,
Flushing, NY.

Maxon Trailer World: 45 Hwy N. 22 W. Union,
New Jersey.

West Coast:
Los Angeles: **Allied Tours West:** 9920 South La
Cienega Bld., Inglewood, Cal 90301.

Five Star Motor Home Rentals: 10646 Venice Bld., Culver City, Cal. 90230.

Holiday Equipmnt Center: 20937 Sherman Way, Canoga Park.

Motor Home Rental: 15092 Harvard Ave., Santa Ana.

Motor Home Centers: 2600 South Park Rd., P.O. Box 240, City of Industry, Cal. 91744.

Motor Homes West: 449 N. La Brea Ave., L.A., Cal. 90036.

San Francisco: **Weslos Recreations:** P.O. Box 789, Vacaville, Cal. 95680.

Winnebago West: 3362 El Camino, Santa Clara, Cal. 95051.

Redwood Travel Town: 7123 Redwood Hwy, Box 46, Cal. 94115.

Rolling Homes: 700 Monument Bld., Concord, Cal. 94520.

N.B. No car-hire or Motor Home company will allow you to cross the frontier into Mexico.

Museums

Without taking you on a 'museum crawl', it really would be a shame to leave the States without visiting a few of the most famous. New York heads the list, but all the major cities house some real treasures (a lot of them from Europe!) in their temples of culture. It's worth knowing anyhow.

National holidays

It's useful to be aware that on the following days and dates, the whole of America shuts down!

New Year's Day: January 1st
Good Friday
Independence Day: July 4th
Labour Day: 1st Monday in September
Veterans' Day: 4th Monday in October
Thanksgiving Day: 4th Thursday in November
Christmas Day: December 25th
There are also lots of holidays observed in various States.

National parks

A whole section of the book deals with the various National Parks.

Newspapers

To get in tune with the scene on the 'fringe' in the States, get hold of a copy of 'Village Voice' or Andy

Warhol's paper 'Interview' or even 'Rolling Stone', all of which are quite widely distributed outside the U.S. For an overall view, the latest copy of 'Time' magazine should put you in the picture.

Photography

Films are expensive in the States (slide films do not include developing). So it's a good idea to stock up before you go, but watch out for some of the security checks at the airport that may damage your film. Take a wide-angle lens if you can: it's the only way to shoot the forest of sky-scrapers or the incredible desert vistas. If you're travelling by car, don't leave films inside if you're parking for more than an hour or two in summer. One good way of keeping them cool is to put them in one of the polystyrene ice boxes sold almost everywhere.

Plane

Flying is still the fastest way of travelling. But you must really be in a hurry and be well off too, because there are hardly any reductions these days, even for visitors, on the American internal airlines. You can ask around, but basically the only reductions available are on some night flights and on so-called 'No-Frills' flights (no in-flight meals) which are quite a bit cheaper on most airlines.

Roller-skates

Roller-skates have really come back into their own in the States and have put skateboards right in the shade! You can hire a pair at the entry to most parks and at Golden Gate Park in San Francisco there are even special paths reserved for roller-skaters. So don't be surprised to see a virtuoso skater bearing down on you, skating backwards at full speed, with his stereo headphones on his head and his transistor in his hand.

Rucksack

If you're travelling by Greyhound, don't take a rucksack with too long a frame (not more than 80cm, or just over 30 inches), or you won't be able to leave it in left-luggage when you stop off.

Shopping

All marked prices in the States are exclusive of tax. Sales tax varies between 4 and 7%, according to the State and the product. So you must always expect to pay more than the marked price. Remember to take it into account when shopping.
Also, don't forget that American plugs may be different to those used at home, as may the voltage,

so if you are taking an electric shaver, hairdryer or whatever, take along an adaptor too. And if you buy electrical equipment over there always check whether it is adaptable for use at home. There are an enormous number of surplus and clothes shops offering really good prices, but watch out for seconds or damaged goods dressed up as bargains ... read the small print on the packaging.

The famous Ray Ban sunglasses are no longer as incredibly cheap as they were, but they are still cheaper than most and come in an enormous range of styles. Records too have gone up a lot, but they are still one of the best things to bring back from the States. You can get the very latest releases, as well as some golden oldies from some wholesale shops (see New York) or 'discount' record stores (see Boston). And of course, you will find an endless variety of 'gadgets' from the most practical to the most eccentric.

For budding cowboys, you can find boots, jeans, shirts, leather gear almost anywhere in the States, especially in the West and Mid-West. Stores take the form of sort of giant supermarkets where all these types of clothes are a lot cheaper than abroad. In Cheyenne, Wyoming for instance, there are about a hundred different kinds of boots for sale, one pair crazier than the next, with painted eagles, steel-capped pointed toes, bevelled heels . . ., and mother-of-pearl buttoned cowboy shirts, leather hats, pants and jackets and belts that are as wild as they are heavy to wear.

As for food, there are markets and supermarkets, like 'Safeway' and 'People's Drug'. Worth knowing that chemist pharmacies operate within the super-markets, are generally quite expensive and that medicines are not reimbursable under your health insurance. The cheapest pharmacies are in the 'Dart' supermarkets.

Survival

Where to turn when all else fails? If you're in town and stuck for a place to sleep, call a switchboard and get the address of the nearest crashpad. In a real emergency, call the operator by dialling 0. In a uni-versity town, go to the campus where you'll always find help and advice.

Telegrams

In the States, unlike other countries, the telegram service is quite separate from the Post Office. You have to go to Western Union offices who handle telegraph communications with the whole world.

Telephone

Terrific! You can call any part of the continental

United States, North to South, East to West, between 17.00 and 23.00 and any time at weekends at really cheap rates. It's also cheaper to dial direct rather than going through the operator (0 on the dial) so keep enough change on you. You don't have to have exactly the right money, the operator will give you change. If you are making an international call, ask the overseas operator when is the cheapest time to do so. If you want the call to be charged to the number you are calling, ask for a 'collect call'. Never hesitate to use the phone: it's a useful, efficient and time-saving way of finding out almost anything you need to know. Use the Yellow Pages, indispensable when looking for a particular service, restaurant, shop . . . you name it! If you are phoning from one town to another, don't forget the three 'area code' digits: each town and sometimes areas within a town have their own code, (212 for New York, 617 for Boston, 312 for Chicago etc.). Some companies and organizations (like the major car-hire firms, hotel chains and so on) have automatic 'collect call' lines: if you dial 800 before the number, the call is free.

Tennis

If tennis is your game, take your racket with you when you go to the States, or buy one there (they are, as a rule, cheaper than elsewhere). You can 'knock a ball about' almost anywhere in the city parks. The per-capita number of tennis courts over there is very high, so having found your court, write your name and the time you want to play on the board at the entrance to the court and then just turn up with your gear.

Time zones

The U.S.A. is divided into four time zones: E.S.T. (Eastern Standard Time), C.S.T. (Central Standard Time), M.S.T. (Mountain Standard Time) and P.S.T. (Pacific Standard Time). There is an hour's difference between one time zone and the next, thus: at 8 o'clock in Los Angeles (P.S.T.), it is 11 o'clock in New York (E.S.T.). For all plane, bus and train time-tables, it's always the local time that is given.

Train

Railway travel is undergoing a re-birth in the States. Crossing the continent in one of the panoramic railway carriages is just as scenic and much less tiring than travelling by road. Some trains even have a cinema and a night-club!

Urban transport

Public transport in American cities leaves something

to be desired. But as distances are always very great and taking taxis is out of the question, it's very advisable to get used to the (complicated) bus and Underground systems. For the bus, you should always have the right money. You put the coins in a glass box when you get on the bus (fares vary depending on area and distance travelled). Drivers are normally nice to foreigners: always ask which way they're going, the fare, etc. Always ask as well for a 'transfer' ticket when paying; this ticket enables you to take free-of-charge a bus going in another direction. For the Underground (Boston, New York, Chicago and San Francisco) you have to use tokens – which you buy in the station and which can also be used on the buses – or tickets from distributors.

Vaccination

There are no specific vaccination requirements for entering the United States, except if you are arriving from a country where there is smallpox, cholera or yellow fever!

Visa

You must be in possession of a valid visa to enter the States (see 'Entry Requirements').

Weather

As a general rule, the summers in America are hot. However, if you are travelling by coach, take along a pullover because the air-conditioning can really be quite chilly. At other times of the year, take along a supply of warm clothes because, except in the South, the winters are very hard. If you are taking two months, say August and September, to tour the States, it's better to start in the North and work your way South, rather than the other way round, to avoid the more dramatic variations in temperature and climate.

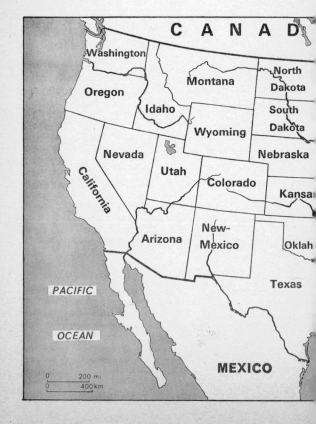

Part II
Sixteen Towns

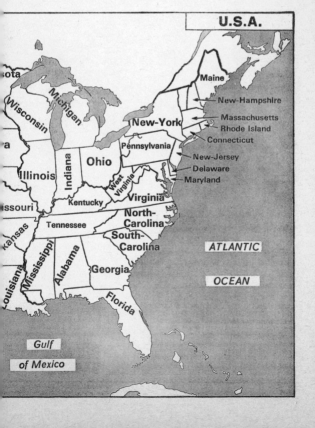

Georgia Institute of Technology   Memorial Arts Center   Swan House

Atlanta
Downtown

| 0 | 0,25 mi |
| 0 | 400 m |

"Six Flags over Georgia" · Wren's Nest

1 Exhibition Hall	9 American Motor Hotel	19 Five Points
2 Robert F. Maddox Hall	10 Peachtree Center Plaza Hotel	20 Joel Hurt Memorial Park
3 Atlanta Downtown Motel	11 Public Library	21 Plaza Park
4 Hilton Hotel	12 Dinkler-Plaza Hotel	22 Historic Lamp Post
5 Regency Hyatt House (Hotel)	13 Inntown Motor Hotel	23 Immaculate Conception Catholic Church
6 Conv. & Visitors Bureau	14 Henry Grady Monument	24 Central Presbyterian Church
7 Merchandise Mart	15 Zero Mile Post	25 State Museum
8 Trailways Bus Depot	16 C&S Bank Building	26 City School Department
	17 Bank of Georgia Bldg.	27 Public Market
	18 Trust Company of Georgia Bldg.	

Kartographie Huber & Oberländer, München

ATLANTA
📷 404
GEORGIA

Since the heroic period of the War of Secession, immortalized by '*Gone with the Wind*', Atlanta has fully entered into the modern world. The capital of Georgia, with its prosperous economy dominates the whole of the Deep South. A local firm made itself world-famous by selling a drink which often symbolises the United States: Coca-Cola. In spite of its impressive hotels, skyscrapers which grow at an astounding rate and the rapid growth in population (more than 1,700,000 inhabitants in the metropolitan area) Atlanta has still managed to keep all the non-chalance and quiet charm which make it a typical Southern town. One notices immediately that Atlanta people are warmer than elsewhere. Racial problems have been if not resolved at least greatly reduced: the mayor of the town of Martin Luther King is black, the city council has a very strong social policy, and the ghettos are not as tough as those of Chicago or New York. Atlanta is certainly a city which deserves a visit.

arriving in Atlanta

Bus

Greyhound: 81 Cain St. N.W. 📞 522.63.00.
Continental Trailways: 200 Spring St. N.W. (in the same block as Greyhound). 📞 524.24.41.

Plane

Bus Marta No 12 will take you downtown from the international airport.

Train

Amtrak: Brookwood, Peachtree Road, N.W. ☎ 874.28.00.

don't panic

Finding your way around

Downtown is not very large and surrounds a main street: Peachtree Rd which goes in a north–south direction. The town spreads for miles round downtown. The houses are set in a veritable forest of magnificent trees. The network of freeways puts the city centre within 15 minutes of anywhere near the city. Uptown is used to describe the residential districts north of Downtown: Buckhead, Brookwood etc.

Transport

Underground: at present only links Downtown with west of the city. In 1980–1 network will be completed.

Bus: Marta has network (the cheapest fares in the U.S. ... but long waits between buses) up to 15 miles round Downtown. Information and maps from MARTA kiosks (W. Peachtree/Peachtree Rd for example). ☎ 522.47.11.
Grayline Tours: ☎ 524.60.86.

Car hire

Dollar Rent-a-Car: 70 Houston St. ☎ 523.66.01.

Econo Car: 31 Baker St. ☎ 659.16.55 and at the airport: 1215 E. Virginia Ave. ☎ 762.88.33.

National: 122 Internation Bld. ☎ 659.73.41.

Rentabug: 3224 Peachtree Rd. NE ☎ 763.23.13.

Refuge

Y.M.C.A.: 145 Luckie St. ☎ 525.54.01. Mixed.
Y.M.C.A.: 22 Butler St. ☎ 659.80.85. Book.

keys to Atlanta

General information

Atlanta Visitors & Convention Bureau: Suite 1414 Peachtree Cain Building, 233 Peachtree Rd NE

(2nd floor) ☎ 659.42.70. There's an information kiosk on Peachtree Center Square.

Travellers Aid: 173 Walton St. NW. ☎ 523.05.85. At the airport: ☎ 766.45.11.

Newspapers

Creative Loafing: weekly; free from Downtown distributors. All the programmes and lots of advertisements.

Gazette: free also, but not as complete.

Atlanta Constitution: Atlanta daily, buy the Sunday edition.

Key and **Where** in the big hotels.

Colleges and Campuses

Emory University: 1380 S. Oxford. Pleasant campus, small restaurants.

Georgia State University: University Plaza is situated Downtown, has a radio station and ride board.

Georgia Technic: 225 North Ave. A rather serious university, but on the other hand has the best ride board if you are looking for a lift to New York or California.

Meeting Places

Five Points Square with its grassy buttes is always crowded, it's the heart of the city.
A lot of young people converge on **Piedmont Park** at weekends. Free concerts in the summer.
Some evenings, if you know how to skate, and even if you don't, the **Omni International** skating-rink is a good place to get to know people.

Survival

The inveterate hitch-hiker won't find much Sixties-style counter-culture in a city like Atlanta. The Peachtree/10th St. quarter around Piedmont Park was the least 'straight' in the city. It's still frequented by the students.

Transport

Rides: Ride Line of Georgia State University's WRAS Station ☎ 658.22.34.

The best ride board is Georgia Tech University's: North Ave./Luckie St. on the ground floor of the Student Center. Advertisements in the paper 'Creative Loafing' ☎ 873.10.53.

Driveaways: AAACON Auto Transport: 180 Allen Rd. N.E. ☎ 256.29.94.
Auto Drive Away Co: 830 Peachtree St. ☎ 881.16.88.

good night

Cheap hotels

Cheaper than the Y.M.C.A., but relatively rough:

Falcon Hotel : (the working man's hotel) 180 Luckie
St. ☎ 524.98.79. Cheap but creepy.

Frances Hotel : 343 Peachtree Rd ☎ 523.75.21.
Equally creepy.

Imperial Hotel : 355 Peachtree Rd N.E. (corner of
Forrest Bld.) ☎ 524.19.41. The best of the lot – clean,
bath and TV.

Georgian Terrace Hotel : 659 Peachtree Rd N.E.
☎ 872.66.71.

Peachtree Manor Hotel : 826 Peachtree Rd N.E.
☎ 874.27.91.

Save-Inn Mid-Town : 1152 Spring St. N.E. ☎
875.35.11.

Tourist hotels

Atlantan : 111 Luckie St. N.E. ☎ 524.64.61.

Dinkler Plaza Hotel : 98 Forsyth St. NW.

More expensive hotels

Peachtree Center Plaza Hotel : Peachtree Rd./
Cain St. ☎ 659.14.00. The best and most expensive.
To see its architecture, take the lift to the 'Top'.
Keep smiling if you are not in evening dress.

Omni International : Marietta St./Techwood Drive.
☎ 659.00.00

Hyatt Regency : 265 Peachtree Rd. ☎ 577.12.34.

Sheraton Biltmore : 817 W Peachtree Rd. ☎ 881.
95.00.

The above three hotels should also be visited for
their architecture.

If you have a car, don't hesitate: motels are the best.
The chain of **'Days-Inn'** are particularly cheap for a
group of 3 or 4 people: if you take the Interstate 85
going north, there are 3 'Days-Inns' (Clairmont Rd,
Stallowford Rd, Chamblee Tucker Rd). 'Days Inns'
in Atlanta ☎ 458.44.44.

getting fed

Downtown there aren't many cheap little restaurants.
You'll have to make do with a sandwich at, for example, **The Sandwich Man :** 57 Forsyth St. in the

Healey Building which is also architecturally interesting.

There are also some good places in Atlanta where you can have a sandwich and listen to music at the same time.

Emporium: in the Great South East. Music Hall in the Broadview Plaza commercial centre (a quarter of an hour by bus (No 71) from Downtown) Piedmont Road/Morosgo Drive. Concerts.

Good Old Days: 1444 Oxford Rd. and also at 3013 Peachtree Rd. Great fried sandwiches served in flower pots. (Closed on Sundays.)

The Gallery: in the Omni International: Marietta St/Techwood Drive. The best sandwich 'spot' Downtown.

Jaggers Old Time: 1577 North Decatur St. The restaurant where students from Emory University meet.

Gabriel's Sub Shops: 128 North Ave. N.W. (near the Tech Hotel).

Pleasant Uptown: in the commercial centre Phipps Plaza, 3500 Peachtree Rd. Not just sandwiches. Go there for lunch. Pleasant decor: plants everywhere, white walls. Sublime Bloody Marys.

Franco's Pizza: 840 Peachtree St. A good pizzeria.

Houlihan's Old Place: in Lennox Square commercial centre. Good for a drink.

Joe Dale's Cajun House: 3209 Taple Drive ☎ 261.27.41. Japanese cooking.

Benihana of Tokyo: 2143 Peachtree St. Tables for eight. The bill is reasonable.

Really different:

The Abbey: 163 Ponce de Leon Ave. N.E. ☎ 881.81.27. The waiters are actually dressed as monks ... Expensive.

The greatest concentration of restaurants in the city are to be found in Underground Atlanta:

The Bucket Stop: 76 Old Alabama St.

Dante's Down the Hatch: 84 Old Pryor St. ☎ 577.18.00. Excellent, and do you know of many restaurants where live crocodiles are part of the decor?

The Old Carriage House Restaurant: 104-B Old Pryor St.

Ricardo's Mexican Restaurant: 52 P. Kensey's Alley.

Rocco's Pizza and Sub Shop: 60D Kensey's Alley. The cheapest in Underground Atlanta.

Rue de Paris: 60 B. Kensey's Alley. Ah! Delicious veal scallops in cream to make a change from all those Big Macs, Burger Kings and the rest of them.

things that everyone goes to see and that you shouldn't miss

Underground Atlanta: 36 Alabama St. (near the Capitol). The tourist trap that cannot and should not be missed. Situated under two Downtown streets, it's an old quarter formerly of ill-repute, and of hardly better repute today after one in the morning. It's crammed with restaurants and noisy clubs. The gas lighting takes you back a century.

Six Flags over Georgia: 10 minutes from Downtown on the Interstate 20. This amusement park must be the maddest in the United States. 'The Great American Scream Machine', and the roller coaster really deserve their names. At night the park is really worth seeing. Try the Great Gasp which is a parachute jump just like the real thing. March to end-November. Every day 10.00 – 23.00.

Cyclorama: Grant Park, Georgia/Clerokle Av. The battle of Atlanta was a decisive turning-point in the War of Secession and is what this circular painting describes with a good dose of lyricism.

Governor's Mansion: 391 West Paces Ferry Rd. ☎ 261.17.76. in Buckhead, a super-chic quarter of Atlanta. Wednesday, Thursday 10.00–12.00; Sunday 15.00–17.00.

Memorial Arts Center: 1280 Peachtree Rd. ☎ 892.36.00. See the High Museum of Art, particularly its Renaissance works and its Impressionists.

Piedmont Park: a magnificent park with green-houses, lake, swimming-pool etc. The weekend meeting place for 'gay' people (amongst others). 10th St. Southern Railway line.

things that everyone goes to see and that can be given a miss

Stone Mountain: in Stone Mountain Memorial State Park, 26 km east of Atlanta. To get there, take bus No. 20 Pryor-Alabama St. An enormous granite boulder (more than 250 m. high) lies right in the middle of the park, like a whale washed up on a beach. The bas-relief on its sides represents the Southern leaders. You can take the cable-railway to get to the top of the block and even a train to go round it (summer only). All Atlanta people will tell you about Stone Mountain.

things that everyone doesn't go to see and which deserve to be seen

Coca-Cola Company: 310 North Ave. (opposite Georgia Tech University). This is the international company's headquarters. Make sure you visit the small museum which retraces the history of this incredible commercial success. You can see in particular the development of the shape of the coke bottle.

Municipal Market: 209 Edgewood Ave. Built in 1923 and modernized in '76. Lots of fresh produce. Good atmosphere.

Swan House: 3099 Andrews Drive N.W. A really handsome house in Italian Renaissance style built in ... 1928! A really fine imitation. Photo exhibition inside.

Fox Theatre: 660 Peachtree Rd/Ponce de Leon Ave. If they haven't yet demolished it, go and see this cinema which looks like a mosque. Inside there is one of the largest organs in the world!

Buckhead: around West Paces Ferry Rd., north of Downtown. This residential quarter with its imposing houses in a forest setting, looking as if they are straight out of '*Gone with the Wind*' is absolutely unique in the United States, and can more than stand the comparison with L.A.'s Beverly Hills.

great scenes

Music

Atlanta has a very good music life based mainly on rock and country-rock.

Great Southeast Music Hall: in the Broadview Plaza commercial centre, Piedmont Rd Morosgo Drive, 10 km. north of Downtown. The best 'spot' in Atlanta for listening to good local or international country-rock. Doc Watson himself is a regular, which is a reference.

The Lullwater: 1545 N. Decatur St. ☎ 377.65.98.

Country Roads: 6400 Hillandate Rd.

The Bistro: 1102 W. Peachtree Rd. Often excellent blue grass. Good place.

Rose's Cantina: 688 Spring St. ☎ 881.02.44. Local groups.

Clubs

North of Downtown:

The Library: 550 Pharr Rd (off Piedmont Rd). Fashionable and elegant club. Unfortunately a bit too 'jet set'.

Colorado Mining Company: 2225 Peachtree Rd. ☎ 351.55.41. Club, restaurant, gaming room.

The Second Sun: 4420 Roswell Rd (north of Buckhead). Teenagers' club, a pick-up place.

Gay bars

(with very good music)

Mother's: Bennett St. behind Harrison's bar (2140 Peachtree Rd).

Union Station: Monroe Drive.

Mural

Really beautiful political mural on the corner of Auburn Ave. and Piedmont Ave. not far from the Greyhound Station: Malcolm X, Angela Davis, Muhammed Ali, Wes Montgomery, Martin L. King and several others.

BOSTON
☎ 617
MASSACHUSETTS

The largest city in New England, Boston is the most European of the American metropolises: the little streets of Beacon Hill, the parks and the low brick houses give it that urban quality which is so seldom found in the United States. The pedestrian isn't a strange animal and there is still a café life. The city of the Irish Catholics is also the biggest student intellectual centre in the United States: it's the Latin Quarter of the country. If possible go there in September, when Boston is an immense campus of some 250,000 students. Lots of pleasant people, of course, rock concerts every week, avant-garde plays, classical music. Two excellent papers such as are only produced on this side of the Atlantic which serve as a cross-roads for everything going on in the young and vital world of Boston. And if you're bored in spite of all that, you still have a very beautiful city, full of charm, to explore. It's more full of history than any other in the United States and has kept, from Benjamin Franklin to John Kennedy, a very solid political tradition.

arriving in Boston

Coach

Greyhound: 10 St. James Ave. ☎ 423.58.10.
Continental Trailways: 10 Park Square. ☎ 482.66. 20.

Plane

From **Logan International Airport** (☎ 567.54.00), public transport is the cheapest: take the Underground at the Airport station, and get off at Government Center station for Downtown (at the airport an MBTA shuttle-service operates for all companies). **Bus Airways Transportation Co.** every quarter of an hour to the main hotels.

N.B. Never take a bus or a taxi if you're in a hurry: there are often traffic jams at Callahan tunnel.

Train

Amtrak: two stations; *South Station*, 145 Atlantic Ave and *Back Bay Station*, 145 Dartmouth St. (near the Prudential Center) ☎ 523.57.20 or 227.00.00.

don't panic

Finding your way around

Thanks to its history, Boston has none of the strict street lay-out found in most American cities. The centre is a park – Boston Common – the old quarter, municipal buildings and the port are on the east side of the park, and on the west is the student quarter of which the heart is Commonwealth Ave. The Charles River separates Boston from Cambridge where you can find Harvard University and the M.I.T., Massachusetts Institute of Technology. On a clear day, take a trip to the top of the Prudential Center. It's very rewarding as there are very few skyscrapers and you get an uninterrupted view over the town. You can get a map from the Foreign Visitors' Center (see later).

Transport

Boston has an appalling traffic problem, so use public transport.

Underground: certainly the best (or rather the least awful) in the United States; there are four lines, blue, orange, green and red. Make the most of it, it's very useful. Open from 5.30 a.m. to 1.00 in the morning. Reduced rates every day from 10.00 hrs to 14.00 hrs and all day Sunday. If you want to go to Cambridge, take the red line and get off at Central for M.I.T. or Harvard Square for Harvard. Connections between lines at Park Street Station, State Station, Government Center and Washington Station.

N.B. MBTA stands for Underground Station: Metro of Boston Transit Authority.

Bus. Zone System. Connections with the Underground, you don't pay twice if you go from one to the other.

Information for Underground and bus: MBTA ☎ 722.50.00.

Taxis

Four main companies:

Checker Cab: ☎ 536.70.00.
Town Taxi: ☎ 536.50.00.
Yellow Cab: ☎ 332.77.00 or 527.55.55.
Boston Cab: ☎ 536.50.10.

Car Hire

American International: 341 Newbury St. ☎ 267.66.61.

Budget: 19 Huntington Ave. ☎ 266.35.37.
Dollar: 39 Dalton St. ☎ 523.50.98.
Econo: 7 Eliot St. ☎ 542.98.00.
National: 183 Dartmouth St. ☎ 426.68.30.
Thrifty: 125 Bremen St. ☎ 569.65.00 (Airport).

Bike Hire

Beacon Hill Bike Shop: 303 Cambridge St.
(MBTA: Charles St.) ☎ 523.91.33.

Boston Bicycle Shoppe: 50 Berkeley St. ☎ 542.31.
45.

Herson Cycle Co: 1250 Cambridge St. ☎ 876.40.00.
The best address of the three, but it's in Cambridge
(MBTA: Harvard).

Refuge

A very wide choice of 'Y's:

Y.M.C.A.: Huntington Branch: 316 Huntington Ave.
☎ 536.78.00. Mixed.

Y.M.C.A.: South Core Branch: 56 Taylor St. ☎
426.22.37. Mixed.

Y.M.C.A.: 140 Clarendon St. (in Cambridge) ☎
536.79.40. Mixed.

Y.M.C.A.: 820 Massachusetts Av. ☎ 876.38.60.
Men only.

Y.M.C.A.: 7 Temple St. (in Cambridge) ☎ 491.60.
50.

In Charlestown:

Y.M.C.A.: Armed Services Branch: 32 City Square
☎ 242.26.60. Mixed.

Youth Hostels:

Brookline Hostel: 45 Strathmore Rd. ☎ 469.03.33.
Summer only. A limit of 3 consecutive nights' stay.

Dorchester Hotel: 1620 Dorchester Ave. ☎ 436.08.
93 (MBTA Fields Corner, red line).

keys to Boston

General information

Foreign Visitors' Center: 15 State St. ☎ 262.48.30.

Visitors' Centers: there are several tourist information centres in Boston:

Tremont St., next to Boston Common Park. The
main one, very centrally placed (MBTA: Park St).

John Hancock Tower: Copley Square (MBTA: Copley).

City Hall Visitor Hospitality Center: City Hall, near the Plaza (MBTA: Government Center).

Traveller's Aid: Airport. ☎ 542.72.86.

International Institute of Boston: 287 Commonwealth Ave. ☎ 536.10.81. Deals mainly with foreign immigrants.

In Cambridge:

Harvard Information Office: Holyoke Center in Harvard Square (Southern side): everything you want to know about the university. ☎ 495.15.73.

Newspapers

The Real Paper and **The Phoenix** are two excellent papers always full of information and advertisements of every kind. Indispensable.

The Globe: particularly the Thursday edition. Supplement of the *Boston Globe*.

At the beginning of every University year, half a dozen Underground papers appear on the campus. **'Harvard Crimson'** is particularly good.

Boston Arts: a supplement of *The Phoenix*. Specially for what to see and what to do in the evening.

Two booking agencies for shows:

Hub Ticket: 110 Stuart St. ☎ 426.83.40.

Tyson Ticket: 226 Tremont St. ☎ 426.26.62.

Colleges and campuses

There are so many colleges on Commonwealth Ave. and Beacon St. that it's impossible to list them all. The first thing to do when you arrive in Boston is to go and see what is happening on the following campuses:

Boston University (known as B.U.) is situated on both sides of Commonwealth Ave. after Kenmore Square. The main student Hall of Residence is at No. 700. The Students' Union is at No. 775 Commonwealth Av. and this is the place to go to make quick contact with the student community and get to know what interesting things are going on.

Northeastern University: less interesting, but useful to know of its existence, on Huntington Av.

Harvard University, in Harvard Square (Cambridge) is an enormous campus on which you can easily get lost if you haven't bought the Holyoke Center map. In any case, most things happen on Harvard Square rather than on the rest of the campus: have a look round the different floors of the Harvard Coop (where the students buy their books and pens). Buying the latest Ginsberg or an old Kerouac can give you the opportunity to meet a lot of nice people.

M.I.T. (MBTA: Central, or across the Charles River on foot via the Harvard Bridge). The campus is on Massachusetts Ave. Go to the Student Center, a modern block opposite the Rogers Building; there's another Harvard Coop in the basement. Excellent self-service restaurant on the first floor. By the way, the American scientific elite don't always have shaved heads, you can also see some genuine 'freaks'.

Meeting places

First of all, of course, the above-mentioned campuses. The whole of the **Kenmore Square** quarter with its snack-bars, pizzerias, record shops (incredible prices at the beginning of the university year!) and clubs is ideal for getting to know people. Similarly all the small streets around **Harvard Square** are full of people and life. (For addresses, see later.) **Boston Common** is full of people over the weekend. The pedal-boats on the lake look like swans. You can have a good time.

Survival

'Crashing' isn't difficult in Boston: begin by exploring Boston University during the day. At night Kenmore Square fills up with freaks and such-like. Have a look at the Phone Book in *'The Real Paper'*.

If you really are in difficulties:

The Salvation Army: 407 Shawmut Ave. ☎ 536. 74.69. Drop-in centre open from 8.00 to 15.00. Very hospitable.

Old West Church Drop-In Center: 131 Cambridge St. ☎ 227.50.88.

To leave Boston

Auto-Driveaway: 566 Commonwealth Ave. ☎ 267.48.36.

Boston Ride Center: ☎ 739.22.00.

---

good night

Student lodging

Northeast Hall: 204 Bay State Rd. ☎ 267.30.42. Near Boston University. From end June to end August.

Boston University Housing and Food Service:
194 Bay State Rd. ☎ 353.35.02. Three nights minimum, a week maximum, summer only, reserve at
least a week in advance. Don't forget Boston Area
Code if you're telephoning from outside the town:
617.

Try your luck in the colleges (unfortunately you normally have to book in advance):

Kenmore Hall: 490 Commonwealth Ave.

Leavitt Hall: 645 Beacon St.

Garden Halls Dormitories: 163 Marlborough St,
Boston, Mass., 02116. Written bookings only.

Other possibilities

If you are staying for a few weeks, contact **'Matching
Room-mate'** 251 Harvard St. Brookline Coolidge
Corner St. ☎ 734.64.69 and 734.22.64. They can offer
rooms or flats to share.
If there are four or six of you, the best idea is to look
for flats to rent on Beacon St. or round Beacon Hill
and even Back Bay (Prudential Center). Agencies
put signs in the windows.

Home Away: 322 Beacon St. ☎ 266.87.55.

Back Bay Beacon Hill: Short-term furnished
apartments for several people and for a minimum of
a few weeks.

Cheap hotels

The Garden House: 168 Canal St. (near North
Station).

Bradford Hotel: 275 Tremont St. ☎ 426.14.00
(MBTA: Boylston).

Essex Hotel: 695 Atlantic Ave. ☎ 482.90.00 (MBTA:
South Station).

Madison Motor Inn: 25 Nashua St. ☎ 227.26.00
(MBTA: North Station).

Terrace Motel: 1650 Commonwealth Ave. ☎ 566.
62.60. Good, particularly if you have a car as it's some
distance from the centre.

Outside Boston itself:

Brookline Motor Hotel: 1223 Beacon St. ☎ 232.75.
00.

Chalet Suisse Motor Lodge: 800 W. Morrissey
Bld. ☎ 287.91.00 (MBTA: Ashmont Station). One of
a chain throughout the U.S.A. Quite good.

Hotel Stanley: 15 Congress St. ☎ 884.90.80 (in
Chelsea – north of Logan airport).

Kirkland Inn: 67 Kirkland St. ☎ 547.46.00 (MBTA:
Harvard in Cambridge). Very reasonable.

Longwood Inn: 123 Longwood Ave. ☎ 566.86.15 (in Brookline).

The Market Place: 200 Beacham St. ☎ 884.86.00 (MBTA: Sullivan Square).

More expensive hotels

Avery Hotel: 24 Avery St. (near Tremont St.) ☎ 482.800.00 (MBTA: Boylston or Essex).

Copley Square Hotel: 47 Huntington Ave/Exeter St. ☎ 536.90.00.

Eliot Hotel: 270 Commonwealth Ave. ☎ 267.16.07 (MBTA: Auditorium).

Fenway Boylston Motor Hotel: 1271 Boylston St. ☎ 267.83.00 (MBTA: Kenmore).

Fenway Commonwealth Motor Hotel: 575 Commonwealth Ave. ☎ 267.31.00 (MBTA: Kenmore).

Hotels for luxury-jean wearers

Surprise, surprise! The Boston Park Plaza offers student reductions. In some cases it can cost less than the above-mentioned hotels.

Boston Park Plaza: Park Square, Arlington St. ☎ 426.20.00 (MBTA: Arlington). Well situated.

Children's Inn: 342 Longwood Ave. ☎ 431.47.00.

Colonnade Hotel: 120 Huntington Ave. ☎ 261.28.00. Next door to the Prudential Center.

Copley Plaza Hotel: 138 St. James Ave. ☎ 267.53.00.

Parker House: 60 School St. ☎ 227.86.00.

getting fed

In addition to the normal range of snack-bar and restaurant chains there is one which is particular to this region: the **'Pewter Pot'**.

There are any number of cafeterias, small restaurants and pizzerias in Commonwealth Ave, in Kenmore Square for Boston, and around Harvard Square for Cambridge.

You can eat well and for a reasonable price at the **Museum of Fine Arts Cafeteria** at 465 Huntington Ave. (closed on Mondays, MBTA: Arborway).

Also excellent: the **M.I.T. Student Center** self-service restaurant in Massachusetts Ave, 150 metres from Harvard Bridge on the Cambridge side.

Some restaurants

Athens Olympia: 51 Stuart St. Greek food.

Charley's Eating and Drinking Saloon: 344 Newbury St. An excellent and well-known Boston restaurant with Victorian decor. Amazingly long bar, well patronized. Open until 2 a.m.

Dunfey's Last Hurrah: Tremont St/School St (MBTA: Park St.) 1900s atmosphere, large salads, moderate prices.

Durgin Park: 30 N. Market St. (MBTA: Haymarket) Really pleasant and relaxed atmosphere (closed on Sundays).

English Tea Room: 28 Newbury St. Very cheap.

Havah Nagila Restaurant: 280 Cambridge St. (MBTA: Charles St). Jewish and Middle-Eastern specialities. Excellent Turkish coffee.

Jacob Wirth's: 31 Stuart St (closed on Sundays). German restaurant with good beer. Style: sawdust on the floor, copper hand-rails on the bar, etc.

Jimmy's Harbor Side Restaurant: 242 Northern Ave. ☎ 423.10.00. Good view of the harbour.

Ken's: 549 Boylston St/Copley Sq. (near the Prudential Center). ☎ 266.61.06.

One Dock Square: 16 North St. (MBTA: Government Center).

No-Name Restaurant: 15½ Fish Pier (MBTA: South Station, on the corner of Fish Pier and Northern Ave). Really worth trying. It's the best seafood restaurant in Boston and isn't very expensive either. From the back room you can watch the boats entering and leaving the port (closed at week-ends).

Union Oyster House: 41 Union St. (MBTA: Haymarket or Government Square). In a building dating from 1742, formerly a shop selling fabrics, this is the oldest restaurant in Boston – a landmark not to be missed.

Specialist restaurants

Soul food

Bob the Chef's: 604 Columbus Ave. (closed on Sundays). Modest decor but genuine Southern cooking. Beans, sweet corn, grilled chops, and (of course) soul music in the background.

Italian

Cantina Italiana: 346 Hanover St. (MBTA: Haymarket).

Fidele's: 30 Fleet St. Superb pasta. Inexpensive.

Giro's: 464 Hanover St. (MBTA: North Station).

Joe Tecce's: 53 North Washington St. (MBTA: North Station). A very well known restaurant which deserves its reputation.

Mother Anna's: 211 Hanover St. Closed on Mondays. Acceptable and cheap.

Anthony's: Pier 4, Northern Ave. ☎ 423.63.63. Fish and shellfish. Good wine.

Chinese

Chinese restaurants aren't very cheap in Boston, you can find them in Chinatown around Harrison Ave/Essex St.

China Pearl: 9 Tyler St. (MBTA: Essex) closed in the evening.

Fung Won: 8 Tyler St.

The Chef: 1003 Saratoga St. ☎ 569.60.66. Cheap, good food. Take-away service.

Restaurants in Cambridge

Cambridge's big advantage is that it has a lot of small restaurants within a small area. So take the Underground to Harvard Square and have a look round:

Averof: 1924 Massachusetts Ave. Lively Greek restaurant.

Barney's: 20 Boylston St.

Bartley's Kitchen: 10 Eliot St.

Bartley's Burger Cottage: 1246 Massachusetts Ave. Cheap. Closed on Sundays.

Casa Mexico: 75 Winthrop St.

Casa Portugal: 1200 Cambridge St. Moderate prices. Quite good Portuguese wine.

Elle's: 71 Mt Auburn St. A great place for stuffing yourself. Always full of students. Try a 'pastrami sandwich'.

The Blue Parrot: 123 Mt Auburn St.

The Hungry Persian: 14A Eliot St. Very cheap.

The Underdog: 6 Bow St. The best hot dogs in Boston; in particular the 'Blasphemy' and the 'C.J. Special'. There are also excellent pinball machines open 11.30–13.00.

The Kitchenette Diner: 168 First St. A small and unattractive looking place from the outside, frequented only by those who know how good it is, i.e. the working-men of Cambridge. Simple cooking, very cheap. Closes at 18.00 hrs.

The Rendez-vous: 24 Holyoke St. (just behind Elsie's) Vietnamese and Greek specialities. Closed at 14.00 from Sunday to Wednesday, at 16.00 from Thursday to Saturday.

The Rendez-vous Lounge: 24 Holyoke St. In the basement of the preceding restaurant, open 17.00–21.00. Closed on Mondays.

The Restaurant: 1001 Massachusetts Ave. Very busy, a good place to meet people.

Legal Seafoods: 237 Hampshire St. (take a Lechmeer bus at Harvard Square). Much used by the student community of Harvard and M.I.T., this restaurant offers sea-food specialities at a reasonable price.

Terra Foods: 1193 Cambridge St. Excellent place to go. Portuguese specialities for next to nothing. Closed on Sundays.

The Garden of the Harvest: 44 Brattle St. Quiet restaurant in a patio.

Wurthaus Restaurant: 4 Boylston St. A choice of more than 100 beers.

Natalle's: 1672 Massachusetts Ave. An Italian restaurant with a student clientele. Cheap.

Iruan: 56 Boylston St. Spanish cooking. Closed on Sundays.

Rather different:

The Hunan: 700 Massachusetts Ave (MBTA: Central). Chinese food.

Joyce Chen's: 390 Rindge Ave. Tuesdays and Wednesdays, 18.00–20.30. 'All you can eat' style of restaurant – Chinese. Recommended.

Autre Chose: 1105 Massachusetts Ave. Maurice, the king of the croissant, had a marvellous idea to open this restaurant-cake-shop which is unique in the United States.

33 Dunster St.: fantastic brunches, and as much as you can eat, on Sundays 11.00–15.00. Unusual décor.

Coffee houses

In Cambridge they are always lively and welcoming. The main ones are as follows:

Algiers Coffee House: 40 Brattle St. A chess and Go club holds meetings in this very pleasant part of Cambridge.

Passion Coffee House: 47 Palmer St. (Harvard Sq.) Good folk music.

The Pamplona: Bow St./Arrow St.

The Coffee Connection: 36 Boylston St. If you want to get away from the awful dish-water which is served up as coffee in the United States, then this is the best without any doubt.

Common Grounds: 15 Pearl St. (MBTA: Central). Pleasant and relaxed. Music on Friday evenings.

things that everyone goes to see and that you shouldn't miss

Where's Boston? 60 State St. 10.00–22.00. Audio-visual presentation of the city and its inhabitants. Conventional, but gives an idea of the Bostonian mentality.

Boston and its history: Very simple: the *'Freedom Trail'* is a kind of bigger version of snakes and ladders, all you have to do is follow the red line on the pavement which begins at the *Visitor Center in Tremont St.* This takes you past all the well-known places of the American Revolution. In particular go and see Boston's oldest house: *Paul Revere House* (1676) open every day 10.00–18.00; *Faneuil Hall* (1742) with its remarkably well-balanced and proportioned architecture, the *Old Corner Bookstore* (1712) where authors such as Thoreau, Emerson and Hawthorne used to meet in the nineteenth century; the *Old State House* (1713) with the balcony from which was read the Declaration of Independence on the 18th of July 1776. These buildings are open every day 9.00–18.00.

Trinity Church and **Copley Square:** this church was built by the architect Henry Richardson in 1877. It's one of the rare examples in the United States of a Roman-style church. Open 8.00–16.00. Entry free. Copley Square is always very lively.

Museum of Fine Arts: 465 Huntington Ave. (10.00–17.00 every day, until 21.00 on Tuesdays and Thursdays, free on Tuesday, closed on Mondays). To get there, get off at Arborway Underground Station, green line, or take a trolley (showing Arborway) at Copley Square. Very good collections of Impressionists and Egyptian Art. In any case, go there if only to see that marvellous Gauguin 'Que sommes-nous? D'où venons-nous? Où allons-nous?' as well as one of Nicolas de Staël's finest works.

Prudential Center: Huntington Ave./Boylston St. Panoramic view from the 'Skywalk'. Deserves visiting.

John Hancock Building: Berkeley St./Copley Square. This skyscraper with its narrow profile has something about it. The architect I. M. Pei hasn't spoilt the site by making maximum use of light reflection. Observation platform on the 60th floor. Open until 23.00 on Sundays.

Beacon Hill: One of the oldest quarters in Boston, situated between the Charles River and Boston Common Park. (MBTA: Government Center.) The paved streets and little brick houses date from the beginning of the eighteenth century. Gas street lights give the final touch to this little island of charm, now very residential. Walk along Mount Vernon St. Information on the history of the quarter at the Tourist Information Center in State House, designed by Charles Bullfinch, architect of the Capitol in Washington D.C. You can visit Nichols House (55 Mount Vernon St) where the writer Henry Adams spent his childhood.

Quincy Market: a covered market built in 1825 and now remarkably restored, where you can find restaurants, small food shops and different boutiques. Busy day and night. A short distance from Quincy Market, the greater part of the Waterfront has been entirely renovated. Pleasant walks along the embankment.

things that everyone doesn't go to see and which deserve to be seen

Museum of Science and Charles Hayden Planetarium: Science Park (MBTA: Science Park) 10.00–17.00, Friday 10.00–22.00, Sunday 11.00–17.00. The main attraction is a giant model of the human heart. Planetarium: until 14.45.

Aquarium: Central Wharf, near Atlantic Ave. (MBTA: Aquarium, blue line.) During the week 9.00–18.00, weekends 10.00–19.00, Fridays open until 21.00. Entrance fee. For once, an aquarium which isn't boring! Underwater divers feed large fish under the admiring gaze of the visitors.

Boston Public Library: Boylston St./Dartmouth St. (MBTA: Copley) 9.00–21.00 during the week, 9.00–18.00 on Saturdays. Go and relax in the little patio of the old part, built in 1895. The extension built a few years ago can't compare with the Renaissance inspired building.

Government Center: City Hall Plaza, Court St./ Cambridge St. Very lively square on summer evenings. Extremely interesting architecture, expressing well the power of government; the tiered steps on the square and the connections between it and the City Hall have been well conceived by the team of architects, contrasting with the stern appearance of the building itself.

Cemeteries: Boston is proud of having some really attractive cemeteries where the graves are engraved tombstones scattered over a lawn, the realm of squirrels and sometimes of lovers; the most important are:
Boston Common, in the corner between Tremont St. and Boylston St; *Granery Burial Ground :* Tremont St. Next to Park Church (MBTA: Park). Those great patriots of the War of Independence, John Hancock,

Paul Revere, Robert Paine and Samuel Adams, are buried here.

Christian Science Center: in the triangle between Massachusetts Ave, Huntingdon Ave and Clearway St. Salt Lake City has its Mormons, Boston has Christian Scientists. This religion is prosperous as is indicated by the complex of buildings on the site. They can be visited from 10.00 to 17.00 during the week and from 12.00 to 17.00 on Sundays. The most interesting is the Mapparium which you can walk through. The Christian Science Publishing Society publishes the *Christian Science Monitor*, a review which is widely read and distributed in the United States and whose political and social influence remains perceptible.

The Visual Arts Center: Quincy St. The only building by Le Corbusier in North America (1961).

The Science College: by José Luis Sert (Professor at Harvard) the architect of the Maeght Foundation at Saint-Paul-de-Vence in France and the Miro Foundation in Barcelona. There is the same genius here in the use of natural light, concrete, and sheer mass. Sert also designed the Holyoke Center and Gund Hall (Department of Architecture) on Quincy St. and Cambridge St. This immense glass-house built in 1969 houses Harvard's School of Architecture. There's no real equivalent of such a building in Europe.

A museum not to be missed: **The Fogg Art Museum,** 32 Quincy St, Harvard University, (weekdays 9.00–17.00, Sundays 14.00–17.00). It's a copy of an Italian Renaissance palace. Remarkable collection of drawings. Unfortunately not all are on exhibition; you have to ask to see those by William Blake whose 'surrealism' which anticipated the movement is striking by its inventiveness and technique.

great scenes

Music

Coffee houses where music is played

The Black Rose: State St./Commercial St. Irish bar.

Store-Phoenix Coffee House: 1120 Boylston St. (MBTA: Auditorium). Have you ever seen a café decorated in Egyptian style before? Good folk music as well.

Sword-in-the-Stone: 13 Charles St. (MBTA: Charles St.) Excellent.

In Cambridge:

Cambridge Folk and Tale House: 863 Main St. (MBTA: Central). Jazz, classical and folk: a bit of everything, different programmes every evening.

Nameless Coffee House: 3 Church St. (MBTA: Harvard). Blues, jazz, folk. Open at weekends only.

Backroom at the Idler: 123 Mt Auburn St, Harvard Square. Folk, jazz and blues.

Reflexions: 10 D. Mt Auburn St.

Clubs

The Ark: 835 Beacon St. (Kenmore Square).

Copperfield's: 98 Brookline Ave. Rock groups.

Dummy's: 967 Commonwealth Ave. Full of young people.

Inn Square Men's Bar: 1350 Cambridge St. Excellent.

Katy's: Kenmore Square. The most popular in Boston.

15 Landsdowne St.: called '15 LSD', this club has got a pretty wild decadent side.

1270 Club: 1270 Boylston St. 'Gay' club.

Together: 110 Boylston St.

Jacob's Ladder: 220 Linnway in Revere (a few miles from Boston on route C1). Club with a swimming-pool.

The Rathskeller: 528 Commonwealth Ave. The club where Boston's rock-groups start out. 'Modern Lovers' and other top 'punk rock' groups cut their teeth here. Sometimes also groups from New York's CBGB come and play here.

The Club: 823 Main St. (in Cambridge): punk rock here also but not so good a selection.

Other good places in Cambridge:

Casablanca: 40 Brattle St. (MBTA: Harvard).

Jack's: 952 Massachusetts Ave. (MBTA: Central) – a favourite club of Cambridge students.

King's: 30 Boylston St. (MBTA: Harvard).

Orson Welles Bar: 1001 Massachusetts Ave. (MBTA: Harvard).

Oxford Ale House: 36 Church St. (MBTA: Harvard).

Speakeasy: 22 Norfolk St. (MBTA: Central). Blues, jazz, soul.

Jazz

Pooh's: 464 Commonwealth Ave. ☎ 262.69.11.

Michael's: 52 A Gainsboro St. ☎ 247.72.62.

Jazz Workshop: 733 Boylston St. ☎ 267.13.00 (MBTA: Copley).

Studley's: Beacon St./Kirkland St. (Cambridge).

Classical concerts

The **Boston Symphony Orchestra** plays in the Symphony Hall: 251 Huntington Ave. One of the most famous orchestras in the United States.

In the summer, many free concerts are held in the Commons of Boston and Cambridge. Consult the *'Real Paper'*. Concerts on a boat: **Concert Cruises**, Water Music Inc. 21 Sherman St (Cambridge). ☎ 492.56.67.

Cinema for film buffs

Excellent cinema-going in Boston where some darkened theatres show very interesting programmes.

Cambridge

The Central Square Cinema: Central Square.

The Brattle Cinema: 40 Brattle St.

Loeb Theater: 64 Brattle St. Alternative, classical and avant-garde.

The Orson Welles Cinema: 1001 Massachusetts Ave.

In Boston itself

Back Bay Screening Room: 19 Arlington St.

Charles Play House: 74 Warrenton St.

Paris Cinema: 841 Boylston St.

Exeter: Exeter St. in Newbury. European films, particularly French and Italian.

Avant-garde theatre

Caravan Theater: 1555 Massachusetts Ave. Cambridge. ☎ 868.85.20 (MBTA: Harvard) Closed from June to October.

People's Theater: 1253 Cambridge St. ☎ 354.94.66. (MBTA: Central then bus to Inman Sq.) Mixed-race troupe.

Pocket Mime Theater: Church of the Covenant, 67 Newbury St. ☎ 266.17.70. (MBTA: Arlington) Season from October to April.

The Proposition: 241 Hampshire St. (MBTA: Central then bus to Porter Sq.)

Shopping

New England Music City: Kenmore Sq. Cheap records.

Cheap Thrills: Commonwealth Ave. Records.

Harvard Coop: at the M.I.T. and at Harvard.

Central Surplus: 433 Massachusetts Ave. (Cambridge). Surplus.

Barnes & Noble: Washington St. Large choice of cheap books and records.

Between Essex St. and Bromfield St. along and around Washington St. are to be found Boston's departmental stores, with the biggest Woolworth's in the world (mediocre quality), the fashionable shop, Jordan's and Filene's – whose sales are famous (the goods are practically given away to customers at the end of the sales).

Haymarket: Blackston St. (MBTA: Haymarket) One of the rare open-air markets in the States. It's held every Friday and Saturday. Good atmosphere: the stalls are mainly run by Americans of Italian origin living nearby in North End.

Etcetera

South End: quarter situated between Columbus Ave. and Harrison Ave. A part of Boston which is developing all the time. There are more than 40 nationalities represented by larger or smaller groups. The Black, Spanish, Syrian and Lebanese communities are very influential. Walk round the streets and discover this less well known side of Boston. Have a look round Chester Square (on Massachusetts Ave., between Tremont St. and Shawmut Ave) Union Park (Union Park St. also between Tremont St. and Shawmut Ave.) or Rutland Sq. (on Rutland St. between Columbus Ave. and Tremont St.) where you'll see so many examples of coherent self-contained accommodation of good quality and yet designed for the less well-off social classes. You can't see this kind of thing from the top of the Hancock or Prudential Building: and so explore the street rather than the roofs (set off from Huntington Ave).

Architecture in Cambridge

Cambridge offers a variety of buildings with an international reputation. Even someone who isn't mad about architecture can spend a pleasant afternoon discovering works by Sert, Pei or Aalto. It's a pity not to appreciate architectural quality when it exists: M.I.T. in front of the Student Center: the Chapel of Eero Saarinen. The light outside enters by reflection off a small lake.
Not far away, near the Charles River, the brick-built University Halls of the Finn Alvar Aalto.

Guided tour of the Campus: at 10.00 and 14.00 by students (at the Admission Office, 108 Rogers

Building). You can visit on your own and ask for a map at the Information Center in the Hall of the Rogers Building. At Harvard: ask for a map at the Holyoke Center, south of Harvard Sq. 1352 Massachusetts Ave.

Trips by boat

Three companies based near the Aquarium (MBTA: Aquarium) offer excursions on the Charles River and around the islands:

Boston Harbor Cruises: Long Wharf. ☎ 227.43.20.

Baystate – Spray and Provincetown Steamship Co: Long Wharf. ☎ 723.78.00.

Massachusetts Bay Lines: 44 Atlantic Ave. ☎ 542.80.00.

Around Boston

Boston and New England

With its six States, Connecticut, Rhode Island, Massachusetts, Vermont, New Hampshire and Maine, New England forms a unity of restful countryside, wild in places, where it's very pleasant to camp in the summer. Many Americans will tell you that in the autumn, when the trees turn a bright red, Vermont is the most beautiful State in the Union.
If you have to make a choice, choose **Cape Cod** as a base. This is a very beautiful peninsula with long beaches of white sand. Local coach companies link up the different towns of New England:

Almeida: 10 Park Ave. ☎ 542.72.42. Check also at the Greyhound Station.

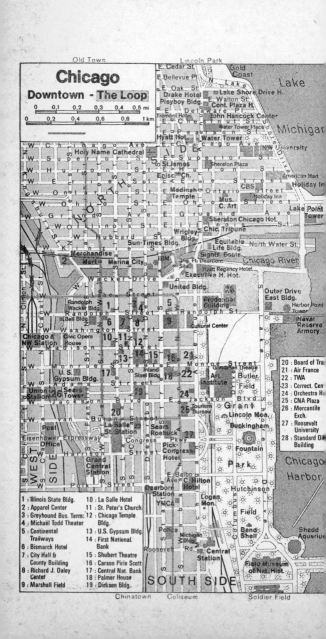

Chicago

Downtown - The Loop

0   0,1   0,2   0,3   0,4   0,5 mi

0   0,2   0,4   0,6   0,8   1 km

1 : Illinois State Bldg.
2 : Apparel Center
3 : Greyhound Bus. Term.
4 : Michael Todd Theater
5 : Continental Trailways
6 : Bismarck Hotel
7 : City Hall & County Building
8 : Richard J. Daley Center
9 : Marshall Field

10 : La Salle Hotel
11 : St. Peter's Church
12 : Chicago Temple Bldg.
13 : U.S. Gypsum Bldg.
14 : First National Bank
15 : Shubert Theatre
16 : Carson Pirie Scott
17 : Central Nat. Bank
18 : Palmer House
19 : Dirksen Bldg.

20 : Board of Tra
21 : Air France
22 : TWA
23 : Correct. Cen
24 : Orchestra H
25 : CNA Plaza
26 : Mercantile Exch.
27 : Roosevelt University
28 : Standard Oil Building

CHICAGO
☎ 312
ILLINOIS

Important stopping point between the East and West Coasts, the second city of the United States doesn't at all correspond to the drab image that people have of it. Chicago is astonishingly beautiful: its sky-scrapers are all superb and sometimes full of the unexpected (Gothic on the sixtieth floor for example), its parks are huge expanses of green, its museums are fabulous and jazz is still very much alive. Chicago has a wide range of different communities: Lithu-anians, Poles, Russians, Germans, Chinese, Italians, and, the largest group of all, the Black community which still largely remains in the very tough ghettos (in the South). The city is also of course a colossus of American and therefore world industry; there are some considerable fortunes and mighty capitalist empires: the Chicago of the legend exists (including the Mafia).

arriving in Chicago

Coach

Greyhound: North Clark St/West Randolph St. ☎ 346.50.00.

Continental Trailways: 20 East Randolph St. ☎ 726.95.00.

Plane

O'Hare International Airport (☎ 686.22.00) and from **Midway** Airport: Continental Air Transport coach service. Transport to the main hotels (in particular the Conrad Hilton which is next to the Y.M.C.A.). It is cheaper to take bus No. 40, the O'Hare express, as far as Jefferson Park and then the train to Downtown.

Train

Amtrak Union Station: Canal/Adams St. ☎ 786.13.33.

don't panic

Finding your way around

No problems: straightforward east-west/north-south layout; State St. separates the east from the west, Madison St. the north from the south; streets are numbered away from these two arteries. 'Downtown' the streets have names. There are a hundred numbers (addresses) for each block (a block covers about 200 metres) and, as for the streets, the numbers begin at State St. and Madison St.

Transport

Public transport: the **Chicago Transit Authority**, immortalized by the pop group of the same name, is a complex system of Underground, elevated train (the '**L**') and bus. Information: ☎ 670.50.00.

Taxis

Yellow Cabs: 1730 S. Indiana St. ☎ 225.74.40.
Flash Cab: ☎ 561.14.44.

Car Hire

Budget: 441 N. State St. ☎ 454.02.27.
Econo: 326 S. Wells St. ☎ 939.60.01.
Drive O'Kar: 645 S. Wabash Ave. ☎ 922.26.48.
Budget: 1025 N. Clark St. ☎ 664.98.00. One of the cheapest.

Refuge

Y.M.C.A.: 826 S. Wasbah Ave. ☎ 922.31.83. Mixed. This Y.M.C.A. merits a few words: it is the biggest, the finest, the most famous in the U.S.A. Since hotels are very expensive in Chicago, and the universities are quite far out from the centre, it is probably your best bet.

Y.M.C.A.: 4251 Irwing Park Rd. ☎ 777.75.00.

Y.M.C.A.: Lawson Center 30 W. Chicago Ave. ☎ 944.62.11.

Y.M.C.A.: 1001 N. Dearborn St. ☎ 332.39.72.

Y.W.C.A.: 37 S. Wabash Ave.

keys to Chicago

General information

Chicago Convention and Tourism Bureau: 332 S. Michigan Ave. ☎ 922.35.30. Twentieth floor. The best place for information.

Civic Center: Clark St/Randolph St. (very near the Greyhound Station). Information bureau in the hall.

Traveller's Aid Society: 327 S. La Salle St. ☎ 435.45.00. Bureaux at the airport also.

The International Visitors' Center of Chicago: 116 S. Michigan Ave. ☎ 332.58.75. For organized groups needing information etc.

Visitor Eventime: the day's events by telephone. ☎ 922.70.00.

Newspapers

The Second City: if you stay more than a fortnight in Chicago, you can buy the '*Chicago Guide Book*' published by this paper.

The Chicago Time Tribune: great for making the time pass on Sundays; good programme page.

Where and **Key:** free in hotels.

Chicago: every other month.

The Chicago Reader: every weekend. Free at the Art Institute school.

Colleges and campuses

As far as these are concerned, Chicago isn't fantastic! The atmosphere isn't the same as at Berkeley or Harvard and the campuses are scattered.

University of Chicago: 55th St. S. to the south, more than 8 kms from 'Downtown'; bus: 4, 28, 55, 59, or train to '59th St.' Station. Around 55th St. S./Woodlawn St.: artist quarter, excellent bookshops, quite a few small restaurants.

Northwestern University: East Chicago St./Lake Shore Drive (two blocks from North Michigan). Worth exploring.

Loyola: Rogers Park; at the back of beyond, 10 kms north of the centre. Take the 'L'.

Roosevelt University: S. Michigan Ave./E. Congress St; a small university.
Behind the Art Institute is the brand-new **School of the Art Institute of Chicago** (SAIC). Advertisement boards. Classical films.

Meeting places

There are two young people's quarters, both situated to the north: **Old Town** (N. Wells St. between 1200 N and 1800 N) and **New Town** (Clark/Broadway, north of Old Town). The first has had its heyday and has been replaced by the second which 'Carnaby Street' type commercialization hasn't yet destroyed. New Town is the student quarter of Chicago, Old Town is mainly full of teenagers and tourists.
On Sundays, base-ball games in **Grant Park,** on the southern side.
Go and get a suntan on the beach in good company at **Oak Street Beach,** three blocks north of J. Hancock. Go round the museums which, in the final analysis, are perhaps what is most interesting in Chicago.

Survival

Counter-culture is very hard to find in what is after all the second city in America!
Try the **Grace Lutheran Church:** 55 W. Belden ☎ 929.35.53.

Loyola University: Sheridan Rd./Devan Ave., near Rogers Park. In theory easier to find amenable people to put you up than in the other universities.

You can sell your blood at the **Interstate Blood Bank:** 2543 W. North St.

Driveaway: *AAACON:* 220 S. State St. ☎ 427.00.86. *Auto Driveaway:* 310 S. Michigan Ave. ☎ 932.36.00.

Legal Aid: Chicago Volunteer Legal Foundation: 19 S. La Salle St. ☎ 332.16.24.

Gay Community Center: ☎ 929 HELP.

Billings Hospital: Near the Museum of Science and Industry. Cheap food if you're broke.

good night

Student accommodation

International House: University of Chicago, 1414 E. 59th St. ☎ 753.22.70. Reserve in advance. Excellent if you have a car since it's far from the centre and from the quarters of Old and New Town.

Vacation Accommodation Center: Midland Hotel, 172 West Adams St. ☎ DE2.12.00.

Inexpensive hotels

In Chicago, the **Y.M.C.A.** is certainly the best solution if you are not staying more than a week and if you are travelling alone.

Warning: these hotels are not in very safe districts.

Astor Hotel: 176 N. Clark St. ☎ 726.06.14.

Allerton Hotel: 701 Michigan Ave. ☎ 787.42.00.

Chicagoan Hotel: 536 N. Rush St. ☎ 787.65.54.

Hotel Wells Grand: 531 N. Wells St. ☎ 337.82.16.

Croydon Hotel: 616 N. Rush St. ☎ 337.67.00.

Tuscany Hotel: 1244 N. Dearborn St. ☎ 787.49.80.

Regency Hotel: 19 E. Ohio St. ☎ 787.49.00.

More to the north:

Acres Motel: 5600 N. Lincoln Ave. ☎ 561.77.77.

Maryland Hotel: 900 N. Rush St. ☎ 664.86.00.

Tropicana Motel: 5440 N. Sheridan Rd. ☎ 275.27.00.

New Town:

Diversey Arms Hotel: 644 Diversey Parkway. ☎ 535.70.10.

More expensive hotels

Ascot House: 1100 S. Michigan Ave. ☎ 922.29.00.

La Salle Motor Lodge: 712 N. La Salle St. ☎ 664.81.00.

Ohio House: 600 N. La Salle St. ☎ 943.60.00.

Travelodge: 125 W. Ohio St. ☎ 467.08.00.

Hotels for well-heeled travellers

(easier to find unfortunately)

Bismarck Hotel: 171 W. Randolph St. ☎ 236.01.23.

Blackstone Hotel: 636 S. Michigan Ave. ☎ 427.43.00.

Conrad Hilton Hotel: 720 S. Michigan Ave. ☎ 427.63.66.

Essex Inn: 800 S. Michigan Ave. ☎ 939.28.00.

Executive House: 71 E. Wacker Drive. ☎ 346.71.00.

Hyatt Regency: 151 E. Wacker Drive. ☎ 565.10.00.

McCormick Inn: 23rd St./Lake Shore Drive. ☎ 791.19.00.

Midland Hotel: 172 W. Adams St. ☎ 332.12.00.

Oxford House Motor Hotel: 225 N. Wabash Ave. ☎ 346.65.85.

Palmer House: 17 E. Monroe St. ☎ 726.75.00.

Pick Congress Hotel: 520 S. Michigan Ave. ☏ 427.38.00.

Ramada Inn: (Downtown) 506 W. Harrison St. ☏ 427.69.69.

---

getting fed

Snack bars and cafeterias

The Y.M.C.A. Cafeteria: 826 S. Wabash Ave, should not be ignored if you're short on money. The same thing goes for the **Museum of National History** cafeteria (large building south of Grand Park). Entry to the museum free on Tuesdays, Thursdays, Saturdays and Sundays. Cafeteria open for lunch; it's in the basement.

Forum Cafeteria: 64 W. Madison St (in Clark St).

Braverman's: 1604 W. Chicago Ave.

Pixley's: Van Buren St/La Salle St.

Pizzeria Due: 609 N. Wabash Ave.

Parkrow Snackshop: E. 11th St near Michigan Ave (a block away from the Civic Center).

Provincial Cocktail Lounge: in the Hotel La Salle: La Salle St/Madison St. Inexpensive sandwiches at lunchtime.

Restaurants

There are more than 6,000 restaurants in Chicago. You can explore the whole gastronomic world in one quarter of this city. The cheapest and nicest restaurants are in Old Town and New Town as well as on North Broadway which is north of W. Diversey Parkway (50 blocks north of the Loop).

American

Eli's: 215 E. Chicago Ave. Good steaks, piano at the bar. Evenings.

Kinzie Steak House: 33 W. Kinzie St. Beef Wellington a speciality.

That Steak Joynt: 1610 N. Wells St. 1890s atmosphere and unbeatable steaks. Piano.

Jacques Garden: 900 N. Michigan Ave. Excellent for brunch on Sundays.

The Berghoff: 17 W. Adams St. Lots of good food washed down with Berghoff beer.

Magic Pan: 63 E. Walton Place. One of the restaurants in the large chain of American creperies.

The Raleigh Room: Michigan Ave/Walton St (in the Drake Hotel). Good food and a beautiful view over Lake Michigan.

The Big Apple and Pancake House: 1260 Deerfield Drive, Highland Park.

French

Gare St Lazare: 858 W. Armitage St (near Halstead St).

La Poele D'Or: 1121 S. Arlington Drive. Good pancakes and omelettes.

Greek

Diana's: 1305 Halstead St. Good place to eat.

Family House: 2421 W. Laurance St. With Louis Katsaros, frozen fish is unheard of, everything is fresh!

Italian

Bruna's: 2424 S. Oakley St. Not just pasta.

Mategrano's: 132 W. Taylor St.

Pizzeria Uno: 29 E. Ohio St. Really good pizzas.

English

Atlantic Fish and Chip Restaurant: 7115 W. Grand Ave. Family atmosphere.

Japanese

Matsuya: 3469 N. Clark St.

Cantonese

Wing Yee's: 2556 N. Clark St.

Chinese

Chump Chinese Food: 507 W. Madison St, Oak Park. Traditional Chinese decor.

Korean

Chosun OK Steak House: 4200 N. Lincoln St. Fish.

Thai

Bangkok: 3525 N. Halstead St. Full of surprises.

Jewish

The Bagel: 3000 W. Devon St. Good family cooking.

Lithuanian

Ruta: 6812 S. Western St. Pleasant surprises.

Swedish

Suea: 5236 N. Clark St.

Hungarian
Hungarian Delight: 3510 W. Irvin Park.

Rumanian
Little Bucharest: 3001 N. Ash St. At the back of a bar, but don't worry – it's very pleasant and quite cheap.

Polish
Patria: 3030 N. Central St.

Czech
Ridgeland Restaurant: 6408 Cormack St/Berwin St. Bohemian atmosphere.

Mexican
A Choza: 7630 N. Paulin St. Really spicy!

---

things that everyone goes to see and that you shouldn't miss

The Art Institute: Michigan Ave/Adams St (Monday, Tuesday, Wednesday, Friday 11.00–16.30, Thursday (free) 10.30–20.00; Saturday 10.00–17.00, Sunday 12.00–17.00. Absolutely marvellous! Without any doubt the finest museum in the United States. The Gauguins and Van Goghs on their own are worth the visit. But there are other things to see: portraits by Picasso, landscapes by Corot, Dalis and Magrittes ... In summer concerts are given on the patio.

Field Museum of Natural History: Roosevelt Rd/ Lakeshore Drive. (Every day 9.00–16.00 in summer, 9.00–17.00 the rest of the year. Open until 21.00 on Fridays (free). Student reductions.) Magnificent stuffed bisons and little dinosaurs devouring each other in perfectly reconstructed settings.

Museum of Science and Industry: 57th St/S. Lakeshore Drive (from the Loop, take a bus going south on Michigan Ave and reckon on at least a 30-minute journey, otherwise take a train from Illinois Central to 59th St). During the week, in summer 9.30–16.00, Sundays 9.30–17.30, the rest of the year 9.30–16.00 and 10.00–16.00. Above all, don't miss the Mathematics Room – Room 15 on the ground floor to the right – with its shapes which plunge into soapy water to show different angles and its super-distorting mirror which makes you look even stranger than you thought you were.

John Hancock Center: 875 N. Michigan Ave. Observation platform open from 9.00 to midnight.

The John Hancock is a surprisingly beautiful sky-scraper: the view from the top is very impressive at night, a place to go and dream ... Ultra-rapid lift: 94 floors in 37 seconds! Half of the building consists of apartments.

Sears Tower: Adams St/Jackson St. From 9.00 to midnight. The tallest skyscraper in Chicago, 103 floors, should also be visited: it is much less original than the Hancock, but the fright you get when you look out of the windows of the top floor has no equivalent. Go up at night – unforgettable. You can visit the offices of the Sears Company during the week at 9.45, 10.45 and 13.45.

Civic Center: Randolph St/Clark St. Another fine building, famous for the giant sculpture by Picasso in the Plaza. (Notice the small-scale model next to it, specially made for the blind.)

Chicago Festival: On the Navy Pier, 600 E. Grand Ave. Annually at the beginning of August. Twelve hours of music over ten days, to suit all tastes.

---

things that everyone doesn't go to see and which deserve to be seen

---

Chicago Police Department: 1121 S. State St. ☎ 744.55.73. In the chemistry lab. you can see a joint 50 cms long and examples of every possible kind of drug ... hunting trophies of the local police. Group visits only, telephone two weeks in advance. Entry free (9.30–15.30).

Adler Planetarium: 1300 S. Lake Shore Drive, on the lake near the Natural History Museum (Field Museum). In summer: Monday to Thursday 9.30–16.30, Friday 9.30–21.00. The Sky Show isn't bad.

Shedd Aquarium: 1200 S. Lake Shore Drive between the Field Museum and the Planetarium (9.00–17.00. Free on Fridays and open until 21.00). Thousands of fish in what is considered to be the biggest aquarium in the world.

Lincoln Park: 2200 N. Lincoln Park on the lake, just north of Old Town, the biggest and most visited park in Chicago. Go there at the weekend to see people.

Architecture: Chicago is the richest city in twentieth century architecture in the U.S.A.; every skyscraper is interesting. There's a very good book on the subject (maps, photos of each building): *Chicago's Famous Buildings,* Arthur Siegel, University of Chicago Press. If you have a car, you can see dozens of major works by Frank Lloyd Wright.

Chicago University: 1212 E. 59th St. (south of the Loop). Amongst the famous buildings, Eero Saarinen's Law School and Wright's Robie House particularly deserve to be seen (5757 S. Woodlawn: 1200 E; visit by appointment ☎ 753.44.29).

The Oriental Institute: 1155 E. 58th St. ☎ 753.24.74. By train as far as 59th St. (from Tuesday to Saturday 10.00–16.00, Sunday 12.00–16.00, entry free.) A very rare collection of beautiful things coming from Egypt, Nubia, Turkey, Iran and Palestine, Assyrian bas-reliefs etc.

'Ethnic' museums: There are five museums in Chicago devoted to five different ethnic groups which are more or less widely represented in the city: Poles, Ukrainians, Lithuanians, Chinese and Africans. If you are interested in the culture of these groups, you'll find a tour of the following places fascinating:

Polish Museum of America: 984 N. Milwaukee (Every day 13.00–16.00). Take a No. 56 bus at the Madison/Michigan intersection.

Ukrainian National Museum: 2453 W. Chicago Ave. (Sundays 12.00–15.00. Entry free.) No. 66 bus from 234 E. Chicago Ave.

Balzekas Museum of Lithuanian Culture: 4012 Archer Ave. ☎ 847.24.41. No. 62 bus from the Loop (13.00–17.00).

Ling Long Museum: 2238 S. Wentworth Ave. The whole history of China from 4000 B.C. to 1900 A.D. Entry free. Take the Lake-Dan Ryan Rapid Transit as far as Cermak-Chinatown. It's one block West then one block South of the Station.

Dusable Museum of African American History: 740 E. 56th Place. ☎ 947.06.00. (Tuesday to Friday 10.00–16.30, weekend 13.00–17.00. Half-price for students.) Take the Dan Ryan Line as far as Garfield Station, then a No. 55 bus going east, get off at Cottage Grove Ave.

Museum of Contemporary Art: 237 E. Ontario St. (Tuesday to Saturday 10.00–17.00, Thursday 10.00–18.00, Sunday 12.00 –17.00.) Half price for students. A very reasonable museum.

And since we're talking of museums, here's an unusual one:

International Museum of Surgical Science and Hall of Fame: 1524 N. Lake Shore Drive. ☎ 642.36.32. Free entry. (Every day except Monday 10.00–16.00.) Make an appointment. The building is an exact copy of the Petit Trianon at Versailles. You'll find inside the history of brain operations from the Incas to the latest discoveries. Take No. 151 bus Sheridan Rd or No. 153 Wilson.

On Ellis St. (between 56th and 57th Street, near the University) you'll find Henry Moore's sculpture **'Nuclear Energy'**. It recalls that it was here that the team of scientists led by Enrico Fermi set off the first controlled nuclear chain reaction on December 2 1942. We know the rest of the story only too well . . .

Archicenter: 310 S. Michigan Ave. (Monday to Saturday 9.00–17.00) Exhibition on Chicago's architecture. Organized visits.

Federal Metro Correctional Center: Van Buren/Clark St. A rather strange skyscraper: prison.

Chicago Sun Times and **Chicago Daily News:** 401 N. Wabash Ave. ☎ 321.20.32. You can visit free the offices of two big dailies. Reserve in advance.

Chicago Tribune: 441 N. Michigan Ave. ☎ 222.39.93. Reserve also.

great scenes

Music

The **Chicago Symphony Orchestra** plays in the summer at the Ravina Pavilion: Highland Park (☎ 782.96.96); in the winter at the Orchestra Hall: 216 S. Michigan Ave (☎ 427.77.11).

Folk

Amazing Grace: 845 Chicago at Evanston ☎ 328.24.89.

Barbarossa: 1117 N. Dearborn ☎ 751.06.24.

Earl of Old Town: 1615 N. Wells ☎ 642.52.06.

Northside Auditorium Bar: 3720 Clark ☎ 327.12.77.

Orphans: 2462 N. Lincoln ☎ 929.26.77.

Somebody Else's Troubles: 2470 N. Lincoln ☎ 953.06.60.

Quiet Knight: 953 W. Belmont ☎ 348.71.00.

Jazz

Backroom: 1007 Rush St.

Jazz Shocase: 901 N. Rush St.

Orphans: 2462 N. Lincoln ☎ 929.26.77.

Blues

Elsewhere on Lincoln: 2960 N. Lincoln ☎ 929.80.00.

Kingston Mines: 2354 N. Lincoln ☎ 525.68.60.

Maxwell Street Market: 14th/Halstead.

Wise Fools Pub: 2270 N. Lincoln ☏ 929.15.10. Get there before 21.00 to get a seat.

Stingray Lounge: 4905 W. Madison ☏ 921.02.42.

Clubs

Generally speaking, most clubs are in Old Town, on N. Wells St. between numbers 1200 and 1550; the expensive fashionable clubs are in Rush St, north of the Loop. The best blues and soul-music clubs are in the southern part of Chicago.

Otto's: 2024 N. Halstead ☏ 528.22.30.

Papa's III: 2432 N. Lincoln ☏ 528.42.60. 16.00–02.00.

Ratso's: 2464 N. Lincoln ☏ 935.15.05.

Vibes: 2251 N. Lincoln ☏ 750.73.60.

Cafe Pergolesi: 3404 N. Halstead.

Geja's: 1248 N. Wells in Old Town.

John Barleycorn Memorial Pub: 658 W. Belden St. ☏ Di8.88.99.

Le Pub: 1936 N. Clark. Good club where you can enjoy a fondue (rather expensive though).

Kingston Mines Company Store: 2356 N. Lincoln. Folk music on Fridays, interesting decor. Theatre, restaurant and folk-music club at the same time.

Ivanhoe: 3000 N. Clark. Rather expensive.

No-Exit Coffee House: 7001 N. Glenwood (in the most northern part of Chicago). Folk music.

The Earl of Old Town: 1615 N. Wells. Folk.

The Store: 1036 N. State. Rock.

The Quiet Knight: 943 W. Belmont. (Closed on Mondays. Entry cheaper on Wednesdays and Thursdays.) Folk and blues.

Soul

The Apartment: 504 E. 75th St.

Barbara's Peppermint Lounge: 3219 W. Harrison St.

Burning Spear: 5523 S. State St.

Mark III: 1615 E. 87th St.

Pepper's: 1321 S. Michigan Ave.

Herman Robert's 500 Room: 33 E. 63rd St.

To find out which singers are appearing in these clubs, read Friday's '*Weekender*' in the *Chicago Sun-Times*. Beware: in Chicago it is prohibited to serve alcoholic drink to minors and the law is strictly respected by the pubs and clubs; always have identity card or passport on you.

Cinemas for film buffs

The Biograph: 2433 N. Lincoln.

McClurg Court: 330 East Ohio St.

Esquire Theater: 100 E. Oak St. (two blocks north of J. Hancock).

Clark Theater: 11 N. Clark St.

Playboy Theater: 1204 N. Dearborn (Friday and Saturday from midnight to dawn).

Marina City Cinemas: in the basement of the famous Marina (300 N. State St). 3 small cinemas (if you're clever you can see the 3 films for the price of one).

Museum of Contemporary Art: 237 E. Ontario St. Film co-op, films made by students.

Art Institute Film Center: behind the Art Institute, Columbus St/Jackson Bld.

Theatres

Chicago City Theater: 333 W. Wisconsin St.

Jane Addams Theater of Hull House: 3179 N. Broadway.

Body Politic: 2261 N. Lincoln Ave. ☎ 871.30.00.

Shopping

Flea Market: Maxwell Street Market, 1300 S. Halstead St. Sundays.

Records at incredible prices

Discount Records: 201 N. La Salle St.

D. and S. Records: 3128 W. Ermitage.

Rose Records: 214 S. Wabash Ave – 765 W. Madison St. The biggest record shop in the world.

Lyon-Healy: 243 S. Wabash Ave. The widest imaginable choice of music scores, if you are looking for something rare (rock, pop, classical etc.).

Books

Kroch's and Brentano's: 29 S. Wabash Ave. ☎ 332.75.00. The biggest bookshop in the world. All the American paperbacks.

A–1 Book Store: 1112 N. State St. Second-hand books.

Richard and Barnes: 1628 N. Wells St. Second-hand books.

Two bookshops with a good selection of books on the cinema:

Barbara Book Store: 434 N. Wells. Open every day.

Bob's News Emporium: 51st St at Lake Park.

The Magnificent Mile

The richest avenue in the world, the **'Magnificent Mile'** is in the part of North Michigan Ave. between Chicago River and Delaware St. There's more money here than anywhere else on the globe; go window shopping.

Etcetera

La Boîte à musique: 835 N. Michigan Ave. Over 500 musical boxes, ranging from two dollars to two thousand.

Ripley's Believe It or Not Museum: 1500 N. Wells St. From mid-day to midnight (in Old Town). The kind of museum which has no equivalent in Europe: a museum of horror, the unusual, the strange and the incredible.

Marina City: in the morning around 7.00–8.00 listen to the squealing of the tyres of cars going down the spiral of the 17 floors of the car park of the very famous towers of Marina City (300 N. State St).

Marshall Field and Co.: Randolph St/State St. Don't miss it! A departmental store with amazing decor.

Free Panorama of Chicago: find a way of getting up to one of the top floors of the Civic Center: Randolph St/Dearborn St. Best time between 12.00 and 13.00.

A motorway going through a post-office? This is practically what you can see at Chicago Post Office: Congress Canal, two blocks from the Sears Building.

Beaches on the Michigan: three beaches for getting away from the stifling heat of a summer's day: Oak St. Beach (1000 N. Lake Shore Drive); North St. Beach (1600 N. Lake Shore Drive) and Fullerton Beach (2400 North Beach St.). Take bus no. 51 or 53.

Street art

'Sound Sculpture': 200 E. Randolph St (in the Standard Oil Building). A musical sculpture by Bertoia.

'Flamingo': by Calder: at the Chicago Federal Center Plaza, Adams/Dearborn St.

'Universe' by Calder: at Sears Tower, 280 S. Wacker St.

'Four Seasons' by Chagall: at First National Plaza, Monroe/Dearborn St.

'Bat Column': at Social Security Center, 600 W. Madison St.

There is also a sculpture of a woman by Picasso: Daley Plaza, Dearborn/Washington St.

Around Chicago

Ravina Festival: Highland Park. ☎ 782.96.96. An exceptional programme of concerts and ballets throughout the summer.

Marriott's Great America: the large amusement park 45 miles north of Chicago, at Gurnee. Take Interstate 94 from Chicago then route 132 (Grand Ave.). Open only at weekends in spring and autumn. Open every day in summer until Labor Day. Roller Coaster with 2 loops!

Rocky Mountain N.P. Cheyenne

Denver
Downtown

0   0,3 mi
0   500 m

1 Catholic Cathedral
2 Wellington Hotel
3 Petroleum Club Bldg
4 Harris Hotel
5 Civic Center Annex
6 Brown Palace Hotel
7 Brown Palace West
8 Security Life Bldg.
9 Paramount Theatre
10 Denver Theatre
11 Masonic Temple
12 Western Savings Ass
13 Albany Hotel

Union Station
Wynkoop St.
Wazee St.
Blake St.
Market St.
Larimer St.
Lawrence St.
Arapahoe
Curtis
Champa
Stout
California
Welton
Glenarm
Tremont

Federal Office Building
Federal Courthouse
Post Office
New Customs House
Tower Merchandise Mart Building
Col. Nat. Bank
Federal Reserve Bank
Larimer Square
Brooks Tower
Telephone Building
City Auditorium
Penny Dept. Store
Police Bldg.
Currigan Convention Hall
Chamber of Commerce
Hospitality Center
YWCA
Hilton Hotel
U. N Square
Bus Center
YMCA
Denham Theatre
Lincoln Towers
Cosmopolitan Hotel Tower
National Bank Center
Capitol Life Bldg.
International House
Texas Bldg
Capitol Annex
State Service Bldg.
Vorhees Memorial

Sherman
Grant
Logan
Lincoln
Broadway

East 20th Ave
East 19th Ave
East 18th Ave
East 17th Ave
East 16th Ave

Heli-Stop
Speer
California
Welton
Glenarm
Tremont
Court
Cleveland Pl

West Colfax Avenue
Galapago
Fox
Elati
Delaware
Cherokee
Bannock
Acoma

U.S. Mint
City & County Bldg
Municipal Bldg
Civic Center
Greek Th.
Art Museum
Public Library
Western Farm

Colorado State Capitol
State Office Building
State Historical Museum
Chapp House Museu

E Colfax Ave
East 14th Ave
East 13th Ave

West Santa Fe Drive
Inca
Cherry Creek Blvd
West 13th Ave
West 12th Ave
West 11th Ave

Broadway
East 12th Ave
East 11th Ave

Colorado Springs

Kartographie Huber & Oberländer, Münch

DENVER

☎ 303
COLORADO

At the foot of the Rocky Mountains, at an altitude of 1600m (whence its nickname of 'Mile High City') the city of Denver attracts the visitor because of its climate, its parks, its open city planning, and its museums devoted to the history of the Far West and Colorado whose capital it is. Denver is also the centre of a region devoted to the joys of nature: skiing in the resorts of Aspen and Vail, outings in the big mountain parks, down-river runs on rubber rafts, horse-riding.

arriving in Denver

Coach

Greyhound and Continental Trailways: 1055 19th St between Curtis and Arapahoe St. ☎ 623.61.11 (Greyhound); 534.22.91 (Trailways).

Plane

From **Stapleton International Airport** to Downtown: bus RDT 64 or else a limousine to the big hotels.

Train
Amtrak: 17th Wynkoop St. ☎ 534.23.71.

don't panic

Finding your way around

All the avenues go in an east–west direction, and the streets in a north–south direction except for Downtown where they go south–east and north–west. Broadway is the north–south avenue which separates east from west. Colfax is a main east–west artery.

Transport

Buses: the town buses, **RTD**, are very efficient. You can get the routes from the Visitor Center. To get a general view of the city centre, obtain a Tourist ride pass which allows you to travel between the most important points from 10.00 hrs to 16.00 hrs. The **DART** (Downtown Area Roundabout) follows a shorter circuit and its fares are cheaper than other buses.
Information RTD and DART, Tel: 778.60.00.

Plane: to go the Aspen Winter Sports Station (Chamonix of Colorado) in 40 minutes, use Aspen Airways. ☎ 398.37.44.

Taxis

Yellow cab: ☎ 892.12.12.
Zone cab: ☎ 861.23.23.
Ritz cab: ☎ 534.52.55.

Car hire

Continental et Aero rent-a-car: 1830 Broadway St. ☎ 861.08.03.

Compacts only: 3970 Monaco Parkway (near the airport) ☎ 388.09.48. 4817 S. Broadway St. ☎ 789. 93.00.

Payless car rental: Sheraton Airport, 3535 Quebec St. ☎ 399.22.01.

Refuge

Central Y.M.C.A.: 25 E. 16th Ave. ☎ 861.83.00. Not the best address!

A.Y.H.: 1579 Franklin St, open from 17.00 hrs. ☎ 832.99.96. Excellent place to stay.

keys to Denver

General information

Denver Convention and Visitors' Bureau: 80 14th St. ☎ 892.15.05

Travellers Aid Society: Union Station. ☎ 861. 79.11 or 832.81.94.

International Hospitality Center: 980 Grant Ave, in the Colburn Hotel. ☎ 832.42.34, intended mainly for a non-student clientele.

If you want to know the weather forecast: ☎ 639. 15.15. To know the time ☎ 639.13.11.

Newspapers and magazines

There are two dailies in Denver: the **Denver Post** and the **Rocky Mountain News**.
Look in the Sunday supplements.

Where free in hotels. The week's programmes and the main restaurants.

Colorado Visitor Review. Small monthly brochure distributed in hotels.

Colleges and campuses

Metropolitan State College: 710 W. Colfax Ave (5 blocks from the Visitors' Bureau).

University of Colorado: there is a branch Downtown 14th St/Arapahoe St (cafeteria, notice-board).

University of Denver: S. University Bld/E. Evans Ave, 8 kms south of Downtown. Take bus No. 8. Lodging possible.

Boulder: take a bus at Denver Bus Center (1 hr. journey). This is the student town.

Meeting places

Larimer Square and **City Park** (take bus No. 20 on 17th St.) are the two most frequented meeting-places: the first gets busy at night, the second should be visited by day.

Surviving

The United Way: Help. ☎ 837.99.99. Colfax Ave.

Legal Aid: ☎ 837.13.13. Broadway Ave.

Ride Line: (fee-paying) Boulder Youth Hostel. ☎ 442.05.22 and Denver Youth Hostel: ☎ 449.66.70 (much further from the centre).

Ride Line: (free) ☎ 893.KBP1. (Rock radio station).

Denver General Hospital: ☎ 893.60.00.

good night

Cheap hotels

Harris Hotel: 1544 Cleveland Place. ☎ 825.63.41.

New Broadway Hotel: 1940 Broadway. ☎ 861.41.63.

Newhouse Hotel: 1470 Grant St (just behind the Capitol) ☎ 861.24.15.

West Hotel: 1337 California St. ☎ 825.22.71.

Family Home: 13280 E. Colfax (far from Downtown) ☎ 344.91.50.

Paragon Motel: 6030 E. Colfax. ☎ 320.93.29.

Rocky Mountain Motel: 6001 W. Colfax. ☎ 237.27.46.

West Court Apartment Hotel: 1415 Glenarm (on the corner of 14th St). Victorian decor and original architecture. ☎ 629.05.03.

More expensive hotels:

Hotel Cory: 1566 Broadway. ☎ 861.82.11.

Denver Travelodge: 1–258 Speer Bld. ☎ 458.54.54.

getting fed

Cafeteria

The one in **Denver Art Museum** (Civic Center) isn't bad at all but relatively expensive.

Sandwiches, coffee houses

Freeweavers Coffee House: 524 E. 17th St. Poetry, paintings.

The Country Sandwich Shop: 1448 Market St.

Muddy Waters of the Platte: 2557 15th St.

Sam's Coffee House: California/16th St.

Maxine's Place: 823 14th St (near Start St.).

Small cheap restaurants

Little Cheese Café: 333 W. Colfax Ave.

New Deli: 13th St (between Vire and Race St).

Around Denver University

Brass Tack: 1700 E. Evans Ave. (Mexican cooking.)

Dolcaminos: 2076 South University Bld.

Fagan's: 1135 E. Evans Ave.

Tico: 1744 E. Evans Ave. (Mexican cooking).

Apple Tree Shanty: E. Colfax Ave. Warm atmosphere.

Restaurants

Casa Bonita: 6715 W. Colfax Ave. (JCRS Shopping Center, near Pierce St, ten minutes from Downtown). A pretty extraordinary Mexican restaurant, music, death dives, puppets ...

Charlie Brown's: Restaurant and Lounge in the Colburn Hotel, 980 Grant St. Cantonese cuisine at reasonable prices.

The Old Spaghetti Factory: 1215 18th St. Very impressive decor (wagon).

The Broker: 17th/Champa. Meeting-place for businessmen at lunch time and the in-crowd in the evening. Free shrimp salad.

Golden Ox: 3130 E. Colfax. Famous for its grilled steaks. 'Old West' atmosphere.

In Larimer Square, bars and restaurants like:

Cafe Promenade, Josephine, The Magic Pan, The Bratskeller with cafe terrace atmosphere.

---

things that everyone goes to see and that you shouldn't miss

Museums

The Denver Art Museum: 100 W. 14th Ave/ Parkway. (Tuesday–Saturday 9.00–17.00; Wednesday 9.00–21.00; Sunday 13.00–17.00), entry free, cafeteria. A museum full of interesting things (Indian art, pre-Columbian art, Far Eastern art). You can walk round it for hours. If you haven't got much time, don't miss the room devoted to the Indian tribes of North Oregon and in particular the exhibition of the different ways of carrying babies on the back.

Colorado State Historical Museum: 200 14th Ave (south of the Capitol). (Monday–Saturday 9.00–16.30; Sunday and holidays 12.00–16.30), entry free. The two models of Denver (one corresponding to Downtown today, the other a reconstruction of the city in 1880) on the ground floor are worth the trip on their own. The diaporamas on the lives of the Indians, the Cowboys and the gold prospectors are real marvels. Exhibition of flora and fauna, and minerals and fossils.

State Capitol: E. Colfax Ave/14th Ave (Monday–Friday, 9.00–15.30), free. A copy of the Capitol in Washington D.C.; interesting for the view it affords from the summit as well as its gold-covered dome.

Larimer Square: 1400 Block Larimer St (between 15th St and 13th St). A block of old Victorian houses which have been repaired and trimmed into tourist restaurants and shops selling gadgets and leather goods. A bit artificial but still worth seeing. Don't forget the bicycle shop, 'Life Cycle'.

Forney Transportation Museum: 1416 Platte St. (9.00–17.00 every day, 11.00–17.30 on Sunday). A bit of everything to do with locomotion.

Denver Botanic Gardens: 1005 York St. (9.00–16.45 every day), free. Bus No. 13. Worth visiting as much for the daisies and other flowers as for the architecture of the greenhouse.

great scenes

Music

There are many clubs in Glendale on Colorado Bld. and Virginia St., e.g. **Bogart's.**

Rock

Mr Lucky's: 555 S. Cherry. ☎ 321.17.50.

Piccadilly: 17th/Broadway. ☎ 839.56.66. You can eat here.

Jazz

Basin Street: Larimer Square. ☎ 573.50.30.

Global Village: 76 S. Pennsylvania. ☎ 778.72.14 (every day except Sunday and Monday).

Greenstreets: 916 15th St. ☎ 255.13.92 (every evening).

Zeno's: 1421 Larimer Square. ☎ 573.50.30.

B.B.C.: 128 Grant St.

Folk

Denver Folklore Center: 608 E. 17th Ave. ☎ 831.70.15.

Clubs

The Broadway: 1260 Broadway. Pleasant place, disco, restaurant, small cinema.

Bentley's: 1128 Grant St. (near 10th Ave. on Capitol Hill). Restaurant and jazz club, sophisticated setting.

The Dove: 2797 S. Parker Road.

Yellow Pages: 1346 South St (corner of 14th St.). Teenagers' disco in the heart of Downtown. Lit-up floor, closes at midnight.

Top Cat: 8800 Federal Bld. Rock, soul, jazz. Monday to Saturday.

N.B. If you have a car, go to **Glendale** the part of Denver where the entertainment is (night-clubs, disco). At the cross-roads of S. Colorado Bld and E. Virginia Ave. Dress up.

Cinema for film buffs

The Flick: Larimer Square/1460 Larimer. ☎ 629. 05.55.

Shopping

Lots of shops on 16th St.

Fred Mueller: Market St/15th. All the gear of the complete cowboy. Bargain sales of jeans.

Denver Book Barter: 919 E. Colfax. ☎ 831.97.68. Practically complete collection of *National Geographics* at derisory prices.

Colorado Comics: 41 E. Colfax, an address for the real fanatic.

Etcetera

Denver Bartending School: 1040 Colfax (on the corner of Downing). A barman's school where you can act as a guinea-pig.

Gart Bros Building: Broadway/U St. Remarkable building dating from the 1920s: it's a copy of a sixteenth-century French house!

Kohlberg's: 1720 Champa St. ☎ 825.45.78. Perhaps a bit expensive but genuine turquoises and jewellery. There are a lot of illicit street vendors so beware of imitation goods.

Mile High Kennel Club: Colorado Bld/E. 62nd Ave. Greyhound races every evening (the dogs, not the buses). You must be over 18.

around Denver

Adventure Bound Inc. organizes trips down river on rubber rafts. Groups of 10 to 15 people. Adventure guaranteed! Book in advance. 6179 S. Adams Drive, Littleton 80121, Colorado. ☎ (303) 771.37.52.

The Mountain Men: 11100 E. Dartmouth, suite 219, Denver 80232. ☎ (303) 750.00.90. Outings and excursions off the beaten path. Send for timetables and prices.

There is a youth hostel at Boulder: 1107 12th St.

High Country Trails: horse rides to Boulder. You can make a trek of several days through absolutely fantastic country (food and accommodation included): 2840 Lakeridge Trail in Boulder. ☎ (303) 444.60.34.

Mount Evans: The highest road in the United States (14,260 feet or 4,300 metres) leads to the top of Mount Evans which gives a very spectacular view over the Rocky Mountains. On a clear day you can see over the Great Plains of the East for hundreds of kilometres. To get there, take U.S. 40 to El Pancho, then S.R. 70 to Bergen Park, S.R. 103 to Echo Lake and finally the S.R. 5 to the top. Return by the S.R. 6 from Idaho Springs.

Estes Park: Beautiful mountain scenery in the Rocky Mountain National Park. Ski-lift to the top of Prospect Mountain (9.00–17.00 hrs from mid-May to mid-September). Estes Park Youth Hostel: Box 1260. 80517.

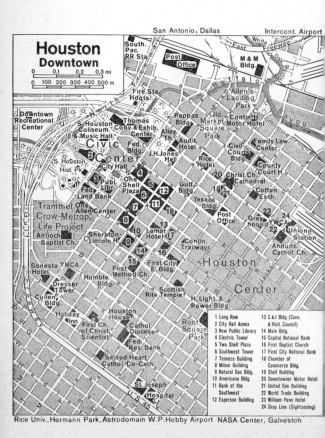

Houston Downtown

1 Long Row
2 City Hall Annex
3 New Public Library
4 Electric Tower
5 Two Shell Plaza
6 Southwest Tower
7 Tenneco Building
8 Milam Building
9 Natural Gas Bldg.
10 Americana Bldg.
11 Bank of the Southwest
12 Esperson Building
13 C & I Bldg. (Conv. & Visit. Council)
14 Main Bldg.
15 Capital National Bank
16 First Baptist Church
17 First City National Bank
18 Chamber of Commerce Bldg.
19 Shell Building
20 Downtowner Motor Hotel
21 United Gas Building
22 World Trade Building
23 William Penn Hotel
24 Gray Line (Sightseeing)

HOUSTON

📞 713
TEXAS

Houston: a fast-developing city, oil capital of the United States, the sixth most densely populated city in the country. It's Texas without cowboys: the astronauts have taken their place. So when you are going through Texas, stop off here to visit the N.A.S.A. centre.

arriving in Houston

Coach
Greyhound: 1410 Texas Ave. ☎ 222.11.61.
Trailways: 1116 McKinney and San Jacinto St. ☎ 759.65.00.

Plane
International Airport, 30 kms north of Downtown – bus.

Train
Amtrak: 902 Washington Ave. ☎ 224.15.77.

don't panic

Finding your way around

The city occupies several square kilometres. The streets and the avenues aren't numbered: all of them have a name. Downtown hinges around Main Street (north–east–south–west) and Texas Avenue (north–west–south–east). Ask for the Exxon map which is pretty clear.

Transport

It's practically essential to have a car in Houston. Public transport (buses), as in Los Angeles, is catastrophic!

Taxi

Yellow cabs: ☎ 236.11.11.

Car hire

American International: 801 Calhoun. ☎ 453.72.57.

Budget: 1925 Milan. ☎ 449.01.45.

Dollar: 3202 Fannin. ☎ 499.01.61.

National Rent-a-Car: ☎ 443.88.50.

Avis: ☎ 659.65.37.

Refuge

All the Y.M.C.A.s in Houston are for men only.

Y.M.C.A. Downtown branch: 1600 Louisiana St. ☎ 224.95.01.

Y.M.C.A. East End branch: 7903 South Loop East. ☎ 643.43.96.

Y.M.C.A. South Central branch: 3531 Wheeler Ave. ☎ 748.54.05.

Y.M.C.A.: 1521 Texas Ave. (Next door to the Greyhound Station.)

keys to Houston

General information

Greater Houston Convention and Visitors' Council: 1522 Main St. ☎ 648.42.00.

Institute of International Education: IA World Trade Center – 1520 Texas Ave (next door to the Greyhound Station). Very pleasant, publishes a list of current exhibitions and cultural activities.

Newspapers and magazines

Houston Chronicle: the local rag. Can be useful for programmes.

Houston Post: another daily.

Colleges and campuses

University of Houston: Calhoun Gulf Freeway. South-east of Downtown. Easy to meet friendly people. Take the Holman bus on Main St and Elgin.

Rice University: Main St/University Bld. South-west of the city-centre. This campus is smaller than the preceding one, and there aren't many people in summer. Take No. 10 bus.

Meeting places

Apart from the campuses: **Hermann Park** (opposite Rice University) and its open-air theatre. **Charles H. Milby Park** (south-east of the city-centre near Freeway Gate and Galveton Road). See also the bars mentioned below.

good night

Very few cheap hotels in Houston. The Y.M.C.A.s (or Y.W.C.A.s) are just as good.

Alamo Plaza Motor Hotel: 4343 Old Spanish Trail (south of McGregor Park). ☎ 747.69.00.

Auditorium Hotel: 761 Texas Ave.

Mill Hotel: 904 Texas Ave. ☎ 223.01.33.

Ramada Inn: 2121 Allen Parkway (west of Downtown).

Monte Hotel: Franklin St/Hamilton St. Take the 'Docks' bus.

Ben Milam: Texas Ave. Not expensive, and opposite the Greyhound Station (dangerous quarter at night).

getting fed

Downtown

The normal snacks, Burger Kings pretty well everywhere. Cafeterias in the Main St department stores.

Fried Chicken: Texas Ave/Travis St.

Lindsey's Cafe: 1314 Prairie St. Inexpensive.

Lou's Bar-B-Q: 307 San Jacinto.

The Montrose Quarter

A lively and inexpensive area between Downtown and Rice University: more than a score of restaurants on Westheimer Rd serving Mexican, Italian, Spanish, Lebanese, French, etc. cuisine.

Alfred's: 2408 Rice Bld. Good food.

Benihama: 1318 Louisiana St. Japanese cuisine. Adequate decor.

Bertha's Genuine: 1710 McKinney. Mexican food.

The Bowery: 500 Louisiana St. Good atmosphere. New York food.

Timmy Chan Restaurant: 2606 Fannin St. Speciality: Polynesian chicken.

Fat Ernie's: Plaza of one Allen Center. Old-fashioned decor.

Domenic: 6707 Harrisburg. Italian restaurant overlooking harbour. Menu based on fish.

To the north

Los Cazuros Taqueria: 2221 Fulton (on the corner of Fulton/Quitman) take Main St. as far as Quitman, 2kms from Downtown. In a quarter which is supposed to be dangerous at night, genuine Mexican cooking, pleasant and inexpensive as well. Excellent place to eat.

bars and pubs

Montrose Quarter

La Bodega: 2402 Mandeil (2 blocks north of Westheimer). Student bar, good place for meeting people.

Prufrock's: 43 Westheimer (from midday to 2 a.m.) Beer and wine. Jeans obligatory.

Near Rice University

Kay's Lounge: 2324 Bissonnet (near Greenbriar St). Hippies and students. Not as pleasant as Prufrock's.

Van's Stampede Ballroom: 1416 Richmond Ave. 'Cowboy' atmosphere, 'Country and Western' music. The beer flows. Not for the too-long haired.

East of downtown

Athense Bar and Grill: 8037 Clinton Drive (near the fort). Greek cooking and dancing. Great atmosphere, clientele a mixture of sailors and young people. Watch your money carefully; it's advisable to be poorly dressed ... and inadvisable for girls to go there on their own.

things that everyone goes to see and that you shouldn't miss

Manned Spacecraft Center – N.A.S.A.: at Clear Lake, 45 kms to the south-east, take highway 45, then No. 1. Greyhound buses go there (9.00–16.00) every day, free entry. All American space flights are guided from here. Film shows. Full-scale model of the moon L.E.M. ☎ 483.43.21.

Astrodome: 10 kms south of the city-centre on South Main St. (bus on Main St.). The biggest covered space in the world. Very impressive. You really should go to a football match (American of course!) and join in the thrills with the 66,000 spectators that the stadium can hold. Reservations and information: ☎ 797.10.00.

Museum of Fine Arts: 1001 Bissonnet (Tuesday–Saturday: 10.00–17.00, Sunday 12.00–18.00, free entry). Excellent collection of Italian and Spanish Renaissance paintings, primitive art from Africa and the Southern Seas, gardens and sculptures.

Hermann Park Zoo: Fannin/N. McGregor Drive. A particularly interesting zoo.

things that everyone goes to see and that can be given a miss

Astroworld: opposite the Astrodome, an inferior version of Disneyland; 23 hectares of attractions (10.00–24.00 everyday in summer; closed January and February).

Bush Gardens: Amusement park situated near Interstate 10, exit Gellhorn (everyday 10.00–18.00).

things that everyone doesn't go to see but which are worth seeing

Rothko Chapel: Barnard St/Yupon St., in the Montrose quarter. A very well-known octagonal meditation centre. Mark Rothko's immense canvases create a very 'cool' atmosphere. It's also an excellent place for meeting interesting people. Open 10.00–18.00. Free.

Port of Houston: Free trip on board the *Sam Houston* along the pass which links the port of Houston to the sea. Departure at 10.00 and 14.00 hrs every day except Monday and throughout September, reserve by phone: CA5.06.72.

Contemporary Arts Museum: 5216 Montrose (Tuesday–Saturday 10.00–17.00, Sunday 12.00–18.00 Free). An average museum of modern art, no more.

Museum of Natural Science and Planetarium: Hermann Park, at the end of Caroline St (9.00–17.00 Tuesday to Saturday, 12.00–17.00 Sunday and Monday). Entry free.

An architectural trip? Go Downtown, some of the buildings are very impressive, e.g. Jones' Hall, Hyatt Regency Hotel (45-minute round trip of the city from the restaurant).

great scenes

Music

Houston Symphony Society: Louisiana. Cheap concerts on Saturday afternoons. Tickets can be obtained from the Institute of International Education: 1 A World Trade Center. Picnic in the open-air with music.

Miller Outdoor Theater: Hermann Park. In summer on Sundays, Tuesdays and Thursdays, free concerts. People take picnics.

Cinema for film buffs

Media Center (Rice University): free performances every weekend. For the programmes: ☎ 528.41.41, extension 1396.

'Gay' bars and pubs

Silver Dollar Saloon: Westheimer St. (1 block east of Montrose Bld).

The Round Table: 507 Westheimer St.

The Pink Elephant: 1215 Leeland St. Good.

The Exile Lounge: 1011 Bell St.

around Houston

Alabama-Coushatta Indian reserve: at Livingston, 120 kms north of Houston on U.S. Highway 59. About 500 Indians live here. You can visit at any time. Special attractions are put on from June to August (Tuesday to Saturday, 10.00–17.00, Sundays 13.00–17.00. Closed Mondays). The most interesting: the museum. Are the Indians themselves a museum population? The game isn't over yet.

Grand Prairie International Wildlife Park: a huge zoo where the animals are free and you can touch the more docile ones. You can get around in a car or in a pedalo (shaped like a hippo!)

Flea Market: 4412 N. Shepherd at Crosstimbers.

The Market Place: 10910 Old Katy Rd. For antiques.

Texas Rodeo: At the Coliseum, 45 kms from Houston. Every Saturday (except in September) at 20.00.

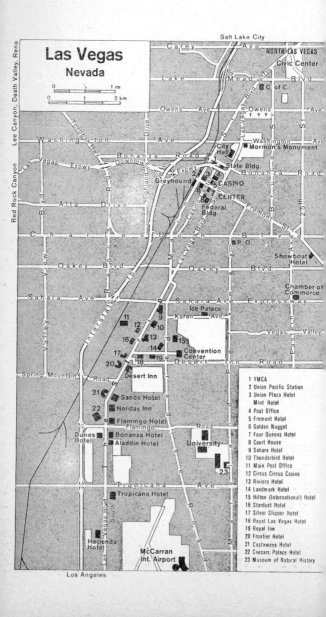

Las Vegas
Nevada

0   1 mi
0   1   2 km

Salt Lake City

Casey Ave.

NORTH LAS VEGAS
Civic Center
C. of C.

Lake Mead Blvd.

Owens Ave.

Owens Ave.

Washington Ave.

Washington Ave.

Bonanza Road

City Hall
Mormon's Monument

Downtown
Las Vegas Expwy.

State Bldg.
Bonanza Road

Greyhound
CASINO
CENTER
Federal
Bldg.

Fremont St.

Alta Drive

Charleston Blvd.

View

Oakey Blvd.

P.O.

Oakey Blvd.

Showboat
Hotel

Sahara Ave.

Chamber of
Commerce

Sahara Ave.

Expressway

Ice Palace
Karen Ave.

Vegas Valley

11
12
9
10
15

16
13
14

Convention
Center

17
20   18   19

Desert Inn Road

Spring Mountain Road

Desert Inn

21
Sands Hotel

22
Holiday Inn
Flamingo Hotel
Flamingo Road

Road

University

23

Dunes
Hotel
Bonanza Hotel
Aladdin Hotel

Tropicana Ave.

Tropicana Hotel

Las Vegas Blvd. South

Hacienda
Hotel

McCarran
Int. Airport

Los Angeles

1 YMCA
2 Union Pacific Station
3 Union Plaza Hotel
   Mint Hotel
4 Post Office
5 Fremont Hotel
6 Golden Nugget
7 Four Queens Hotel
8 Court House
9 Sahara Hotel
10 Thunderbird Hotel
11 Main Post Office
12 Circus Circus Casino
13 Riviera Hotel
14 Landmark Hotel
15 Hilton (International) Hotel
16 Stardust Hotel
17 Silver Slipper Hotel
18 Royal Las Vegas Hotel
19 Royal Inn
20 Frontier Hotel
21 Castaways Hotel
22 Caesars Palace Hotel
23 Museum of Natural History

Lee Canyon, Death Valley, Reno

Red Rock Canyon

LAS VEGAS

☎ 702
NEVADA

The sound of money as you have never heard it before. Take the start of 'Money' by the Pink Floyd and repeat it 100,000 times: that's the sound of Las Vegas. Visually, it's mile upon mile of neon lights, bizarre hotels, and weird casinos. The pinnacle of vulgarity, kitsch at its most extreme ... Still, you should at least go there once. Paradoxically Las Vegas is the cheapest city in the States ... As long as you don't gamble of course! The best time to arrive in this desert-city is at night-fall; this is when Las Vegas is at its most fascinating.

arriving in Las Vegas

Coach

Greyhound: Union Plaza Hotel, 110 S. Main St. ☎ 392.26.40.
Continental Trailways: 217 N. 4th St. ☎ 382.70.86.

Plane

McCarran International Airport, 13 km from the city-centre. Bus service.

don't panic

Finding your way around

Las Vegas can be divided into two main parts:

Downtown: Main St. and the popular casinos.

The Strip: Las Vegas Boulevard a few kms south of Downtown; this long boulevard is made up of one ultra-luxury hotel-casino after another.

Transport

Take a bus to go from Downtown to the Strip. It's practically essential to have a car in Las Vegas if you are staying more than one night and if you intend to do the rounds of the casinos.

Car hire

Aero Rent-A-Car: 3244 Mel Ave. ☎ 735.33.44.

Avis: McCarran Airport. ☎ 739.55.95.

Hertz: McCarran Airport. ☎ 736.24.60.

Refuge

No Y.M.C.A. or Y.W.C.A. in Las Vegas.

---

keys to Las Vegas

Before anything else, a small piece of advice: don't get caught by the gambling fever. You lose every time, or nearly. Besides, it's just as interesting and much less risky to watch other people gamble.

General information

Las Vegas Convention and Visitors' Authority: Convention Center. ☎ 735.23.23.

You will be given a whole bundle of vouchers for free breakfasts, free shows, free cocktails, vouchers and tokens for gambling machines, etc. This is the bait. Take advantage of it: for example you can eat breakfasts (plentiful and free) all day long. These vouchers are also available at casinos – the best from Mr Suys Casino (opposite Stardust).

Las Vegas Chamber of Commerce: 2301 E. Sahara Ave. ☎ 457.26.64.

Colleges and campuses

University of Nevada Las Vegas: 4500 Maryland Parkway, east of the Strip.

Meeting places

Everywhere! The proximity of so much money abolishes many frontiers ... and creates others.

Survival

The **Greyhound Station,** with its fairly soft carpeting, is almost like a hotel! No problem food-wise. If you're in desperate need of money don't be afraid to beg a dollar off an old American lady who has just won 50. But do so before she loses ten times over what she has just won.

good night

If you can stay awake, you don't have to go to bed at all in Las Vegas as the city never stops. The hotels in South Main St and in Downtown generally (around the Greyhound Station) are the cheapest.

The Apache Hotel: 407 S. Main St.

Sal Sager: Main St/Fremont St.

Las Vegas Club Hotel: Main St./Fremont St.

Victory Motel: 318 S. Main St.

Virginia Rooms Motel: 319 S. Main St.

Western: 899 E. Fremont St. ☎ 384.46.20.

El Cortez: 600 E. Fremont St. ☎ 385.52.00.

Circus-Circus: 2880 Las Vegas Bld. ☎ 734.04.10.

getting fed

In Las Vegas, it's a question of getting *well* fed; go for example to the **Mint** (100 Fremont St.) and eat as much as you want for a set price. **The Carousel** is another good place. On the Strip, amongst others: the **Silver Slipper Casino.** You can eat for next to nothing in most of the casinos. **Caesar's Palace** is a must, and the **Circus-Circus** (fantastic).

things that everyone does and that should be given a try (at least once)

Risk a symbolic dollar in the slot machines (but know when to stop!). If you gamble very prudently you can have a great time in Las Vegas. You should try **Caesar's Palace** and the **Circus-Circus.**

great scenes

Free view of the city: take the lift at the bottom of the *Mint Hotel* (100 Fremont St). It takes you to the roof and a super-de-luxe restaurant: excellent view on your way up. Best done at night. In the same place you can visit the wings of the Casino (*'Behind-the-Scene-Tour'*). Everyday, every half-hour, 10.00 to 19.00 Free. You must be over 21 (or look it).

A pretty special casino: the Circus-Circus of the Hotel Spa Casino. N.B. If you're not travelling in jeans, there is a guided visit of the casinos and cabarets which lasts ... eight hours, is expensive but includes evening meal, drinks and tips.

Gray Line Tours: 1406 S. Commerce St. ☎ 384. 12.34.

A museum worth visiting: *Natural History Museum:* 4505 Maryland Parkway (Monday–Friday: 11.00–17.00 Saturday: 10.00–12.00, Sunday: 14.00–17.00, entry free). Indian craftwork, desert snakes, exhibitions devoted to the early pioneers.

Desert Research Institute: 4624 Maryland Parkway (every day: 9.00–17.00, entry free). If you are fascinated by the desert sands.

around Las Vegas

Lots of things to see in the region and advisable to have a car (hitching isn't easy hereabouts and during the summer, after half an hour in a temperature of 40° Centigrade, you will have melted).

National Wildlife Range Desert: 45 kms to the north-west, on U.S. Highway 95. You can see desert moufflons (wild sheep) (every day: 9.00–17.00).

Hoover Dam: 50 kms to the south-east on U.S. highway 93. A famous dam mentioned in all the geography books. You can visit the dam and the power-station (every day: 7.00—17.00).

Fire Valley National Park: 50 kms to the north-west on the 1–15, then 34 kms to the south-east on the NEF 40. A spectacular panorama: red and purple rock formations, petrified trees. There are also sculptures left by the early natives.

Kingman: in Arizona, 178 kms to the south-east on U.S. Highway 93. Particularly to be seen: the ghost towns, relics of the Gold-rush. Also: London Bridge (near Lake Havasu) entirely rebuilt on the spot!

Death Valley: 210 kms west of Las Vegas: since the building of properly signposted road, crossing it is no longer as hazardous as it used to be (providing your own transport is reliable). The colours are most beautiful early in the day. You are given a map at the entrance to the National Monument. Make a point of seeing Zabriskie Point.

LOS ANGELES
☎ 213
CALIFORNIA

L.A.? It's even more incredible than its reputation. It's the place where miles and miles of film are produced every year, where there is saturation broadcasting of ready-made music in order to sell millions of records, where giant advertising boards give a regular rhythm to travelling in town; it's nearly a world on its own. With extravagant Hollywood, filthy-rich Beverly Hills, poverty-stricken Watts, carefree Santa Monica, intellectual Westwood and dozens of other districts, Los Angeles (like New York, that other extreme of the United States) is a fascinating patchwork of different cultures and ways of life. It's everything but a city: mile upon mile of detached houses, a network of eight-lane motorways, and its only limits the desert and the ocean.

---

arriving in Los Angeles

Coach

Greyhound: *Downtown:* 6th St./Los Angeles St. *In Hollywood:* 1409 Vine St.

Continenetal Trailways: 601 Main St. (opposite Greyhound).

Plane

Los Angeles International Airport: Century Bld/ Sepulveda Bld. Bus and airport coaches via the following terminals:

Downtown : **L.A. Hilton (6th/Figueroa), Greyhound Station. Biltmore, Bonaventure, Hyatt Regency.**

Hollywood : **Holiday Inn, Sheraton Universal, Roosevelt Hotel, 30 Universal City Plaza.**

Beverly Hills : **Century Plaza, Beverly Hilton.**

Wilshire District : **Ambassador.**

West L.A.: **Westwood Holiday Inn.**

---

don't panic

Finding your way around

A good detailed map is essential here; the one sold at Texaco petrol stations appears to be the best. L.A. is made up of a large number of districts: Hollywood is the best-known of course, Beverly Hills, Venice, Highland Park, Watts, Santa Monica ... Downtown is the centre of the immense spread of the city, where the Freeways cross over each other; like all Downtowns in the States, it's becoming derelict. Santa Monica and Venice are two districts of L.A. on the Pacific: worth going to for the long lively beaches. Whilst the former is safe, the second can be quite dangerous at night: what used to be mainly an artists' village in the sixties has become more and more a favourite place for junkies who have turned it into what isn't always safe territory.

The level of crime is supposed to be the highest in L.A. Westwood, above Santa Monica Bld, and between the Pacific and Beverly Hills is perhaps the nicest district in L.A. and one of the few, with Hollywood and Downtown, where the pedestrian isn't considered to be some kind of strange animal. The U.C.L.A. campus is the centre and Westwood the principal artery. Watts is the Black ghetto, unfortunately so well-known for the violent riots that broke out there in 1964.

Transport

In Los Angeles there isn't much choice; either you have a car or you don't, and quite honestly it's better if you do. This is why, for once, we give below a wide choice of car-hire companies' addresses.

Car hire

Car hire companies are concentrated in three parts of L.A.: the International Airport, Downtown and Hollywood. In view of this, and also that you nearly always have to return the car to the pick-up point, it's important to choose carefully. Downtown in particular is best only if you have decided to leave by Greyhound or Trailways coach.

Airport

Hertz: International Airport. ☎ 1(800) 654.31.31.

Avis: 33 World Way. ☎ 646.56.00.

Budget: 9775 Airport Bld. ☎ 645.45.00.

Econo: 5657 W. Century Bld. ☎ 776.61.84.

Dollar: 6141 W. Century Bld. ☎ 645.93.33.

Payless: 4730 W. Century Bld. ☎ 641.11.31.

Downtown

Hertz: 924 W. 7th St. ☎ 1(800) 654.31.31.

Avis: 1207 W. 3rd St. ☎ 481.20.00.

Budget: 550 W. 5th St. ☎ 627.13.43.

Budget: 701 S. Figueroa/7th St. opposite the Hilton. ☎ 627.13.45.

Alfa: 922 W. 7th St (opposite the Hilton, on the same parking lot as Budget, has 4 or 5 Volkswagens; if you're lucky enough to get one, the rate of hire must be the lowest in L.A.)

Dollar: 727 S. Figueroa. ☎ 623.24.04.

Thrifty: 3355 Wilshire Bld. ☎ 381.78.68.

Hollywood

Hertz: 7047 Hollywood Bld. ☎ 1(800) 654.31.31.

Avis: 7000 Hollywood Bld. ☎ 467.00.74.

Dollar: 6819 Hollywood Bld. ☎ 466.63.87.

Allstate: 6935 Hollywood Bld. ☎ 466.82.41 (the cheapest in Hollywood).

If you have someone to drive you to the car-hire company to pick up a vehicle, it's advisable to go to a company not situated in one of these three districts. Look up Automobile Rental in the Yellow Pages. Enquire at American International (situated at Inglewood) and Ideal Rent-a-Car. Don't forget that the big companies have reverse charge telephone numbers (but these are often busy): Hertz: (800) 654.31.31. Avis: (800) 331.12.12. Budget: (800) 228.96. 50. Econo: (800) 874.50.00.

Buying a car

You can find a second-hand Volkswagen or Volvo (on the campus or in the newspapers, particularly the Sunday *L.A. Times*.)

Driving in Los Angeles

Driving in L.A. is something of an art, if not a philosophy: it's important to realise that the Freeways are almost always the quickest way of going from A to B (even if you only have 3 kms to do). They do have rush hours though (17.00–18.00) which are to be avoided. Everybody drives at the same speed in an unbroken procession: let yourself be carried along by it, breaking the speed limit is very severely punished by the cops. 'On surface' driving (as opposed to the Freeways which pass over the city) is slower and interrupted by traffic lights at every cross-roads. Parking is also a real problem in spite of the size of the city.

Taxi

In view of the distances involved, this must be considered as a last resort. Two big companies control L.A.:

Yellow Cabs: ☎ 481.23.45.

Red and White Cabs: ☎ 654.84.00.

Hitch-hiking

Not really advisable in L.A. where not having a car is considered as a sign of degeneracy (readily understandable after having spent an hour in the city).

Bus

A reasonable means of transport for those who are *very* patient. The bus station is the same as for the Greyhound (6th St/Los Angeles St, Downtown). Zone-based charges. Information: ☎ 626.44.55.

Walking

Above all, do not underestimate distances on the map: it takes more than an hour to go from Hollywood to the L.A. County Museum and yet they appear to be so close together on paper! In the final analysis, the best way of getting round in L.A. is to meet people ... who have one or two or three cars and who will drive you round or lend you a vehicle. It's not a bad idea to hire something for three or four days, just long enough to get to know people and understand how L.A. works.

Refuge

Hollywood Y.M.C.A.: 1553 N. Hudson Ave. (100m from Hollywood Bld). The best placed, in the centre of Hollywood. ☎ 467.41.61. (Greyhound Station not far: 1409 Vine St.)

Y.M.C.A.: 8015 S. Sepulveda Bld. ☎ 776.09.22 (the nearest to the airport, 3 nights maximum stay).

Y.M.C.A.: 206 6th St. (6th floor).

Hollywood Studio Club: 2155 Lodi Place. ☎ 465.31.66 (women only).

Ammon Hennacy House of Hospitality: 605 N. Cummings St. ☎ 264.81.44.

In towns contiguous to L.A.:

Long Beach

Y.M.C.A. Downtown Branch: 600 Long Beach Bld. ☎ 437.35.34.

Y.M.C.A.: 550 Pacific Ave.

Armed Services Y.M.C.A.: 151 Queens Way. ☎ 436.96.40.

Pasadena

Y.M.C.A.: 2750 New York Drive. ☎ 793.31.31.

Y.M.C.A.: 235 East Holly St.

Y.M.C.A.: 78 North Marengo Ave.

keys to Los Angeles

General information

International Institute: 435 S. Boyle Ave. ☎ 261.41.71.

Los Angeles World Affairs Council: 900 Wilshire ☎ 628.23.33. Advice bureau for foreign visitors.

Traveller's Aid: 646 S. Los Angeles St. ☎ 625.25.01.

Hospitality International: 500 Lucas Ave. ☎ 481.80.00 and 682.26.28. Information for students.

Greater Los Angeles Visitors' and Convention Bureau: 505 S. Flower St. ☎ 628.31.01. Weekdays till 17.00 hrs, Saturday 16.00 hrs.

For shows: **Ticket Mart Booking Office:** 1303 Westwood Bld. ☎ 479.55.01.

Newspapers and magazines

The Calendar supplement of the Sunday edition of the **Los Angeles Times** is a pretty exhaustive source of information about the week's programmes. You'll need a bag, or even a wheelbarrow, to carry it around!

Free, but of limited interest (in hotels and reception centres): **Key** and **Where**.

And the **L.A. Weekly,** which gives details of shows, concerts, etc.

Colleges and campuses

U.C.L.A. (University of California, L.A.): in Westwood between Beverly Hills and Santa Monica, on Sunset Bld. A magnificent campus with an incredible cinema department complete with numerous studios. There is a garden of contemporary sculpture near the Art Center, and an inverted fountain near the Physics Department. Go to the Ackerman Union cafeteria (on the right following Westwood Bld, in the campus, opposite the stadium).

U.S.C. (University of Southern California): Jefferson Bld/Flower St., nearer Downtown. Smaller than U.C.L.A. but still a pretty busy campus.

Cal Tech (California Institute of Technology): In Pasadena (California Bld/Hill Ave). Really only for those whose interest is in science, otherwise you might not find the atmosphere to your liking).

Meeting places

There aren't many pedestrians-only quarters in L.A.: Hollywood Bld. and Sunset Bld. (between Hollywood and Beverly) are the busiest arteries; from 20.00 hrs onwards they are inhabited by rather strange individuals out to make themselves noticed and who can even be alarming. There are lots of bars, restaurants (expensive) and shops selling records, books and T-shirts as well as a few large drugstores. The heart of Hollywood is at the crossroads where *Highland Ave* and *Hollywood Bld* meet. *Westwood* is the best place for meeting people: see list of restaurants below. In summer the young people go to the beaches, the nearest being *Santa Monica* (with its pier which has resisted all the attacks of town-planners and promoters, one of the least artificial places in L.A.) and *Venice* (a track for cyclists runs between these two beaches). To the south, next to each other, are *Long Beach, Laguna Beach* and *Dana Point*, all of which are favourites for surfing. There are also some very beautiful beaches to the north, particularly *Ventura* and its sand dunes which you can drive around in a 'buggy'.

Disneyland (see later) is a place where cars are banned; it's possible to meet interesting people.

For details of all important meetings (political, mystic, religious, musical, sportive, etc.) keep an eye on the *Free Press*.

Survival

A few useful telephone numbers:

Directory enquiries: 411

Weather: 554.12.12.

Police: 625.33.11.

Fire brigade, hospital, ambulance: 384.31.31.

Services of various kinds: 481.21.33. See also addresses given by the *L.A. Free Press.*

For a place to sleep for one or two nights, dial 627. 48.61, the number of the *Catholic Information Center* (809 S. Flower St., open 9.30–17.30, Monday to Friday, and until 13.30 on Saturdays).

Jorge Estrada: ☎ 474.92.07 (495 Dalehurst Ave, 5 minutes from U.C.L.A.) In summer you can find students who will put you up in the 'fraternities' near the U.C.L.A. campus (see below). On the campus itself concentrate on the Ackerman Union and around it

U.C.L.A. Helpline: ☎ 825.76.46 (10.00–02.00 hrs).

Free Clinic: Hollywood Sunset Free Clinic: 3324 W. Sunset. ☎ 660.24.20.

You can sell clothes and other objects at: Challenge Thrift Stores, 5920 S. Broadway.

KLOS Community Switchboard: ☎ 870.87.16. From Monday to Friday (15.00–02.00 hrs). From midday onwards over the weekend. Help and advice.

Cheap Food at Farmers' Market: 3rd Ave/Fairfax.

Jobs: look for a job as waiter in one of the small restaurants in Westwood.

Traveller's Cheques: American Express Office: 723 W. 7th St., L.A. California: 90017. ☎ (213) 488.13.01.

Leaving L.A.: Consult the *Ride Board* on Floor B of the *Ackerman Union*.

Ride Center: 1610 Argyle St (in Hollywood). ☎ 461. 38.29.

Look in the *L.A. Times* under the 'Transportation-Auto' section of the Classified advertisements; they also show all the Driveaways, e.g. *Free Cars to San Francisco:* ☎ 674.56.33.

Drive a new car to San Francisco: ☎ 225.71.01 (every day 9.00–17.00, except Wednesdays, Saturdays and Sundays).

Auto Driveaway: 4800 Melrose. ☎ 666.61.00.
A useful hint: P.S.A. is the cheapest company in California (☎ 776.01.25). If you are going to San Francisco it works out hardly more expensive than the bus.

---

good night

Student accommodation

U.C.L.A.'s Fraternities Houses: enquire about available room at the Student Union, on the campus. Most of them are on Gayley Ave, and the little streets giving on to it (Landfair, Strathmore). They have signs in Greek letters on the front. Very inexpensive in summer and you can rent by the week or month. One condition 'sine qua non': you have to be accepted by the titular members of the Fraternity. Possible only in summer. Particularly recommended: No. 543 Landfair Street, ☎ 478.70.29.

On the campus itself, the only Hall of residence which takes temporary students is **Rieber Hall**, 310 De Neve (☎ 825.22.75). Breakfast included but not cheap for a University residence.

Cheap hotels

The cheapest are in Downtown and therefore not nearly so conveniently placed as the Hollywood Y.M.C.A.

Downtowner Motel: 944 S. Georgia St. ☎ 627.20.03

Figueroa Hotel: 939 S. Figueroa St. ☎ 627.89.71.

Holiday Lodge Motel: 1631 W. Third St. ☎ 483.49.20.

Jerry's Motel: 285 S. Lucas Ave. ☎ 481.09.21.

Milner Highland Hotel: 813 S. Flower St. ☎ 627.69.81.

Motel de Ville: 1123 W. 7th St. ☎ 624.84.74.

Oasis Motel: 2200 W. Olympic Bld. ☎ 385.41.91.

Rainbow Hotel: 536 S. Hope St. ☎ 627.99.41.

Royal Host Motel: 901 W. Olympic Bld. ☎ 626.62.55.

Royal Pagoda Motel: 995. N. Broadway. ☎ 223.33.81.

San Carlos Hotel: 507 W. 5th St. ☎ 628.22.91.

In Hollywood

Bahia Motel: 5265 Sunset Bld. ☎ 466.85.21.

Saharan Motor Hotel: 7512 Sunset Bld. ☎ 874.67.00.

Hollywood Downtowner Motel: 5601 Hollywood Bld. ☎ 464.71.91.

Hollywood Highland Motel: 2051 N. Highland ☎ 851.30.00.

In Beverly Hills

Devonshire Lodge Motel: 7575 Beverly Hill Bld. ☎ 936.61.54.

Cheap motels

Geneva Motel: 321 W. Manchester. ☎ 677.91.71.

Regalodge Motel: 200 W. Colorado.

Royal Pagoda Motel: 995 N. Broadway. ☎ 223.33.81.

Mission Inn: 3649 7th St, Riverside. ☎ (714) 784.03.00.

getting fed

In Los Angeles the hamburger is king, you can't get away from it! Among the thousands of places where you can buy them one must give a special mention to **Tommy's** (Downtown, Beverly Bld/Rampart Bld) which serves up something a bit better than the everyday article. You really should try Julius Oranges orangeade (stalls everywhere in L.A.). If you get fed up with living off hamburgers, hot-dogs and such-like, there's no lack of restaurants! Among the cheapest are:

Brown Derby: 9537 Wilshire Bld.

Maison Gerard Restaurant: 224 S. Beverly Drive. French food.

Edward's Steak House: 9600 Flair Drive.

Cristal Hollow: 600 Ave of Champions. Soup and salad.

Red Onion Casa Maria: 3301 Atlantic. Mexican food.

Boston Deli Resori: 650 S. Flower St. Good breakfasts.

Bruno's Restaurant: 3838 Centinela Ave. Italian food in the setting of a Roman palace.

Compari's Italian Restaurant: 8600 S. Sepulveda Bld. Sit in a 'Ben Hur' chariot.

Dario's Delicatessen: 410 Ord St. Sandwiches, lasagne, pizza ...

Dunes Restaurant: 5625 Sunset Bld. Near the studios.

El Pueblo: 201 N. Los Angeles St.

Golden Temple: 7910 W. Third St. Vegetarian food.

Googie's Restaurant: 501 W. Fifth St. You can have breakfast at any hour of the day.

Mike's Lunch Box: 621 S. Figueroa St. Cheap breakfast.

Restaurants in Westwood

Westwood Village is packed with good restaurants with a very relaxed atmosphere. The following are two classics:

Alice's Restaurant: 1043 Westwood Bld, a very well-known meeting-place in L.A.

Yesterdays: 1056 Westwood Bld (opposite Alice's). Superb decor, incredible sandwiches: quite simply a 'must'.

Less sophisticated than the two preceding:

Mario's: 1001 Broxton Ave. A little Italian restaurant which in the space of a few years has become a big Italian restaurant.

Restaurant Mifune: 11617 Santa Monica Bld. A cheap Japanese restaurant for students not far from Westwood.

Unusual restaurants in L.A.

Café Figaro: 9010 Melrose Ave. Restaurant frequented by the student and artistic intelligentsia of L.A. Excellent sandwiches in an original setting.

Nature's Health Cove: 1010 Broxton Ave Macrobiotic restaurant.

La Strada: 3000 Los Feliz. Italian singers sing opera whilst you eat: quite unusual and worth the detour.

The Old Venice Noodle Company: 2654 Main St (in Santa Monica). Worth going to for the extraordinary decor and the spaghetti, which is of an equally high standard.

French restaurants

Café Brasserie: 8704 Sunset Bld. (in Hollywood). Very reasonable prices.

L'Auberge: 7574 Sunset Bld.

Maison Gerard: 224 S. Beverly Drive.

Robaire's: 348 S. La Brea.

The Bicycle Shop Cafe: 12217 Wiltshire Bld (especially for its onion soup).

Japanese cooking

Tokyo Kaikan East: 337 E. First St. Downtown, in Little Tokyo, one of L.A.'s best and most authentic Japanese restaurants.

---

things that everyone goes to see and that you shouldn't miss

Disneyland: At Anaheim, 40 kms south of Downtown. If you haven't got a car take bus 800 (or the Greyhound for Santa Ana and get off at Anaheim). In summer, open every day 9.00 to 1 a.m., and the rest of the year, Wednesday to Friday, 10.00–18.00, Saturday and Sunday, 9.00–19.00. Not particularly cheap. Disneyland deserves to be seen for many reasons, the most important being that you can really enjoy yourself there. It's a triumph of ersatz and illusion; from this point of view the pavilion set up by General Electric is fabulous. In the first ten years after its foundation in 1955 Disneyland had more than 50 million visitors! Don't miss in particular 'The Pirates of the Caribbean', the most spectacular attraction by far: spell-binding and not easily forgotten. N.B. If there are several of you, it's very easy to find cheap accommodation in one of the hundreds of motels which surround Disneyland.

L.A. County Museum: Hancock Park (on Wilshire Bld). Tuesday to Friday, 10.00–17.00, Saturday and Sunday 10.00–18.00. Excellent museum of modern art together with a marvellous collection of pre-Columbian art. See also in the park the skeleton of a dinosaur lying in a lake of oil.

Farmer's Market: 3rd St/Fairfax Ave. Masses of agricultural products from more or less everywhere, perhaps the only place in L.A. where you can see good natural food neither tinned nor wrapped in cellophane!

Huntington Library: at San Marino, north-east of Downtown, near Pasadena (park entrance at 1151 Oxford Rd). Every day, except Monday, 13.00–16.30. Free. Closed in October. Remarkable for its extremely beautiful park with views over L.A. and the collections of incunabula (including Gutenberg's Bible) and manuscripts in the museum. Admirers of the poet and painter William Blake and his visions will be very interested to know that the biggest collection in the world of his paintings is to be found here. (You have to apply to see it). (N.B: the famous California Institute of Technology is 500 metres north of it and has a cafeteria).

J. Paul Getty Museum: 17985 Pacific Coast Highway (one mile north of Sunset Bld in Malibu). Monday to Friday, June to September, and Tuesday to Saturday, October to May, 10.00–17.00. Entrance free. Reconstruction of Pompeii's Villa dei Papyre. Quite a fair collection of antique sculptures and paintings (Rembrandt, Rubens, Raphael, Boucher).

Motorama, 'Where cars are the stars': 7001 Hollywood Bld. Just next to the famous Graumann's Chinese Theater. 10.00–22.00 and 11.00–22.00 at weekends. This unusual museum has on show specimens of the most extravagant cars that the cinema in Hollywood has ever produced as well as some very fine old bangers.

---

things that everyone goes to see and that can be given a miss

---

Universal Studios: Studio City, north of Hollywood. Take the Hollywood Freeway (101) and leave it at Lankershim Bld. Visiting from 10.00 to 17.30.

Very disappointing; a typical tourist trap and you won't learn much about the cinema. The Warner Studios (Burbank Studios, see later) are more interesting.

Knott's Berry Farm: A few kilometres before Disneyland at Buena Park, this is a reconstruction of an old American town. Perhaps not worth while going so far to see; you might as well go straight on to Disneyland.

Capitol Records: Vine St/Hollywood Bld. The headquarters of the famous record company can be visited on Tuesdays and Thursdays. Free but not fantastic.

Graumann's Chinese Theater: 6925 Hollywood Bld. Footprints of very famous stars of the cinema on the pavement. Amusing but nothing special.

Hollywood Wax Museum: 6767 Hollywood Bld. Every day 10.00–midnight. Friday and Saturday until 2 a.m. Not particularly impressive; the wax effigies of stars are not very well done. On the other hand the automaton, which is often at the entrance, is really worth seeing.

Olvera Street: Downtown opposite the station, a Mexican street 100 metres long: the real tourist-trap to be avoided at all costs.

---

things that everyone doesn't go to see but which are worth seeing

---

Alligator Farm: 7671 E. La Palma Ave, Buena Park (opposite Knott's Berry Farm). Every day 10.30–21.00 in July and August and until 17.00 for the rest of the year. Entrance fee. Some 1,000 alligators and crocodiles await you in this rather special kind of 'farm'.

Movie World: 6900 Orange Thorpe Ave, Buena Park (take the San Diego Freeway). Every day, 10.00–18.00. Many rare specimens of the history of the cinema.

Movieland Wax Museum and Palace of Living Art: 7711 Beach Bld. (10 mins from Disneyland), 10.00–22.00. Remarkable place where you can see among things a wax reproduction of Michelangelo's 'David'.

Burbank Studios: 4000 Warner Bld, Burbank. Much more interesting than the Universal City studios. The Columbia and Warner Brothers Studios really show you what Hollywood represents and how it works. To visit them you have to reserve by phone: ☎ 843.60.00, extension 1744. Monday to Friday.

Exposition Park: Exposition Bld/Figueroa Bld.

This is where you can find the California Museum of Science and Industry, the Natural History Museum, and the famous Coliseum Stadium built for the Olympic Games of 1932. Visiting every day except Monday, 10.00–17.00.

The architecture of Los Angeles

Los Angeles is immensely rich in architecture; you can find every kind and variety of style often in close proximity to each other. On the same avenue you can see side by side Swiss chalets, pagodas, Gothic manors, Mexican 'haciendas' and a whole range of architectural eccentricities: a real paradise for lovers of kitsch. In L.A. the 'villa', and the lifestyle it implies, reigns supreme. Great architects have left imposing works: not to be missed are the houses of *Frank Lloyd Wright, Rudolph Schindler, Charles Eames* and particularly those of *Richard Neutra* which, built on piles and with their immense bay windows, have become the archetype of the modern Californian villa.

Other things to see in Los Angeles

Watts Towers: 1727 E. 107th St. (one block from Wilmington Ave, 15 mins by car east of the international airport). These towers, strangely like the work of the Catalan Gaudi, were built by Simon Rodia, a character mad enough to have spent three-quarters of his life creating alone and unaided a wild kind of architecture, having nothing to do with recognized norms, out of rubbish (bottles, plates, tins, old iron, etc.).

Wayfarers' Chapel: Palos Verdes, one mile east of Marineland. Entrance free every day 11.00–16.00. This chapel built entirely of glass by F. L. Wright is a real marvel.

Pacific Design Center: Melrose Ave/Robertson Ave. Designed by the currently most popular architect in L.A., Cesar Peli. Particularly worth seeing: the immense covered gallery on the top floor.

1800 Fairburn St (on the corner of Little Santa Monica): a work by Charles Moore – for many the greatest contemporary American architect – which is a psychoanalyst centre.

Hotel Bonaventure: 5th St/Figueroa (Downtown). A grandiloquent work by John Portman. Interesting and prestigious architecture.

N.B. One of the only bookshops on the West Coast specializing in architecture: Hennesy and Ingalls Inc, 11833 Wilshire Bld.

Parks: There are many parks in L.A. and most of them are worth having a stroll around: *Barnsdall Park* (between Sunset and Hollywood Bld to the east), *Rancho Park* (south of Hollywood between the Santa Monica Freeway and Baldwin Hills), *Griffith Park.*

Little Venice on the Pacific: try and see it before the promoters transform the little canals into marinas for millionaires.

Self Realization Fellowship Lake Shrine: 1790 Sunset Bld., Pacific Palisades. Every day except Monday, 10.00–17.00 (500 metres from the Pacific). It's designed for meditation and so a calm reigns there which is difficult to find elsewhere in L.A. The windmill-shaped chapel is rather strange.

---

great scenes

Music

Musical activity in L.A. never stops: the best Pop groups give concerts in the famous *Hollywood Bowl* (2301 N. Highland Ave) in summer. Two other celebrated Pop centres: the immense *Forum* (at Inglewood, near the international airport) and the *Santa Monica Civic Auditorium* (at Santa Monica 500 metres from the beach). The Bowl gives fine classical concerts with the L.A. Philharmonic directed by Carlo Maria Giulini. Very good concerts also at the Greek Theatre. (South side of Griffith Park). Finally, free concerts at Exposition Park and Lincoln Park on Sundays at 14.00 hrs.

Clubs

Many clubs in which every kind of modern music can be heard (from hard rock to soft rock as well as folk-music and free jazz) but prices are often high. The most famous are on Sunset Bld.

Whisky a Gogo: 8901 Sunset Bld. No minors.

Galaxy: 8917 Sunset Bld. Rock.

Gazzarri's Hollywood a Gogo: 9039 Sunset Bld. Rock.

Roxy: 9009 Sunset Bld. Rock.

Mardi Gras: 2424 Wilshire Bld.

Shelley's Manne Hole: 1608 Cahvenga Bld. Jazz.

Windjammer: Marina del Rey (on the Pacific, near Venice). Soft rock.

Troubadour: 9081 Santa Monica Bld. (Beverly Hills). Jazz, blues.

The Intersection: 2735 S. Temple. Folk.

Cinema for film buffs

You should really go at least once to the cinema as Los Angeles is *the* city of the 'Seventh Art'.

Nuart Theater: Santa Monica Bld.

Encore Theater: Melrose Ave/Van Ness Ave.

The Vagabond: 2509 Wilshire Ave; a cinema specializing in 'revivals' of the 1930s. Now and again they show the uncut version of Tod Browning's 'Freaks'.

Fox Venice Theater: 620 Lincoln Bld (in Venice).

Beverly Canyon: Beverly Hills.

The Los Angeles Cinematheque: 104 S. Vermont Ave. ☎ 384.00.93.

Films made by students are shown at **Royce Hall** on the U.C.L.A. campus.

If you have a car go and eat popcorn in one of L.A.'s numerous 'drive-in' cinemas.

Bookshops for film buffs

Cherbrokee Bookshop: 6607 Hollywood Bld.

Larry Edmunds Bookshop: 6658 Hollywood Bld. 10.00–18.00. Monday to Saturday.

Bar

Casey's Bar: 1109 Glenden Ave (Westwood). Always full to overflowing after 21.00 hrs. Much favoured meeting-place of smart Hollywood society.

Shopping

Hermosa Reptile and Wild Animal Farm Inc: 21 Pacific Coast Highway, Hermosa Beach. Cameleons, large lizards, tortoises, pythons, iguanas, boas etc. are the speciality of this shop which has a large number of customers.

Thrift Shops: 235 S. Broadway, 11550 Santa Monica Bld. and 7918 Santa Monica Bld: thrift shops (not to be confused with the chain of shops called 'Thrifty') are shops whose proceeds go to charity. Those of L.A. are well-known for the finds that can be made.

Arco Plaza: 505 S. Flower St. (Downtown). The biggest underground commercial centre in the United States. Los Angeles is the town with the largest number of shopping centres in the world, some of them, like this one, worth seeing. See also *Carson Mall*, 250 Carson Mall, **Carson**, where the architecture is imitation Maya.

Universal News Agency: 1655 N. Las Palmas (20 minutes from Hollywood Bld.). This news agency keeps an impressive collection of newspapers from all over the world. Open in the evening and on Sundays.

Aaron Brothers: 900 La Brea Ave. A large bazaar which sells confiscated goods of every kind.

Street murals

The biggest, maddest and most magnificent in the whole of the United States is the one on the wall of Farmer John's meat factory, Vernon Ave/Soto St. south of downtown.

There is an excellent little mural at Venice, 30 metres from the beach on Brooks Ave.

The street mural which has been the most publicised is 'the Isle of California' on Butler Ave, close to Santa Monica Bld, and 4 blocks west of the San Diego Freeway. Painted in 1971 by a group called the 'Los Angeles Fine Art Squad', it's a symbolic criticism of American society.

There is a shop selling musical instruments which has been painted all over on the corner of Sunset Bld and Vista St.

MIAMI
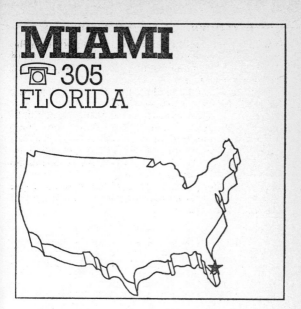
☎ 305
FLORIDA

In the bottom corner of Florida, in the kingdom of the coconut trees and fine sandy beaches, a town has sprung up well-known for the hordes of rich tourists in flowered shirts and brightly-coloured shorts who invade it every winter. But Miami is not just that. One has to distinguish, in fact, between Miami Beach, that incredible row upon row of white concrete houses with private swimming pools which stretches for miles alongside the ocean, and Miami itself which has a large colony of Cuban refugees and is one of the biggest ports in this part of the world. It isn't just Biscayne Bay which separates the millionaires' paradise and the second town of the 'Sunshine State'.

arriving in Miami

Coach

Greyhound: 275 N.E. 1st St. ☎ 377.95.77. Miami Beach: Cillons Ave.

Continental Trailways: 99 N.E. 4th St. ☎ 373.65.61

Plane

Miami International Airport: 11 kms north-west of the city. Regular bus service to Downtown.

Miami
Downtown

0 ———————— 0,5 mi

0 ———————— 800m

1 Temple Israel of Greater Miami Reform
2 First Church of Christ Scientist
3 Mount Sinai Baptist Ch.
4 New St. John's Baptist Ch
5 Mount Zion Baptist Church
6 Central Baptist Church
7 First Methodist Sanctuary
8 Miami-Metro Tour. Bur.
9 Biscayne Terrace Hotel
10 First Christian of Miami C
11 New Everglades Hotel
12 Gesù Catholic Church
13 Greyhound Bus Terminal
14 YMCA
15 Ponce Product Building
16 First Federal Building
17 Columbus Hotel
18 McAllister Hotel
19 One Biscayne Tower

Hialeah, Airport

Julia Tuttle Causewa

Amtrak Station

Civic Center

Airport, Hialeah, Orlando

Dorsey Branch Library

Biscayne Park City Cemetery

Miami Museum of Modern Art

Historical Museum of South Florida

Flagler Memorial Library

Trinity Episcopal Church

Venetian Causeway

MacArthur Causew

East West Expressway

Biscayne

Heliport

Watso Park

Greater Bethel Church

Post Office

Orange Bowl Stadium

Freedom Tower

Auditorium

Torch of Friendship

New

Port o

Miami

Scottish Rite Cathedral

Old Fort Dallas

Lummus Park

Fla. E. Coast RR Station

Main Post Office

Dade County Court House

Columbus Monument

Bayfront Miami Library Park Band Shell

W. Flagler

E. Flagler St

Federal Bldg

Du Pont Bldg

YWCA

Biscayne Blvd

Miami River

Bay

Brickell Park

Coral Gables, Everglades, Key West Seaquarium

Kartographie Huber & Oberländer, Münc

Train
Amtrak: 2206 N.W. 7th Ave and 23rd St. ☎ 371.
66.11.
112

don't panic

Finding your way around

This is very simple in Miami: a straightforward grid system with numbered streets and avenues and one main boulevard, Biscayne Bld. Miami Avenue separates east from west, and Flager St south from north. As in New York the avenues go north–south and the streets east–west.

For Miami Beach it's even simpler: everything is on Collins Avenue which goes north–south. The perpendicular streets are numbered, the first one being the one which is the furthest south.

Between Miami and Miami Beach there are five causeways, two of them having tolls (Broad Causeway and Venetian Causeway).

Transport

In view of the mediocre bus system, don't hesitate to hire a car in Miami, particularly since there are many things to see in the region. Here is a list of the cheapest companies:

Abott Motors: 2925 N.W. 36th St. ☏ 635.99.65.

Budget: 824 Biscayne Bld. ☏ 374.31.95.

Dollar: ☏ (800) 421.68.68.

Greyhound: 1620 Collins Ave (Miami Beach). ☏ 871.33.20. Special mention for the Greyhound company which for Florida only hires out cars at cheap rates.

Way-Lo: 1100 Biscayne Bld in the Howard Johnson Hotel. ☏ 358.65.65.

Sears: 1300 Biscayne Bld. ☏ 379.54.11.

Refuge

Y.M.C.A.: 40 N.E. 3rd Ave. ☏ 374.84.87.

Y.W.C.A.: 100 S.E. 4th St. ☏ 377.81.61. This one is mixed.

keys to Miami

General information

Greater Miami Chamber of Commerce: 1200 Biscayne Bld. ☏ 377.47.11.

Miami Department of Publicity and Tourism: 499 Biscayne Bld. ☏ 377.54.61.

Miami Convention Bureau: Municipal Building, 1700 Washington Ave (Miami Beach). ☎ 534.75.11.
Traveller's Aid: 2190 N.W. 7th St. ☎ 643.57.00.

Colleges and campuses

South of Downtown and south-west of Coconut Grove is the **University of Miami.** There is a ride-board if you are looking for a lift north.

Meeting places

Go to the **Coconut Grove,** a district situated a few kilometres south-west of Downtown; this is the young people's quarter and it's very easy to make friends in all the little restaurants and bars. The atmosphere is really 'cool'. All the yachts sailing for the Caribbean leave from the **Dinner Key Marina.** It isn't difficult during the high season (autumn, winter) to find a post as a skipper. If you are competent!

good night

If you haven't got time to go as far as Coconut Grove, there are inexpensive hotels, such as the following, Downtown around the Greyhound Terminal:
Boatwright Hotel: 25 N.E. 7th St. ☎ 374.87.57.
Leaminton Hotel: N.E. 1st St/3rd Ave. The cafeteria is very good.
Urmey Hotel: 34 S.E. 2nd Ave.
McAllister: 10 Biscayne Bld. ☎ 374.61.51.
Travellers: 4767 N.W. 36th St. ☎ 880.36.61.

Miami Beach:
Poincinia Hotel: 1555 Collins Ave.
Dunes: 17001 Collins Ave. ☎ 947.75.11.

things to see in Miami

Seaquarium: Rickenbacker Causeway (15 mins from Downtown). Flipper the Dolphin still lives here.
Miami Museum of Modern Art: 381 N.E. 20th St (closed on Mondays, open the rest of the week 10.00–17.00). Not comparable to the other museums of modern art in the United States but very dynamic none the less.
Vizcaya Art Museum: 3251 S. Miami Ave. South of Rickenbacker Causeway. A palace full of European art treasures set in a beautiful park.

Serpentarium: 2655 South Dixie Highway. Poisonous snakes bred by a lover of the King Cobra.

Museum of Science and History: 3289 S. Miami Ave. Mainly interesting for the part devoted to the native populations of Florida.

Parrot Jungle: 11000 S. W. 57th Ave. A tropical park full of parrots.

The Cuban Quarter ('Little Havana'): a little town in itself south-west of the city where English is a foreign language.

around Miami

Everglades National Park: see the chapter on 'National Parks'.

Key West: take U.S. Highway 1 which runs for 180 kms from one little coral island to another. Key West, a town much favoured by artists, writers and every kind of drop-out, is on the last island. Hemingway was largely responsible for popularizing the place: try imagining his 'old man' hunting the swordfish off the coast . . .

in Florida

Walt Disney World: near Orlando in the middle of Florida (Highway 192 and 254). Even more extraordinary than the famous Disneyland of Los Angeles' Disney World is as big as a town. The hotel that the monorail runs through is very impressive. There are so many attractions that you really need to stay at least four or five days to see them all. Disney World also deserves attention because of the declared ambition of its organizers and creators to build a town of the future which would do away with all the present contradictions. American visitors from big cities with enormous urban problems often fly in to live for a while in a mythical universe where the American dream has at last become reality. Accommodation around Disney World: many motels including some belonging to the Days Inn chain which are among the cheapest.

J. F. Kennedy Space Center: on the coast, 46 miles east of Orlando or from Interstate 95. The main interest of this launching-base for the historic flights to the moon lies in visiting the V.A.B. (Vehicle Assembly Building) which is still the biggest building in the world. It is amazing and makes you feel giddy just to go inside. There is also the

N.A.S.A. museum, very well set out and very informative.

Daytona Beach: North-east of Florida, on the coast. This town, known for its Formula 1 motor-car races, has one of the nicest beaches in the United States, except that in the high season (Easter) it tends to be over-crowded with young people. However, it's an ideal spot for making friends when hitch-hiking.

Fort Lauderdale: 30 minutes north of Miami, nick-named 'the American Venice', a town designed for holiday-makers. The beach along North Atlantic Bld is calmer than those of Miami. Lots of good night-clubs for lovers of the night-life: Pier 66, Plagpen and the Rapp Lounge.

NEW ORLEANS

☎ 504
LOUISIANA

A surprising town, famous for its French Quarter (or Vieux Carré), its Creole cooking, its Dixieland jazz and its burials. Its Spanish architecture is a complete break with every other style to be seen elsewhere in the United States and takes you back a hundred years into the past. The vegetation composed of magnolias and liana-hung trees soon gives you the blues, and the 'Cajun' music remains as strange as it's beautiful. New Orleans slowly bewitches you when you stay there for a while. It's also a very big port, the second in the country after New York.

arriving in New Orleans

Coach

Greyhound: Loyola Ave/Howard Ave (2101 Earhart Bld). ☎ 525.93.71.

Continental Trailways: 1314 Tulane Ave. ☎ 525.42.01.

Plane

Moisant International Airport: 18 kms away. A town bus runs to and from the centre of the city every half-hour. If you are in a hurry there is a hire-car service to the main hotels.

New Orleans
French Quarter/Vieux Carré
Business District

0   0,3mi
0   500m

Greyhound, Internat. Airport

Dramed Stadium

N. Orleans St.
St. Ann St.
Dumaine St.
N. Robertson St.
Lafitte Ave.
Villere St.
Marais St.
Treme Ave.
Orleans St.
St. Ann St.

Municipal
Auditorium

Cultural
Center

Beauregard
Square

Roman St.
N. Derbigny St.
St. Louis Cemetery
Canal St.

Housing Project

Old St. Louis Court Bldg.
St. Louis Cemetery
Our Lady of
Guadalupe
Church

Municipal
Court

Museum "Sold
of the Sou

Orleans St.
St. Ann St.
Burgur.

Toulouse

Mardi Gras
Museum

Peter

Tabarry
Theatre

S. Robertson St.
Villere St.
S. Prieur St.
Iberville St.
Marais St.
Treme St.
Crozat St.
N. Basin St.
Bienville St.

Wax
Museum

St. Louis

Grima House

21
26
19
18
17
16
15

St. Katherine
Church

Simon Bolivar
Mon.

Joy
Theatre

Athletic
Club

Burgundy

Jazz
Museum

22
23
24
25

Charity
Hospital L.S.U.
Medical Center
Tulane
Medical School

Continental
Trailways

ELK

Saenger
Theatre

Lowe's
State Theatre

Audubon
Bldg.

Dauphine

Old
Absinthe
House

Wildlife
Museum

26

Veterans Hosp.

Public
Library

Orpheum
Theatre

Common St.

Boston
Club

Bourbon

Iberville St.

Royal St.

27

Monteleone
Hotel

Home of Sie
de Bienvil

Louisiana
State Bldg.

Supreme Court Bldg.

Duncan,
Plaza.

Gravier

Jesuit
Church

Holiday
Inn

City Hall
Civic Center

Public Service
Bldg.

Cotton
Exchange

Kolb's Restaur. C.

U.S. Custom
House

Mariti
Muse

Civil Courts
Bldg.

Hibernia
Bank (Tower)

Union St.

Gateway Bldg.

Common St.

International House

Canal St.

Poydras

Lafayette

Western
Union

Masonic Temple

Chamber of
Commerce

Medallion Towers

Liberty
Monumen

Federal
Building

Federal Reserve
Bank

Charles St.

Poydras

Board of Trade

Rivergate
Exhibition
Center

Post
Office

Girod

Scottish Rite
Temple

Gallier Hall

Lafayette
Square
Federal
Bldg.

Magazine St.

Tchoupitoulas St.

Julia

Plaza
Towers

O'Keefe

Baronne

Carondelet St.

Camp St.

U.S. Federal
Courts

Commerce St.

St. Peters St.

Fulton St.

Lafayette

Union
Station

St. Charles Ave.

St. Patrick's Church

Pontchartrain Expressway

Lee Circle

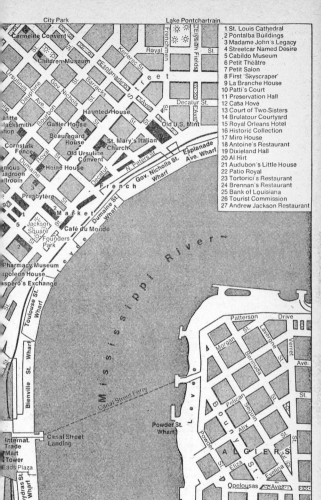

Train

Union Passenger Terminal: 1001 Loyola Ave.
☎ 586.00.27.

don't panic

Finding your way around

The New Orleans that you can hope to visit in a few days is only a tiny part of the enormous city that stretches around the Mississippi; the French Quarter is made up of a grid system of streets situated north of Canal St, the shopping artery of the city. Here the streets have names – mainly French.

Transport

The tramways run along Canal St and St Charles Ave. Information ☎ 529.45.45. Free map of the network.

Bicycle hire: 1029 Royal St, 1006 Royal St, 736 Orleans St.

N.B. New Orleans is best seen on foot: everything is concentrated within a small radius.

Refuge

Y.M.C.A. Lee Circle Branch: 936 St Charles Ave. ☎ 568.96.22. One floor reserved for girls.

keys to New Orleans

General information

Tourist & Convention Commission: 334 Royal St. ☎ 522.87.72. Free coffee. Open every day from 9.00 to 17.00 hrs.

Newspapers and magazines

Figaro: a weekly with the programmes of all the shows.

Today in New Orleans: free in hotels.

Colleges and campuses

Tulane University: St Charles Ave/Exposition Bld. New Orleans' main University; a few bars in the quarter where students meet, on the Campus, a 'ride-board' in the Students' Union and a cafeteria. To get there take the tramway on St Charles Ave.

Meeting places

During the day: around Jackson Square in the centre of the old town. In the evening and at night all activity is concentrated in a few streets of the French Quarter: Bourbon St, Royal St, and Dauphine St. The further you go from Canal St the stranger the people you meet. During the day only a few tourists lend a little life to this quarter.

Survival

Go round the little shops in the **French Quarter**, a number of them have notice-boards.

Baptist Mission: 201 Magazine St. Crashing (men only).

Nose Switchboard: ☎ 524.93.14.

Auto Driveaway: 201 Kent Ave. ☎ 885.92.92. Take the air-terminal bus on Tulane Ave.

good night

The cheapest: there are a few small hotels (rather grubby-looking from outside) on St Charles Ave and on Carondelet, west of Canal St. Here are the addresses of three of them:

Chalmette Hotel: 808 Carondelet.

Le Dale: 749 St Charles Ave. ☎ 523.87.00.

Imperial Hotel: 609 St Charles Ave.

There are often rooms available in Bourbon St (100 metres from Canal St).

Very well-placed but rather more expensive:

Hotel Toulouse: 506 Toulouse/Decatur. ☎ 522.30.35.

More expensive hotels

Lasalle Hotel: 1113 Canal St. ☎ 523.58.31. Not too far from the French Quarter.

Nine-o-five Royal Hotel: 905 Royal St. ☎ 523.02.19.

Hedgewood Hotel: 2427 St Charles Ave. ☎ 895.97.08.

If you are travelling by car, go to one of the cheap motels on Airline Highway (between Downtown and the airport). For example:

Home Sweet Home Motel: 4231 Airline Highway. ☎ 835.59.46. Easily the cheapest.

Keystone Motel: 8825 Airline Highway. ☎ 721.14.77.

Sherwood Motel: 1015 Airline Highway. ☏ 833.94.94.

Nearer the Vieux Carré and nearly as cheap:
Crescent Motel: 3522 Tulane Ave. ☏ 486.57.36.

Inexpensive motels on Chef Menteur Highway (90 East) north-east of the Vieux Carré:
Del Mar Motel: 8542 Chef Menteur Highway. ☏ 242.27.70.
Park Plaza Motel: 4460 Chef Menteur Highway. ☏ 944.45.31.

getting fed

Most restaurants in the Vieux Carré are very expensive, but there are still a few which most people can afford:
Acme Oyster House: 724 Iberville St. Sea-food specialities.
Baronne Taverne: Canal St/Baronne St.
Bozo's: 2713 St Ann St.
Café créole: 624 Bourbon St.
Coffee Pot: Peter St/Bourbon St.

Poor Boys (sometimes called 'Po-boys')
These are enormous sandwiches costing next to nothing which really fill you up.
Mother's: 401 Poydras St. The recognized Po-Boy specialist. A must if you are short of money: make a nice change from the Burger King.
Martin's Poor Boy Restaurant: 1940 St Claude Ave.
Clarence & Lefty's: 1934 Almanasta St.

Mexican cooking:
Pancho's Mexican Buffet: 918 Gravier St.

Tripe specialities:
Roma's: 1003 Decatur St.

Good cheap restaurants, centrally situated
Asia Garden: 530 Bourbon St. Cantonese cooking.
The Bon Ton: 401 Magazine St. Cajun.
Bonanza Sirloin Pit: 131 St Charles Ave.
Café Maspero: 440 Chartres St.
Castillo's Mexican Restaurant: 620 Conti St.

Felix's Restaurant: 739 Iberville St. Oysters at the bar.

Gin's Mee Hong Restaurant: 739 Conti St. Cantonese.

Homes Pot Pourri Restaurant: 130 Bourbon. Young people's restaurant with sophisticated decor (antiques, plants, mirrors etc), and reasonably priced menu.

Maison Blanche Department Store: 901 Canal St.

Messina's Oyster House: 200 Chartres St.

The Original Mellus Bar: 622 Conti St. Rice and red beans, toasted sandwiches.

Place D'Armes Hotel: carriage café: 625 St Ann St.

Crêpes:

St Louis St Crêpe Shop: 817 St Louis St.

Outside the French Quarter:

French Market: 1008 N. Peters. On the banks of the Mississippi, a market with cafés, restaurants and street-vendors.

El Ranchito Restaurant: 1811 Elysian Fields Ave (closed on Tuesdays). The oldest Mexican restaurant in New Orleans.

Dooky Chase Restaurant: 2301 Orleans Ave.

Spaghetti Eddie's Warehouse and the Boston Bar: 1017 Pleasant St.

Where to buy local produce:

Chez Hélène: 1540 N. Robertson St.

Buster Holmes: 721 Burgundy St.

Dooky Chase: 2301 Orleans Ave.

things that everyone goes to see and that you shouldn't miss

The French Quarter: One's attention is drawn by the charm of the forged ironwork balconies which adorn every house. It's really worth spending hours wandering round the Vieux Carré and having a discreet look at the patios and backyards. A few places of interest:

On Royal St:

at **127:** the first Carnival Ball took place here in 1857.

at **334:** originally the Old Bank of Louisiana, built in 1826.

at 400: on the 1st floor you can visit the **Louisiana Wildlife and Fisheries Museum** (8.30–17.00, closed at weekends, entrance free). Collections of animals native to Louisiana.

at 403: lived Étienne de Bore, Louisiana's first sugar merchant; his plantation was on the site of the present Audubon Park.

at 437: lived the inventor of the first cocktail, a chemist.

at 520: the patio of this house built in 1816 is open to the public.

at 700: notice the elegance of the balconies (1835).

at 1132: the house of James Gallier Jr, an architect responsible for many buildings in New Orleans.

On Chartres St:

at 440: gentlemen discussed business (i.e. sugar, cotton, slaves), around an absinthe or two.

at 538: began in 1788 the fire which destroyed nearly all of the Vieux Carré.

at 1113: Beauregard House, dating from 1826, has been restored. Can be visited 10.00–16.00 hrs.

at 1114: see the Ursulines Convent (1845).

Jackson Square: a very 'Montmartre, Place du Tertre' type atmosphere (and indeed some of the artists come from Montmartre).

Le Cabildo: opposite Jackson Square, Louisiana State Museum (every day except Monday, 9.00–17.00). Under the arcades go and see one of the very first submarines (with pedals!).

Jazz Museum: Bourbon St/Conti St in the Royal Sonesta Hotel. You can sometimes listen to old recordings. (During the week, 10.00–17.00; Sundays, 13.00–17.00. Closed on Mondays.)

---

things that everyone doesn't go to see but which are worth seeing

Certain old houses are especially worth seeing:

Maison Miro: 529 Royal St (dates from 1727, rebuilt in 1788).

House of Doctor le Monnier: 640 Royal St (1811, first building in the Vieux Carré to have more than two floors).

Pontalba Apartments: on the north and south sidewalks of Jackson Square (1849, the oldest apartment blocks in the United States).

House built in 1850: 525 St Ann St. Can be visited.

Hermann-Grima House: 820 St Louis St. Built in 1831 this house is remarkable for its contemporary furniture, its two interior courtyards, and its stable (now converted). Weekdays 10.00–16.00; Sundays, 13.00–17.00. Closed Wednesdays.

Pontalba Historical Puppetorium: 514 St Peter St in Jackson Square (every day, 10.00–18.00). An unusual history museum: puppets re-enact the life of the pirate Jean Laffite and the history of the city up to the battle of New Orleans.

Voodoo Museum: 739 Bourbon St (every day, 10.00–13.00). (If there are several of you, try haggling over the entrance fee.) A unique collection of 'trinkets' and other more or less authentic machines having been used by voodoo cults.

Pharmacy Museum: 514 Charles St (Tuesday to Saturday, 10.00–17.00). Alembics, balloon-jars, test-tubes, steel syringes etc; the complete panoply of the perfect nineteenth-century apothecary can be seen in this small museum.

The docks: at the end of Canal St: interesting walks to be had along these busy docks, where coffee, bananas and other exotic products are unloaded. Take advantage of the Ferryboat which is free; you can cross the Mississippi without having to go on the two-hour excursion on the river which is unexciting and expensive.

Place Beauregard: Voodoo rites were practised here. It's claimed that jazz was born in this square.

St Louis Cemetery: near Basin St, at the end of Conti St. Worth seeing for its above-ground-level burial chambers.

Superdome: an immense covered stadium (the biggest in the world). Can be visited at 10.30, 13.30, 15.30. Behind Canal St, going towards Loyola Ave.

New Orleans Museum of Art: City Park. Take a bus on Canal St and ask for the museum (some distance away). Everyday, 10.00–17.00, Thursdays 13.00–21.00. A small unexceptional museum but worth while if only for the bus journey (Esplanade Ave in particular).

great scenes

Music

As far as jazz is concerned, New Orleans is more than disappointing. The French Quarter is crammed with striptease clubs. But there are two great places:

Preservation Hall: 726 St Peter St. (on the corner of Bourbon St). Far and away the best place for jazz.

Your Father's Moustache: Bourbon St. Always full, good atmosphere.

Festival calendar

Mardi Gras: this is the time to be in New Orleans when the whole city spends a wild week dancing, parading, drinking, etc.

Spring Fiesta: visits to plantations, patios and houses in the Garden district are organized for two weeks from the first Friday after Easter onwards. Information from 529 Ann St. ☎ 581.13.67.

Jazz and Heritage Festival: every April, a series of musical and gastronomic events. Not to be missed. For more details, write in advance to: Festival Headquarters: 424 Barracks St, New Orleans, L.A. 70116. ☎ 522.47.86.

Theatre

Two of New Orleans black community's theatres are worth getting to know:

Free Southern Theatre: 1240 Dryades St (on the corner of Erato). ☎ 581.50.91. Most performances are free. The troop is 'politically engaged'.

Dashiki Project Theatre: 2135 Second St (on the corner of Loyola Ave). ☎ 283.44.64.

Shopping

Community Flea Market: Barracks/French Market Place. At weekends, all day. Right next to the famous 'Streetcar named desire'.

Aunt Sally's Praline Shops: 810 Decatur. Excellent. A little-known speciality in New Orleans. Excellent pralines also at **Dupree's Gift Shop:** 524 Royal St.

Two shops have a very wide choice of kites:

The Kite Shop: 542 St Peter St (Jackson Square).

Kites of All Nations: 603 Royal St.

Rare jazz records:

Duke's Palace: 214 Royal St (in the Monteleone Hotel).

The Riverband Shopping Area: St Charles Ave/Canal St. A dozen or so fashion and craft shops gathered together under this name at the end of St Charles Ave (take the tram).

Bars

Two very old bars where you can order an 'anis' (if not an 'absinthe' which has been illegal for a long time).

Old Absinthe House: 240 Bourbon St.

Old Absinthe Bar: 400 Bourbon St.

Other pleasant spots:

Cosimo's: 1201 Burgundy St.

La Boucherie Bar: 330 Chartres St.

Maxwell's Plum: 400 Burgundy St.

The Pearl: 119 St Charles St.

Maple Leaf Bar: 8316 Oak St.

around New Orleans

Calmette National Historical Park: 9.5 kms to the east; site of the battle of New Orleans (1815). The reception centre is a restored house dating from before the Revolution. (Every day, June to August, 8.00–18.00, September, 8.00–17.00; entrance free).

Lake Pontchartrain: 3.2 kms away. You cross it on a fly-over highway 39 kms long, the longest road over water in the world. Amusement park, beach.

Cajun Festivals: in the country of the 'bayous', where the Acadians live, there are many festivals. At the end of April the suckling pig festival at Mansura; Cajun crayfish festival at the beginning of May at Breaux Bridge; Cajun music festival in April at Abbeville.

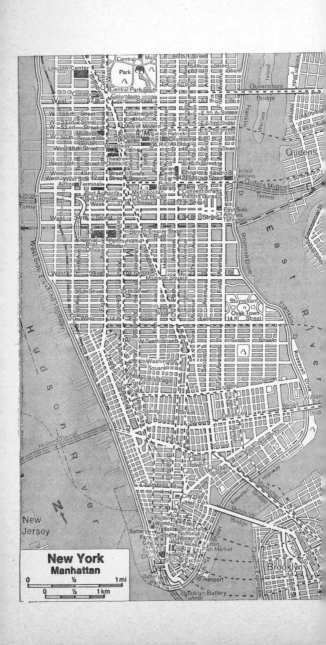

New York
Manhattan

0   ½   1 mi

0   ½   1 km

NEW YORK

☎ 212
NEW YORK

'New York is hell'. Most people arrive with this idea firmly in their heads and look askance at everything. It's fashionable to spend only a few days, or even hours, here before getting as quickly as possible on the road to the West. To do so is to deprive oneself of one of the most remarkable experiences in city living that one could ever hope to have: a world where all kinds of extremes exist side by side, and where the intensity of life struggles with the disproportionate coldness of the buildings. New York: you love it or you hate it. In any case your mind is quickly made up.

New York is not a smaller or more concentrated version of the U.S.A.: no other city in America can be compared to it; a New Yorker is a being different from all other Americans, and not just because of the accent. More cosmopolitan than any other metropolis in the world, with its Jewish, Irish, Italian, Cuban, Puerto-Rican, Chinese, Russian, Hungarian etc. colonies, it offers a spectacle of an astonishing variety: it would take months to get to know all the quarters of Manhattan, and yet Manhattan is only one of the five big boroughs of New York city together with the Bronx, Queens, Brooklyn and Richmond. So the only problem is: where to start?

129

arriving in New York

Coach

Greyhound and Continental Trailways: Port Authority Terminal 8th Ave/41st St W. ☎ 594.20.00 (Greyhound); 730.74.60 (Continental).

Plane

From J. F. Kennedy Airport: from 5.15–21.30 the buses of the Carey Company run a service every 15 minutes to the East Terminal in Manhattan (1st Ave/37th St). After 21.30, there is a bus about every 45 minutes. On average the journey lasts three quarters of an hour. Taxis are much more expensive and therefore only a good idea if you are in a group or four or five. If you are on your own you would do better to pay a few dollars more for a trip by helicopter (New York Airways) which will take you to the Wall Street Heliport in less than 15 minutes. If you haven't got much luggage, the cheapest way to get to Manhattan is to take a bus Q10 as far as the New York Subway. Rather rough, however, as a first contact with the U.S.A. and best avoided at night. At the airport itself white and yellow buses run continually to and from all the terminals.

From La Guardia Airport: Bus Q33 to Roosevelt-Jackson Heights where you take the subway.

From Newark Airport: Carey bus as far as West Side Airlines Terminal/2nd Ave/42nd St.

Connections with La Guardia and Newark international airports: Carey buses link J. F. Kennedy with La Guardia every hour from 7.45 to 13.15, and every half-hour from 13.15 to 21.15. Salem Transportation Inc. runs a limousine service to Newark Airport about every 90 minutes from 12.00 to 19.30. At J. F. Kennedy Airport, Hertz, Avis and National car-hire counters are to be found in the hall of the General Aviation Terminal.

Train

Amtrak: *Grand Central Terminal*: 12 W. 51st St. ☎ 532.49.00.

Pennsylvania Railroad Station: 7th Ave/W. 33rd St. ☎ 736.60.00.

don't panic

Finding your way around

You will probably stay in Manhattan, the island with

130

which New York is always identified, forgetting that Brooklyn, Queens, the Bronx and Richmond are also part of New York City. Knowing your way around is essential in the town of the famous right-angled layout of streets and avenues, all of them numbered, which was designed in 1811. It's very easy to understand how this system works: it's not very poetic, but very practical for finding addresses and particularly for judging distances.

The avenues run north–south and the streets east–west. They are numbered in the direction of east to west for the former and south to north for the latter. East and West Manhattan are separated by Fifth Avenue. Broadway is an artery which is an exception to the grid system: it runs diagonally from the north-west to the extreme south of the island. An address can be given:

According to its number: in the case of a street it's always followed by West (W.) or East (E.) depending on which side of Fifth Avenue it's situated. (The numbers get bigger from Fifth Avenue onwards.) For example: 90 E. 42nd St.

Sometimes according to its location with regard to both avenue and street, either because the address is at an intersection, or because it's in one of the four contiguous blocks (a method used in conversation to situate a restaurant, bank etc). For example: 7th Ave/134th St. When the address is on an avenue (for example, 1233 5th Ave), you can use a small conversion table to work out at which street level it's situated. You can find this at the beginning of the Yellow Pages directory.

New Yorkers always use three keywords to indicate the three zones which divide Manhattan from north to south: *Uptown* (the northern part from 59th St to the end of the island), *Midtown* (the middle part from 14th St to 59th St) and *Downtown* (the southern part from 14th St to the southern tip). The streets are nearly all one-way: west–east for those with even numbers, and the contrary for the others. As for the avenues, the traffic goes in the direction south–north for those with even numbers, and north–south for those with odd numbers, including Broadway.

Finally, there are two avenues which don't have a number: Madison Ave (between Park Ave and 5th Ave) and Lexington Ave (between Park Ave and 3rd Ave). Park Ave is always used instead of 4th Ave. Sometime 6th Ave is called Avenue of the Americas. From Central Park onwards, 11th Ave becomes West End Ave, 10th Ave Amsterdam Ave, 9th Ave Columbus Ave, and 8th Ave Central Park West. Downtown things get complicated: the chessboard isn't regular.

Transport

Bus: The routes follow the main avenues and streets. Always have the right money or else a Subway token; there is only one fare for any distance travelled. The fare is half-price at weekends from 18.00 on Saturday until midnight on Sunday. There are two bus circuits (Culture Bus 1 and 2) operating on the basis of a daily set fare at weekends and on national holidays from 10.00 to 18.00 hrs. You can obtain the itineraries (with the most important points of the town) from the Visitor Center (90 E. 42nd St).

Subway: Buy a token in the station and ask for a map, essential to find your way round this extremely complex network run by three companies: IND (independent), IRT (Interborough Rapid Transport Co.) and BMT (Brooklyn and Manhattan Transit Co.). Be careful: There are express trains and local trains. To be frank, the New York subway doesn't enjoy a very favourable reputation. It's certainly advisable not to hang about in the passageways after midnight and it's true that no other Underground in the world is noisier or dirtier. You should, however, take the 'sub' at least once, if only to discover what a mobile exhibition of popular art is, the most magnificent living anthology of graffiti, 'underground' art in the literal sense: all the coaches are covered with graffiti and slogans sprayed on (in the depots at night) by gangs of youths. For bus and subway you can telephone for information to the **N.Y. Transit Authority:** ☎ 330.12.34.

Taxi

The famous **Yellow Cabs** are very expensive, but a little taxi-ride round New York is better than any fairground merry-go-round! Furthermore, at certain times of the night there's no other way of getting back home. Above all don't forget to give a 15% tip; failure to do so will provoke a hostile or even violent reaction.

Bicycle

Definitely not advisable except in Central Park.

On foot

If you have the time, without doubt the best way of seeing New York. Allow yourself one day for Greenwich Village and Soho, two more for Midtown, a fourth for Central Park and the beginning of Uptown etc. A word of warning: only cross the road at pedestrian crossings and when the sign shows 'walk'. New York isn't London and car-drivers (not to mention taxi-drivers who show no mercy) are not indulgent.

A reminder: count a minute's walk per block when

going in a north–south direction and three minutes per block in a 'crosstown' i.e. east–west direction.

Car hire

Before hiring a car in New York, bear in mind that you will spend a lot of money in parking meters and different carparks. There is practically nowhere where you can park free in Downtown and Midtown. Avoid parking in front of fire hydrants and in 'Tow Away' zones: both of these can prove expensive.

Here are some car-hire companies:

Avis: 217 E. 43rd St. ☎ (800) 331.12.12.

Hertz: 310 E. 48th St. ☎ (800) 654.31.31.

Cheaper:

Alpha: 304 Pearl St. ☎ 755.90.00.

Alpha-Gaines: 902 2nd Ave. ☎ 421.11.55 and 141 W. 54th St. ☎ 247.42.42.

Dollar: 225 W. 34th St. ☎ 279.05.85.

Econo: 231 E. 43rd St. ☎ 686.49.21.

National: Hilton Hotel (6th Ave/53rd St). ☎ (800) 328.45.67.

New Castle: 407 E. 61st St.(between York Ave. and 1st Ave). ☎ 753.74.64.

Refuge

Y.M.C.A. Vanderbilt: 224 E. 47th St. ☎ 755.24.10.

Y.M.C.A. West Side Branch: 5 W. 65th St. ☎ 787.44.00.

Y.M.C.A. McBurney Branch: 215 W. 23rd St. ☎ 741.92.26.

Y.M.C.A. Harlem Branch: 180 W. 135th St. ☎ 281.41.00.

Y.M.C.A.: 138 E. 28th St. ☎ 685.51.41.

Y.M.C.A.: 8th Ave/51st St. ☎ 216.37.00.

The Y.M.C.A. West Side Branch is definitely the least unpleasant.

Y.W.C.A.: 135 E. 52nd St. ☎ 753.42.00

---

keys to New York

General information

New York Convention and Visitors Bureau: 90 E. 42nd St. ☎ 687.13.00. Situated opposite Grand Central Station: provides a full tourist information service. Open every day, 9.00–18.00 hrs.

133

New York City Information Center: a small kiosk (Broadway/42nd St. ☎ 221.98.69) in Times Square where you can obtain in particular the information sheet devoted to jazz concerts, *Jazz Interactions*.

Council on International Education Exchange: 777 United Nations Plaza (at the east end of 46th St). Very useful for students (and others). Publishes brochures and information sheets several times a year. It's also the place to go to book your return flight if you are on a C.I.E.E. charter (entrance is on 44th St. Take the lift on the right).

Rand McNally Map Store: 48th St; between 5th Ave and 6th Ave. The best shop for maps and guides to New York. Some maps are free.

Texaco and **Exxon:** give away free (but less and less often) maps of the U.S.A. and town-guides to New York. **Texaco** is very close to Grand Central Terminal: Lexington Ave/42nd St. **Exxon** is at 6th Ave/49th St.

Exxon Touring Service: 1251 6th Avenue/50th St. ☎ 398.30.00.

Newspapers and magazines

The **Sunday New York Times** with its 'art and leisure' supplement is the best guide to the week's events in New York. Reading the Sunday New York Times is the traditional occupation of millions of New Yorkers on Sunday.

The **Village Voice** is the New York weekly *par excellence*. As well as providing full coverage of shows it also includes articles which are always interesting. There is also **Soho News**, an excellent weekly guide to what's happening in the artists' quarter.

Andy Warhol's Interview: the smartest, most snobbish and most typically New York of the city's monthly reviews. Everything you could wish to know about show-biz, the stars, glamour.

Punk: For those who love 'garage rock'. Very specialized.

A very different kind of weekly is **Cue**, mainly devoted to restaurants.

There is also that high-class magazine, the **New Yorker.**

Given away free of charge in hotels is **Key Host,** a small brochure which lists theatre-shows, exhibitions in museums etc. And finally, if you want to get to know the New York-Babylon world of sex, **Screw** is obviously the best introduction.

Post

The General Post Office, open every day, is on 8th Ave/33rd St.

Colleges and campuses

N.Y.U. The University of New York is in the centre of Greenwich Village: the buildings are on the southern side of Washington Square Park.
The famous and rather select **Columbia University** is on Broadway/116th St; really friendly atmosphere in the Halls of Residence around the campus.

Meeting places

First and foremost, **Greenwich Village;** i.e. some of the main streets and those around them: Mc-Dougal, Bleecker St., Greenwich Ave.
Apart from Greenwich and its Washington Square, there is **East Village** between Broadway and 1st Avenue and between 14th St and 2nd St. Not quite what it was in the sixties, but you never know ...
Have a look round Tompkins Square and St Monk's Square. Two museums are very popular for making social contacts (i.e. picking-up girls): the MET and particularly the MOMA with its open-air cafeteria in a garden full of sculptures.

Soho and its bars for artists in search of a nostalgic bohemia is worth visiting; you can meet some interesting people.

Rockefeller Center: Manhattan's number-one meeting place. At lunchtime it's always bursting at the seams.

The boats and ferries are always good places for getting to know people (see later under New York Skyline).

Central Park: there is always something on: in summer, for example, free plays and concerts.

The 'Singles Bars', meeting places for young New Yorkers, are on the first three avenues between 60th and 70th St. See also the list of pubs and restaurants.

Survival

First and foremost, look through *Village Voice* which is a mine of information.

Look at the notice-board in Columbia University; go to the **Loeb Student Center** in Washington Square.

If you want to head away from New York towards the Californian dream-world, there are two 'Driveaway' companies:

Aaacon Auto Transport: 230 W. 41st St. ☎ 354. 77.77.

Dependable Car: 130 W. 42nd St. ☎ 840.62.62 (20th floor).

See also advertisements in the *Voice* for cheap bus journeys.

There are also two 'ride centers': ☎ 279.38.70 and Green Tortoise: 101 Crosby.

Three useful telephone numbers if you run into trouble: 411 for general information, 911 for the police, 330.12.34 for information about the subway.

---

good night

Student accommodation

C.I.E.E. New York Student Center: William Sloane House, 9th Ave/W. 34th St. ☎ 695.51.33. 1, 490 rooms! Reductions for students.

International Student Residence: Columbia University, Johan Jay Hall, Broadway/116th St (Bus M.104 or else subway IRT on 7th Ave). In June, July and until mid-August, puts up foreign students. Telephone in advance 280.27.75.

International Student Center: 38 W. 88th St. ☎ 787.77.06.

International House: 500 Riverside Drive. ☎ 678. 50.00. Open in summer and very pleasant; you can meet other students from all over the world.

(Relatively) cheap hotels

It's impossible to find a really cheap decent hotel in New York, but some of them have rooms without air-conditioning which are cheaper. If you stay for at least six days you can also get a cheap weekly rate.

Barbizon (women only): Lexington Ave/63rd St. ☎ 838.57.00.

Clinton: 19 W. 31st St. ☎ 279.40.17.

Diplomat: 108 W. 43rd St. ☎ 279.37.07.

Earle: Washington Square (Waverly Place). ☎ 777.95.15.

Irving Hotel: 26 Gramercy Park South (20th St/ 3rd Ave). ☎ GR5.62.63.

Kenmore: 145 E. 23rd St. ☎ 475.38.40.

Lincoln Square: 166 W. 75th St. ☎ TR3.30.00.

Martha Washington (for women only): 30 E. 30th St. ☎ 689.19.00.

Opera: Broadway between 76th St and 77th St. ☎ 787.19.00.

Pickwick Arms: 230 E. 51st St. ☎ 355.03.00. No air-conditioning.

Rio Hotel: 132 W. 47th St. ☎ 757.38.70.

Rosoff's: 147 W. 43rd St. ☎ JU2.32.00.

Stanford: 43 W. 32nd St. ☎ 563.14.80.

Sutton East: 330 E. 56th St. ☎ 751.17.00.

Webster: 40 W. 45th St. ☎ MU2.43.90.

York: 488 7th Ave (between 36th and 37th St). ☎ 868.26.70.

Relatively expensive hotels

Carter Hotel: 250 W. 43rd St. ☎ 947.60.00.

Chelsea Hotel: 222 W. 23rd St. ☎ 243.37.00.

Edison: 228 W. 47th St. ☎ 246.50.00.

George Washington: Lexington Ave/23rd St. ☎ 475.19.20.

Martinique: Broadway/23rd St. ☎ 736.38.00.

Times Square Motor Hotel: 255 W. 43rd St. ☎ 354.79.00.

Tudor Hotel: 304 E. 42nd St. ☎ 986.88.00.

Wales: 1295 Madison Ave/92nd St. ☎ 876.60.00.

Wellington: 7th Ave/55th St. ☎ 247.39.00.

If you are planning on staying for some time have a look at the classified advertisements in *Village Voice* under the heading 'Room-mates': you can often find cheap flats to share. There are also a number of advertisements in the *Sunday New York Times*.

---

getting fed

If all you want is something quick to eat between visiting a museum and a skyscraper, you will find plenty of snackbars, sandwich bars, cafeterias etc. Good value for money, for example, are the chains of shops called '*Chock Full O'Nuts*', '*Nathan*', '*Zum Zum*', which can be found more or less everywhere in Manhattan. (Avoid as far as possible the '*Bun and Burger*', a chain of restaurants whose hamburgers, without being better than elsewhere, are terribly expensive, as well as the '*Bagel Nosh*' chain which charges very high prices for very ordinary sandwiches.) But there are other ways and means of spending as little as possible than going to the above-mentioned restaurant chains whose awful food can tire even the most hardened.

A general principle if you want to eat well and inexpensively is to eat 'ethnic' food, i.e. Chinese in

Chinatown, Italian in Little Italy, German in York-town, Jewish in Midtown etc. (see later).

A useful tip for the whole of the United States but particularly for New York: in many coffee-houses and some restaurant-cafeterias you can get a large breakfast for a cheap price at any time of the day; at the weekend you can get a good 'brunch special' around 13.00–14.00 hrs in restaurants which advertise it outside.

Also useful to know: the cafeterias of a large number of museums have something to offer, in particular:

The Cafeteria of the Museum of Modern Art: 11 W. 53rd St. Excellent: eat well and inexpensively in an island of calm in the very centre of Manhattan. Go there on a Wednesday when entrance to the museum is practically free.

The Cafeteria of the Metropolitan: 82nd St. Very ordinary in comparison (it's in the basement) but entrance to the museum is practically free: you give what you want. Very useful if you are in the district and feeling hungry.

On fine weekends in **Central Park** barbecues are set up on the main paths: you can get a quarter-chicken for next to nothing.

Finally, there is one chain a cut above the others where you can get a good cheap steak, and that is **Tad's Steak House.** Here are some of the addresses where they can be found: 154 W. 34th St, 18 E. 42nd St, 7th Ave/48th St and 172 W. 72nd St. A cheap way of eating is to have a hot-dog at any time of the day, like the natives, and then have a steak in the evening in a Tad's.

A different case altogether: **Belmore Cafeteria,** Park Ave/28th St. A 'luncheonette' which is depressing to say the least, but it's open 24 hours a day. All the Manhattan taxi-drivers go there.

Restaurants

If you are rich enough you can eat really well in New York: just go to one of the restaurants recommended in papers such as *Cue* or the brochure *Key Host* which is distributed in hotels and tourist information centres. But you can still eat very well (and often in a very pleasant setting and atmosphere) for a generally moderate price in the following restaurants:

Midtown East Side

Amy's: 210 E. 23rd St. Inexpensive chain of restaurants.

Curacavi: 819 2nd Ave (between 43rd and 44th St).

Elaine's: 1703 2nd Ave. Very fashionable and so quite expensive.

Jack's Nest: 310 3rd Ave (between 23rd and 24th St).

The Madhatter: 1485 2nd Ave. Kind of easy-going, well-bred-student atmosphere; always full in the evenings.

Friday's: 1152 1st Ave. Large portions in a restaurant frequented by 'singles'.

Yellowfinger: 3rd Ave/61st St. Rather expensive given the quality but is still an institution among the 'singles' restaurants'.

There is a large number of small restaurants on Lexington Ave, 3rd Ave and, above all, 2nd Ave, where, between 72nd St and 86th St, you can find many Hungarian restaurants such as:

L and H Bakery and Restaurant: 1588 Second Ave (between 82nd and 83rd St).

Midtown West Side

Beggar's Banquet: 105 W. 44th St (near 6th Ave). Excellent choice of salads.

The Market: 411 9th Ave and also 572 11 Ave.

Mamma Leone's: 239 W. 48th St. A classic.

There is a large number of interesting restaurants around the Lincoln Center on Columbus Ave from the 62nd to the 70th St. From 70th St onwards you come into the quarter which is much favoured by Columbia University students and young people in general: Upper West Side. There are quite a lot of small Chinese and Cuban restaurants.

Uptown

At our place: On Broadway, between 94th and 95th St.

The Symposium: 544 W. 113th St.

La Tablita: Columbus Ave/75th St. Argentinian cooking, rather expensive.

Green Tree: Amsterdam Ave/111th St. Hungarian and very pleasant.

Downtown

The domain of the good small restaurant and bar-restaurant begins where the grid system becomes less regular, i.e. south of 14th St on the West side.

Greenwich Village:

Many good addresses on Bleecker St; amongst others:

Nobody's Restaurant: 163 Bleecker St.

Pink Tea Cup: 310 Bleecker St. (Fried chicken, beans.)

A good address nearby:

Café Feenjon: 105 McDougal St.

Soho:

Spring St Bar: 105 Spring St (on the corner of West Broadway). One of the high spots of Soho's 'bohemia'. Serves excellent sandwiches and salads.

Chinatown:

Without any doubt the best quarter as far as gastronomy is concerned. Furthermore, it's seldom expensive: take a stroll along Bayard St and the little streets round about.

Bobo's: 20 1/2 Pell St.

Chef Ma's: 10 Pell St.

Nom Wah Tea Parlor: 13 Doyers St.

Szeshuan Chinese Restaurant: 40 Bowery St.

Little Italy:

The restaurants here are marvellous!

Ferrara: 195 Grand St (on the corner of Mulberry St). A famous café where you can get Italian ice-cream and patisseries.

Forlini's: 93 Baxter St.

Giambone: 42 Mulberry St.

Lombardi: 53 Spring St.

Leonardo's: 169 Mulberry St.

Luna's: 112 Mulberry St.

Paolucci's: 149 Mulberry St. (One of the cheapest with Leonardo's.)

Umberto's Clamhouse: 129 Mulberry St. Very well-known because very cheap in view of the quality of the food.

Lower East Side and East Village

Caldron: 306 E. 6th St. Very fashionable little macrobiotic restaurant (closed at weekends).

Katz's: 205 E. Houston St. Jewish specialities ('Deli': beef sandwiches).

Other restaurants

Some of the bar-nightclubs listed below also have a restaurant (but don't expect anything special: salads, cooked meats, sandwiches, steaks).

Here are some recommended addresses:

McSorley's Old Ale House: 15 E. 7th St. (near 2nd Ave). Good beer in an Irish atmosphere.

Oyster Bar and Restaurant: in Grand Central Station. The widest choice of oysters in the United States (rather expensive unfortunately).

Maxwell's Plum: 1st Ave/64th St. The gathering-place for the New York intelligentsia; have a cocktail here on a Saturday evening around 21.00 hrs.

---

things that everyone goes to see and that you shouldn't miss

Famous places

Times Square: Broadway/42nd St. Begin with this condensed version of all that is extreme in New York: this court of miracles should be seen at nightfall, in drizzle, when the neon lights of the advertisement hoardings, porno cinemas, cafeterias with aluminium counters, sex-shops and massage-parlours light up to present a unique spectacle where the main roles are played by poverty, drugs and the most way-out vices. Emerging from the Subway at Times Square around 21.00 hrs is an experience not to be missed.

Rockefeller Center: 5th Ave (between 48th St and 51st St). The complete opposite of Times Square and yet it's only two or three blocks away. In the centre of Midtown, the Rockefeller Center is primarily a group of 1930 skyscrapers housing the headquarters of very big companies (e.g. R.C.A. with the main building). New Yorkers use it as a place for meeting people, not only businessmen but also people doing their shopping during the day; in a way it's Manhattan's forum with its open-air café closed in by the four walls of a patio. Make sure you read the magnificent entirely humanist and slightly paternalistic prose of Mr Rockefeller on the big plaque opposite the fountain.
From 9.00 to 19.00 hrs you can visit the NBC studios or the whole of the Center. There is an Observatory at the top. Behind the RCA Building on the Avenue of the Americas is Radio City Music Hall which puts on shows tailor-made for tourists.

Wall Street: to the extreme south of Downtown, a little street perpendicular to Broadway. The awesome impression of being stuck in a split in the granite at the foot of façades which loom over you, is only equalled by the frenzy of the little men in black or grey suits who gamble with the whole world's capitals, running from one building to another as if the end of the world was nigh. The New York Stock Exchange is on the corner of Wall Street and Broad St. From an overhead bay you can watch one of the most impressive spectacles in New York, the liveliest play imaginable: the 'Trading Floor', in other words the very heart of the sacred monster: Grand Capital. Once you have seen this you have understood half of the United States (entrance free, 10 00–15.30 hrs). For those who like contrasts: go to Wall St twice, the first time during the week around 17.00 hrs. and the second during the weekend at any time. You will hardly believe it's the same place.

Central Park: from 59th St to 110th St between Central Park West and 5th Ave. Few cities can boast of having a park of some four kilometres long by 800 metres wide in their very centre. In the summer at weekends it's as if everybody has come for a stroll. Many kinds of activity go on here, from the most official (free classical music concerts, Shakespeare plays) to the most occult, as well as the most everyday (picnics, red balloons, cycling, boating ...). The musical side is perhaps the most exciting: there are lots of groups, some improvised some not, playing jazz, reggae, rock, African music, Cuban music etc.

A reminder by the way: it really is true that it's inadvisable to go for a walk in Central Park after 21.00 hrs.

New York seen from above

The forest of skyscrapers soon makes the visitor want to have a global view of the city. There's no lack of viewing points:

World Trade Center: Trinity Pl/Liberty St. Apart from the helicopter (see later), the towers of the World Trade Center afford the most fantastic view of New York. When visibility is good it will take your breath away: you have the whole of Manhattan at your feet and the boroughs of Brooklyn, Queens, Richmond and the Bronx are also perfectly visible. The 107th and top floor of the South Tower is open to the public but isn't free (open until 21.30 hrs). There is a restaurant (very expensive) on the top floor of the North Tower. From an architectural point of view, the Towers, with their narrow windows and Gothic touches in the lower part, are not particularly impressive.

Empire State Building: 5th Ave/33rd St. The Empire is now almost an antique with its 380 metres (as against 420 for the WTC Towers). Open every day until midnight. Has an observatory but you have to pay to get in. Think of King Kong when you are up there. N.B. If there are only a few dollars left in your jeans pockets, it's easy enough to find a skyscraper you can get to the top of free; all you have to do is be discreet and sure of yourself: once in the lift just press the buttons to the the top floor and there between the offices you are bound to find a magnificent view over Manhattan. For example: the Chase Manhattan Bank (in the Financial District). Best time: on a Friday at 16.30 hrs.

Helicopter trips: a little extravagance not easily forgotten – if you can afford it.

Island Helicopters: ☎ 683.45.75. Heliport: 34th St on the East River. Choice of flights lasting from 5 to 25 minutes (9.00–17.00 hrs).

Hel-Aircopters: 12th Ave/30th St. ☎ 695.05.20.

New York skyline

The New York skyline is particularly striking. To fully appreciate it you have either to cross to the other side of the East River via Brooklyn Bridge or the Subway and walk along Brooklyn Heights esplanade or take one of the following boats:

Staten Island Ferry Boat: as it costs next to nothing you can easily afford the little cruise which goes from the extreme South of Manhattan to Staten Island.

Circle Line: Pier 83 (43rd St, on the Hudson River) ☎ 563.32.00. Complete tour of Manhattan. Sailings every 45 minutes from 10.00 to 17.30 hrs in summer. Marvellous cruise but a bit long: three hours.

Statue of Liberty Ferry (see section 'Things that everybody goes to see and that can be given a miss').

Museums

The Metropolitan Museum of Art (often called by Americans 'The Met') : 5th Ave/82nd St (10.00 to 16.45, closed on Mondays, open until 20.45 on Tuesdays and 11.00–16.45 on Sundays). The American equivalent of the Louvre. Some real masterpieces: Botticelli's 'St Jeremiah's Last Communion', Vermeer's 'Woman at the Window' and 'Woman with Jug', Gauguin's 'Orana Maria', Van Gogh's 'Arlésienne with books', some Courbets and a Breughel. Between the collection of Egyptian antiques, Italian paintings, the department of Medieval Art, Spanish paintings (including some fine Grecos), you could spend whole days here. But don't let these prevent you from going to see the children's museum in the basement – it's very instructive.

The Guggenheim Museum: 5th Ave/89th St (open 11.00–17.00 hrs, closed on Mondays, open on Tuesdays until 20.00 hrs, free Tuesday evening). The building itself is an architectural masterpiece by Frank Lloyd Wright. What it contains is an excellent collection of modern art. A very wide collection of paintings by Kandinsky (180 works by one of the pioneers of abstract art) and a good number of paintings by Paul Klee. See also the Justin Thannhauser collection of Impressionists.

The Museum of Modern Art (the 'Moma'): 11 W. 53rd St (close to 5th Ave). Friday to Tuesday, 11.00–18.00; Thursday, 11.00–21.00. On Tuesdays you pay what you want to or can afford. Closed on Wednesdays. Has two famous paintings by Picasso: 'Les Demoiselles d'Avignon' and 'Guernica' and two huge paintings by Monet, 'Les Nénuphars' – fantastic! Also works by artists belonging to the Pantheon of modern art such as Van Gogh, Cézanne, Braque, Chirico, Dali etc., as well as those belonging to the school of contemporary American art such as Rothko, Newman, Pollock, Warhol etc. Next door and on the same side of the street the 'Moma' has opened a shop with a very wide choice of art books and photos.

The Whitney Museum of American Art: Madison Ave/75th St (closed on Mondays; open 11.00–18.00 hrs, 12.00–18.00 hrs on Sundays, and until 22.00 hrs on Tuesdays, free Tuesday evenings). This museum is devoted exclusively to contemporary American art. Worth seeing because, like all painting, American painting reflects very well the society of which it is the product: note, for example, the importance of the car for the hyper-realists. Note also the architectural quality of the building designed by Marcel Breuer.

---

things that everyone goes to see and that can be given a miss

---

The Statue of Liberty: This work by the Frenchman Bertholdo is very fine, but particularly when seen from a distance. During the summer there's a real crush to climb the last steps up to the crown (the return journey by ferry from Battery Park takes in all at least two hours).

St Patrick's Cathedral: 5th Ave/50th St. Some people might like it. Has air-conditioning. Quite amusing for a Gothic cathedral ... Opposite a statue of Atlas carrying the world on his shoulders.

United Nations: 1st Ave/44th St. The interior isn't as good as the exterior which could have been much worse (have a look at the buildings nearby). Guided visits by international hostesses who are – it goes without saying – charming.

Lincoln Center: Broadway/9th Ave. A group of theatres which owe their prestige to their productions (world-famous opera, New York Philharmonic Orchestra etc.) and not to the neo-classic type of contemporary architecture of the buildings. Only worth going to see, therefore, for the performances.

things that everyone doesn't go to see but which are worth seeing

Public Library: 5th Ave/42nd St. (Every day from 10.00–18.00 hrs except Sundays.) One of the few peaceful spots in Midtown, New York's Public Library seems a bit of an enigma in the middle of the perpetual bustle which surrounds it. A nice comfortable place to escape.

The Frick Collection: 5th Ave/70th St (open June to August, 10.00–18.00, Wednesday to Saturday; 13.00–18.00 on Sundays, entrance free; September to May, Tuesday to Saturday). A small museum devoted particularly to Renaissance works. Worth visiting for two first-rate paintings by Vermeer.

Natural History Museum: Central Park West/79th St. (Every day 10.00–17.00, 11.00–17.00 on Sundays; no set entrance fee.) A remarkable collection of dinosaur and mammoth skeletons, amongst others. There are few museums in the world as fabulous as this one, if only for the body of a transparent woman.

The Hayden Planetarium: Central Park West/81st St. Two blocks from the Natural History Museum of which it's the Department of Astronomy. (Every day 11.00–17.00, Sundays 13.00–17.00; performances every hour during the weekend.) Like in all the planetariums – too often neglected by adults – you are bound to enjoy yourself. Sometimes they put on a laser show with music. ☎ 724.87.00.

architecture in New York

There are so many skyscrapers that it's difficult to make a choice. There are some, however, that deserve to be recognized as being among the major architectural achievements of this century:

Seagram Building: 375 Park Ave/53rd St. Many people think that this is the finest skyscraper in New York. And there is no lack of arguments in favour; the architect Mies Van der Rohe has carried out to the full his ideas on the purity of form using steel structures and glass walls to produce in 1958 a building whose elegance has rarely been achieved elsewhere. One of its original aspects is to have devoted a third of the land (at the price that it is here!) to a square, between the building and Park Ave. Behind, however, there are two small buildings which seem to have been added on (in one of them, Philip Johnson, the architect who collaborated with Mies on this project, has designed one of New York's smartest restaurants, 'The Four Seasons').

145

Ford Foundation Building: 2nd Ave/42nd St (not far from Grand Central Terminal). Really worth seeing; it's built round a tiered interior garden. (Architect: Kevin Roche, 1967.)

Chrysler Building: Lexington Ave/42nd St. This skyscraper built in 1930 is remarkable for its steel steeple which reflects the slightest ray of sunshine.

Solow Building: 9 W. 57th St. A skyscraper with rounded forms is so rare that this one is worth mentioning.

Tired of building uninteresting skyscrapers, some very rich Americans have developed a nostalgic taste for medieval architecture. Thus Rockefeller has had a reconstruction of a twelfth-century French cloister built in Fort Tyron Park, on a hill to the extreme north of Manhattan:

The Cloisters: (Tuesday to Saturday, 10.00–17.00, Sundays 13.00–17.00). A journey in time and space far, far away from the modern world. Really enjoyable even if you are not a historian. Concerts of medieval music on Sunday afternoons.

museums for understanding America

Museum of the American Indian: Audubon Terrace, Broadway, between W. 155th St and W. 156th St (Tuesday to Sunday, 13 00–17.00. If New York is for you only a halting-post to the Far West where you intend picking up the trail of Geronimo and Cochise, then why not visit this museum which is perhaps the most important on the culture and history of the Indians of the two Americas?

Museum of American Folk Art: 49 W. 53rd St (not far from the 'Moma'; Tuesday to Sunday, 9 30–17.30). Everything to do with American arts and crafts from their early beginnings.

districts and boroughs

Harlem

More or less from 110th St (north of Central Park) to 155th St between St Nicholas Ave and the East Bank of Manhattan. So many things, true or false, are said about Harlem that the best thing is to go there and see for yourself: in any case, the 'black ghetto' really is a ghetto, and whites don't receive a warm reception. But if there are several of you, you can always go and listen on Sunday to one of the numerous gospel' services which take place in the quarter's churches – the atmosphere is amazing. To be on the safe side, go to Harlem by car if you are on your own. There is an agency which organizes three-hour tours: Penny Sightseeing Company: 303 W. 42nd St. ☎ 247.28.60. Suitable for those wanting to visit Harlem as they would a zoo. Especially worth seeing: the **Studio Museum in Harlem**; 2033 5th Ave (Tuesday to Friday: 10.00–18.00, weekends 13.00–18.00, entrance free), the **Puerto-Rican market, La Marquetta,** between 110th St and 116th St on Park Ave.

Brooklyn

Take the Subway, or cross Brooklyn Bridge. From a population point of view, the borough of Brooklyn is one of the biggest cities in the United States (2.6 million inhabitants). It's also one of those which has the greatest number of different ethnic groups (Blacks, Italians, Jews, Greeks, Arabs, etc.).
The **Brooklyn Museum** (188 Eastern Parkway) is worth seeing. The famous **Coney Island** beach, in the southern tip of Brooklyn, is a world in itself, with its popular attractions and boulevard atmosphere: a popular place for those interested in taking photos of the local fauna.

Queens

Population-wise (2 million inhabitants) Queens is New York's second borough. Don't miss the **City Panorama** in Queens Museum (Meadows Park): a faithful small-scale reproduction of Manhattan with more than 800,000 buildings reproduced down to the last detail. **Shea Stadium**, a circular stadium holding some 55,000 people is also in Queens.

Bronx

North of Manhattan, a borough often synonymous with extreme urban poverty. Black and Puerto-Rican minorities live here in pretty desperate conditions. **Bronx Zoo** is considered to be one of the biggest in the world. A good place for a stroll on a sunny weekend (free at weekends; open 10.00–17.00).

great scenes

Music

Whether it be for classical music or rock, jazz, free-jazz, 'ethnic' (Cuban, African etc.) or punk, New York has a variety and a vitality which has certainly no equivalent in the world: music bursts out everywhere, from the concerts in Central Park to the jam-session during one of those jazz evenings in private flats. Those who have music in their blood, soul or under their skin will spend many a blessed hour in New York City.

Classical music

Lincoln Centre: Broadway and 65th St. Various activities including:

Metropolitan Opera House, home of the Metropolitan Opera Company. Expensive, but you can get 'standing-room' tickets.

Avery Fisher Hall, performances of all kinds of music and the place to hear the New York Philharmonic.

Juilliard School of Music, performances are given by the most gifted pupils in all fields of music. Often free admission.

Jazz

More jazz is played in New York than any other kind of music. If you stay more than a week you are almost certain to see some of the greatest jazz players. There are more than a hundred jazz clubs. Here is a selection. Some of them also put on rock and folk music; telephone in advance to find out which artists are on the bill, as well as the entrance fee which varies depending on the fame of the performer. Not cheap in any case.

In Manhattan:

All's Alley: 77 Greene St. ☎ 226.90.42.

Cellar: 70 W. 95th St. ☎ 866.12.00.

Eddie Condon's: 144 W. 54th St. ☎ 265.82.77.

Fat Tuesday's: 17th St/3rd Ave. ☎ 533.79.02.

Gregory's: 1149 First Ave (near 63rd St). ☎ 371.22.30.

Jazz Forum: 50 Cooper Sq. ☎ 477.26.55.

Jazzmania Society: 14 E. 23rd St. ☎ 477.30.77.

Jimmy Ryan's: 154 W. 54th St. ☎ 205.95.05. One of the best known.

Michael's Pub: 211 E. 55th St. ☎ 758.22.72.

Storyville: 41 E. 58th St. ☎ 755.16.40.

Tin Palace: 325 Bowery (near 2nd St). ☎ 677.97.27.

Village Gate: Bleecker St/Thompson St. ☎ 982.92.92. Rock and folk music also.

Village Vanguard: 7th Ave/11th St.

Jazz is sometimes played in the Lincoln Center and in certain churches (St Peter's Church: 55th St/

Lexington Ave for example). Look in *Village Voice*. The following organization provides up-to-date information on the activities of New York's jazz clubs:

Jazz Interactions: 527 Madison Ave, Suite 1615. It publishes a sheet (*Jazz in New York*) with the week's programmes which is distributed in the tourist kiosks (in Times Square). You can also telephone: 421.35.92.

Also popular

The Bottom Line: 15 W. 4th St.

The Other End: 147 Bleecker St. Good rock club.

Really different

Infinity: 654 Broadway. One of the biggest, most expensive and wildest nightclubs in New York.

12 West: 12 West End Ave (on the waterfront, west side, Downtown). One of New York's most important 'gay' clubs. Males only allowed.

Columbus Ave and Amsterdam Ave, from 65th to 80th St: the 'gay' quarter. Good restaurants and fashion boutiques.

Cinema for film buffs

New York is very far from equalling a capital city such as London in the choice of films which it offers every week, but there are plenty of excellent American films and classics of the cinema which can be seen and seats are cheap. Two films are often shown for the price of one.

The Public: 425 LaFayette St.

Bleecker Street Cinema: 144 Bleecker St. ☎ 674.25.60.

Theater 80: 80 St Mark's Place. ☎ 254.74.00.

Quad Cinema: 34 W. 13th St. ☎ 255.88.00.

Carnegie Hall: 7th Ave/56th St. The large cinema in the famous Carnegie Hall is a favourite with film buffs; it shows classics by such as Fritz Lang, Pabst and Griffith. Watch the programmes in *Village Voice*.

Museum of Modern Art: 53rd St near Fifth Ave.

Theatres

Between the major successes appearing on Broadway (between 44th St and 49th St) and those playing off-Broadway (around the Village) there is a wide choice.

For the latter, go and see what's on at:

Cubiculo: 414 W. 51st St.

Mama: 74 E. 4th St.

Ontological-Hysteric Theater: 80 Wooster St.

Afro-American Total Theater: 49 W. 32nd St.

Shopping

Shopping in New York is a really enjoyable exercise in view of the infinite variety of rare and unusual things that can be bought in the relatively small perimeter of Downtown and Midtown Manhattan. Fifth Ave is the artery of the big luxury shops, first and foremost of which is Saks (5th Ave/49th St). The cut-price departmental stores, such as Macy's, Korvette and Gimbels, are around Herald Square (6th Ave/34th St). Bloomingdale's, between Lexington Ave and 3rd Ave and 59th St and 60th St is a very well-known departmental store. All art galleries and famous couturier's shops are to be found on Madison Ave from 55th St onwards going north. The complete opposite to these luxury businesses is Delancey St in the heart of Lower East Side, which is a kind of flea-market cum permanent bazaar. At the weekend you'll be surprised at how crowded it is. Greenwich Village has 'underground' bookshops, second-hand clothes shops, little record shops, 'head shops' (everything for the accomplished smoker) etc., in short the classic businesses of a 'student-artist' quarter. 47th St in the centre of Midtown, must be the street where there are more diamonds per square yard than anywhere else in the world. Worth having a look at. The best guide if you want to buy anything in New York is, of course, the 'Yellow Pages' directory. Below is a more modest list of useful addresses:

Records

Disc-o-mat: 474 7th Ave (between 36th St and 37th St). The best.

Sam Goody's: 3rd Ave/43rd St.

Village Oldies: 149 Bleecker St. See also House of Oldies: 267 Bleecker St.

Record Hunter: 5th Ave/42nd St.

Books

Barnes and Noble: 5th Ave/18th St. An enormous choice of books on offer. Some real bargains.

Brentano's: 5th Ave/46th St and near the Village: W. 8th St/University Place.

Doubleday: 5th Ave/53rd St.

Scribner's: 597 5th Ave.

Rizzoli: 5th Ave (between 57th St and 56th St).

New York's most fashionable bookshop. People go there as much to be seen as to look at the books on art. A complete selection of European papers and journals.

Specialist bookshops:

East Side Bookstore: St Mark's Place/2nd Ave. Politics, sociology, ecology.

Supersnipe Comic Art Emporium: 1617 2nd Ave.

The Science Fiction Shop: 56 8th Ave (in the Village two blocks south of 14th St). The bookshop for the science-fiction fanatic.

Cinemabilia: 10 W. 13th St (between 5th Ave and 6th Ave). ☎ 989.85.19. Terry Ork's bookshop is quite simply the best in New York for the cinema. When Truffaut comes to New York he does his shopping here.

Wittenborn: 101 Madison Ave. The best specialist in books on art and architecture.

Murals

There are some really beautiful ones in Manhattan:

On 8th Ave between 40th St and 41st St just opposite the Bus Terminal, near a carpark.

On 25th St, nearly on the corner of Lexington Ave: a house painted for the architect James Doman by Amado Ortiz.

On Delancey St, on the corner of Bowery. An impressive Cuban wall describing the battle of a poor family for decent accommodation. The work of the City Arts Workshop.

On Delancey St and Forsyth St: a mural several storeys high.

On the corner of **Rivington St and Christie St** not far from Delancey St, a really prodigious allegorical mural.

On the border of **Chinatown**, a three-dimensional mural depicting a 'Chinese' street in New York (Canal St/Allen St).

On the corner of **Bleecker St and LaFayette St** (south of Washington Square), a magnificent mural painted by Mel Petarsky in 1970.

On W. 3rd St: a big 'abstract' mural near Mercer St.

Foot hockey

An original sport played only in the immense slippery corridors of Madison Square Garden during the breaks between ice-hockey matches. Join in with the teenagers who are mad keen on this game. Enormous bets are made at the same time in the Penn Station coffee-shops.

Main festivals in New York

The Chinese New Year: end of January–beginning of February (Chinatown).

New Year's Day: January 1. At midnight (December 31) people gather at Times Square.

St Patrick's Day Parade: March 17. Parade of Irish Catholics on 5th Ave.

May Day: May 1. Celebration in Union Square.

Spanish-American Day: 1st Sunday in May. Parade of Spanish-Americans on 5th Ave.

Puerto-Rican Day: 1st Sunday in June. The Puerto Ricans' turn to parade along 5th Ave.

San Gennaro Feast: 2nd fortnight in September. The liveliest festival in New York. 'Little Italy' on Mulberry St and Grand St becomes one big fair with some uproarious stands.

Steuben Parade: New Yorkers of German origin parade down 5th Ave on the last Saturday of September.

Columbus Day: October 12, national holiday, parade of the Italians down 5th Ave.

---

around New York

The State of New Jersey isn't just a land of industry and pollution with hideous factories: it has also preserved 200 kms of white-sanded beaches. **Atlantic City,** on the 'Garden State Parkway' is a busy resort. In the very north of the State of New York, 30 kms from Buffalo, are **Niagara Falls,** still as romantic and wild in spite of the outrageous tourist exploitation that they have to contend with. 12 hours by coach from N.Y. city. N.B. The Falls themselves are in the province of Ontario in Canada.

PHILADELPHIA

☎ 215
PENNSYLVANIA

Philadelphia, the town where the Declaration of Independence of the United States and the Constitution of the Union were signed, is today a very large metropolis which really must be visited if you are going from New York to Washington. The historic centre of Philadelphia is rich in monuments inseparable from the past of the American nation. Thanks to the efforts of the city council, the rights of the pedestrian, as in Boston, are also respected. The University of Pennsylvania lends life to the whole of one of the city's quarters, on the other side of the Delaware River.

---

arriving in Philadelphia

Coach
Greyhound: 17th St/Market St. ☎ L08.48.00.
Continental Trailways: 13th St/Arch St. ☎L09.31.00.

Plane
From the **International Airport** take the Airport Express bus: cheap, operates every half-hour from 7.00 to 23.00 hrs and from 6.00 to 22.30 in the Downtown to Airport direction.

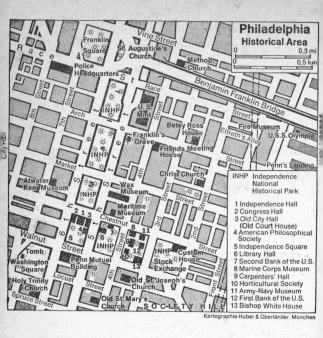

Kartographie Huber & Oberländer, München

Train

Amtrak: Penn Central: 30th St/Market St. ☎ 824. 16.00.

don't panic

Finding your way around

The City Hall is in the centre of a grid system going from east to west from the Delaware River to the Schuylkill River and beyond. The streets going north–south are numbered from the Delaware River onwards. The streets going east–west have names, the main street being Market St. The historic part is situated around Chestnut St between 6th St and 2nd St: so it's impossible to get lost.

Transport

SEPTA bus and subway : There are two kinds of very useful 'rover' tickets for the visitor (every day in summer, and the weekend only from November to March):

Cultural Loop: a one-day 'rover' ticket with which you can take the bus as and when you like on a circuit going round the city's most interesting sites. Ask for the map at the Visitor Center.

Taxi

Taxis are expensive and difficult to find at night.

Car hire

Budget: 18th St/J. F. Kennedy Bld. ☎ 92.39.00.

National: 1714 J. F. Kennedy Bld. ☎ L07.17.60.

Refuge

Y.M.C.A.: 1421 Arch St. ☎ L09.14.00. (Must be the most expensive in the States!)

Y.M.C.A.: 2027 Chestnut St. ☎ L04.34.30.

A.Y.H.: Chamounix Mansion, W. Fairmount Park. ☎ 878.36.76. Far and away the best.

keys to Philadelphia

General information

Convention and Visitors' Bureau: 1525 J. F. Kennedy Bld. opposite City Hall. (Everyday 9.00–17.00; 9.00–17.00 Monday to Friday in summer.) ☎ 864.19.76.

Traveller's Aid: 1218 Chestnut St. ☎ 922.09.50.

Council for International Visitors: Civic Center Museum, 34th St/Civic Center Bld. ☎ 879.52.48. Provides assistance for foreigners. Interpreters. Contacts with families.

Information on cultural events: ☎ 864.19.90.

Newspapers and magazines

Spot Lite: a weekly guide found in hotels.

Inquirer: Weekly guide to concerts, films etc. Free from Visitor's Bureau.

Colleges and campuses

One very important University: **Pennsylvania University,** on the other side of the Schuylkill River (Subway: 33rd St). If you have the time to visit it (i.e. if you are staying more than three days) catch a 42 bus on Chestnut St.

Meeting places

The Parkway, a long esplanade lined with trees which goes from the City Hall to the Museum of Art is Philadelphians' favourite place for a walk. Many activities in summer: street plays, folk-music festival, exhibitions, puppets etc.

Survival

To leave Philadelphia: **Auto Driveaway**: 225 S. 15th St. ☎ 735.66.85.

---

good night

If you are staying for less than a week, accommodation is Philly's weak point: everything is very expensive and the student is reduced to choosing one of the centres listed under 'Refuge'.

In summer, if you are staying for at least a week, don't hesitate:

Penn University's Fraternity Houses on Locust St and 36th St. Very cheap for a week or more. Try in particular the **Phi Gamma Delta**: 3619 Locust St. If you can afford it, here are the addresses of the two cheapest hotels in the town centre:

St Charles Hotel: 1935 Arch St.

Apollo Hotel: (opposite the former).

More expensive hotels:

Franklin Motor Inn: 22nd St/Parkway. ☎ 568.83.00.

Hamilton Motor Inn: Chestnut St/39th St. ☎ EV6.52.00.

Howard Johnson's Motor Lodge: 11580 Roosevelt Bld. ☎ H04.95.00.

For those who are lucky enough to have a car there is a cheap motel at Cherry Hill in New Jersey on Highway 38: **Colonial Motor Lodge**: Cherry Hill. ☎ 663.01.00.

---

getting fed

The University of Pennsylvania quarter (34th St to 36th St) is the best for eating cheaply; but there are a few other reasonable places:

American Flame: Jupiter St/Walnut St.

Bain's Cafeteria: 215 S. Broad St. Jewish specialities.

China Boy: 901 Race St.

China City: 932 Race St.

Chocho: 1824 Ludlow St. Japanese cooking.

Chuckwagon: 1616 and 811 Chestnut St. Sandwiches. Superb beer.

Dr Watson's Pub: 216 S. 11th St.

Freddy's Restaurant and Pizzeria: 21st St/ Chestnut St. Student atmosphere.

Happy Paradise: 204 N. 10th St.

The Happy Rooster: 118 S. 16th St.

Harry's American Bar: 1918 Chestnut St. Expensive but worth it. Good American food (giant salads etc.)

Jasmine Inn: 1008 Race St.

The King's Inn: 312 Race St.

Pop Edwards: 1624 Market St. Close to the City Hall; excellent.

Steamship Ltd: 104 Chestnut St. Sea-food.

things that everyone goes to see and that you shouldn't miss

Independence Hall; Chestnut St between 5th and 6th St on Independence Mall (everyday 9.00–20.00, entrance free). Built between 1732 and 1756 to the plans of Andrew Hamilton and Edmond Wooley, this handsome building is the most historic in the United States, since it's here that the Declaration of Independence was signed in 1776 in the presence particularly of Benjamin Franklin, George Washington and Thomas Jefferson, to name the most famous.

Liberty Bell: on Independence Mall, opposite Independence Hall, in a glass pavilion (everyday 9.00–18.00). Itself the symbol of liberty, this bell which dates from 1752 was the first to announce the Declaration of Independence of the United States of America.

Franklin Court: Orianna St (a little street parallel to 4th St and close to both it and Chestnut St). Everyday, 9.00–19.00, entrance free. On the site of Benjamin Franklin's last house. An exhibition in an underground museum devoted to the numerous inventions we owe to this man of many parts who wasn't afraid to become 'politically engaged'.

City Tavern: 2nd St/Walnut St. (11.30–21.30 closed Mondays.). As faithful a reproduction as possible (including the waiters) of Philadelphia's most famous tavern in the 1770s. The names of the regulars at that time were: Washington, Jefferson ... (Drinks quite expensive; go there for breakfast).

Betsy Ross House: Four blocks from Independence Hall, in Arch St/3rd St. (Everyday, 9.00–17.00; entrance free.) The house of the seamstress whose major work is well-known: the American flag.

Philadelphia Museum of Art: 25th St/The Parkway. (9.00–17.00, closed Mondays; free Sunday mornings.) An immense museum which has some remarkable art treasures. You must see the astonishing rooms in which a Far Eastern temple and palace have been entirely reconstructed, and the one in which a cloister of the Abbey of Saint-Genis in Les Fontaines-du-Roussillon is exhibited in its entirety, including the fountain and greenery. You have to go to Philadelphia to be able to admire the twelfth-century porch of the Abbey of St Laurent-de-Cosse (Nièvre, France): whatever next! Admirers of Marcel Duchamp, that great surrealist iconoclast of the twentieth century, will be interested to know that three-quarters of his work is in this museum.

Fairmount Park: the biggest municipal park in the U.S.A., it begins behind the Museum of Art. Lots of things to see: the Japanese House and Garden, the Samuel Sculpture Garden, the Azalea garden (2,000 plants), the Memorial Hall (with a scale-model of the centenary exhibition in 1876) and above all ten magnificent colonial residences. There is a special bus service to the park in summer.

things that everyone doesn't go to see but which are worth seeing

Afro-American Historical and Cultural Museum (Black History Museum): 7th St/Arch St. (Everyday, 10.00–17.00; entrance fee.) Inaugurated in 1976, this small museum devoted to Black American culture and its links with Africa is very educational: it's a pity that more room hasn't been left for black American art, but don't let this prevent you from going in.

Perelman Antique Toy Museum: 270 S. 2nd St (Everyday, 9.30–17.00; entrance fee.) The biggest collection of old American toys in the world: no fewer than 3,000 toys! Grown-up children love it!

Franklin Institute Science Museum: 20th St/Parkway. (Everyday, 10.00–17.00; entrance fee.) One of those museums where you can touch, experiment, see, hear etc.

Chinese Cultural and Community Center: 125 N. 10th St. (Monday to Friday, 11.00–16.00.) In a rather strange building, a small but very active Chinese cultural centre (exhibitions, concerts) where you can even have a meal. Excursions to Chinatown leave from here. (☎ WA3.67.67. for more information.)

Second Bank of the United States: Chestnut St. between 4th St and 5th St (9.00–17.00; free). A partial copy of the Parthenon in Athens! Unique as an example of 'neo-classical' architecture.

Pennsylvania Academy of the Fine Arts: Broad St/Cherry St. (April to December: Tuesday to

Saturday, 10.00–17.00, Sundays, 13.00–17.00; entrance fee.) A building in the finest Victorian style, housing a large collection of American paintings.

Barnes Foundation: 300 N. Latches Lane (20 minutes by bus from Market St). ☎ M07.02.90. Telephone for an appointment. Philadelphia really isn't for people who don't like museums! Here is another one, but it houses one of the finest private collections in existence. All the big names: El Greco, Monet, Renoir, Cézanne, Degas and Picasso, but also the anonymous creators of the magnificent African sculptures on view here.

great scenes

The least that can be said is that Philadelphia's night-life isn't fantastic. But you can spend a pleasant evening listening to a concert or seeing an old film. The only clubs worth going to are in the student bars on Walnut St between 34th St and 38th St.

Main Point: 874 Lancaster Ave (north-west of the University): the best club for folk-music, rock and jazz around.

The Onion: Walnut St/34th St. Cellar.

Smoky Joe's: Walnut St/38th St.

PHOENIX

☎ 602
ARIZONA

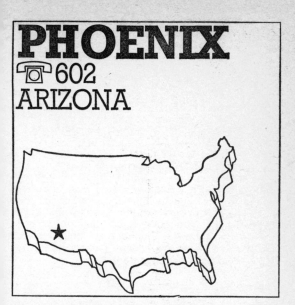

Arizona's biggest city is a miniature Los Angeles, minus the Pacific, and the role of the car is just as important. It's also an oasis in the middle of a desert. Some streets are lined with giant cacti, and swimming pools are everywhere. There are also golf courses which are watered night and day. Phoenix owes its incredible development to being the sunniest place in the U.S.A. During the summer the temperature can reach 40°C and more in the shade. With its 700,000 inhabitants, Phoenix is first and foremost an immense residential and leisure centre.

But for the traveller it's mainly a base for exploring Arizona, one of the most attractive States in the U.S. with its rich archaeological past, including the ruined buildings of the Pueblo Indians, and the Mexican influence in the south.

arriving in Phoenix

Coach

Greyhound: 525 E. Washington.
Continental Trailways: 433 E. Washington.

Plane

Sky Harbort: The city is so wide-spread that Phoenix airport is almost within its boundaries. Car-hire companies are at the Terminal.

don't panic

Finding your way around

There is one main north–south axis: Central Ave. All north–south streets are numbered from this Avenue onwards. There is one main east–west axis: Van Buren St. and all east–west streets have a name.
Downtown, the town centre, is around the Central Ave/Washington St intersection.
Camelback Mountain is a small mountain in the northern part of the city. East of Camelback lies Paradise Valley, the residential quarter of Phoenix. The University of Arizona is at the southern end of the city, at Tempe. You can get good maps of Phoenix and Arizona from the Chamber of Commerce (805 N. 2nd St) and from the Arizona Transport Highway Department (2010 W. Encanto Bld).

Transport

To be frank, difficult if you haven't got a car. There are buses, but not many of them, and journeys can be very long, even in Downtown. As for hitch-hiking, Phoenix is one of the worst places for it in the United States, and in the summer when the weather is very hot it's not much fun either.

Car hire

Allstate: Near Phoenix Airport. The cheapest. ☎ 275.75.86.
Avis: at the Airport. ☎ 273.16.15.
Hertz: at the Airport. ☎ 254.70.51.

Refuge

Y.M.C.A.: 350 N. 1st Ave (one block west of Central Ave and four blocks from Washington St). ☎ 253.61.81. One of the better Y.M.C.A.s in the United States and probably the cheapest. Mixed, one floor being reserved for girls.

keys to Phoenix

General information

Chamber of Commerce: 805 N. 2nd St. ☎ 254.55.21.

Valley of the Sun Convention Bureau: 2701 E. Camelback Rd. ☎ 956.62.00.

Colleges and campuses

The University of Arizona is at Tempe, southeast of Downtown.

Meeting places

Downtown on Central Ave, McDowell St and where sporting events take place (Big Surf, for example).

---

good night

Hotel prices are reasonable during the low season which is from May to November.

Student accommodation

Arizona State University: Moeur Building in Tempe. Enquiries: Room 124 or telephone 965.35.15.

Hotels

There are a few cheap hotels Downtown:

Hotel Apache: 515 N. Central Ave (one block from the 'Y'). ☎ 254.11.27.

Marshall Hotel: 19 E. Washington. ☎ 262.98.85.

Moderately priced hotels

Arizona Ranch House Inn: 5600 N. Central Ave. ☎ 279.32.21.

City Center Hotel: 600 W. Van Buren. ☎ 252.40.61.

Motels

This is the ideal accommodation in Phoenix if there are two or more of you. The motels are grouped together on Van Buren St (motel row).

Desert Rose Motel: 3424 E. Van Buren St. ☎ 275.44.21.

Desert Star Motel: 4120 E. Van Buren St. ☎ 275.57.46.

The motels on Grand Ave are a little more expensive.

Bali-Hi Motor Hotel: 1515 Grand Ave. ☎ 252.67.01.

Coliseum Inn: 1600 Grand Ave. ☎ 254.51.71.

---

getting fed

An address to remember if you want to eat cheaply: The **Y.M.C.A. cafeteria:** 350 N. 1st Ave.

Other good, and rather more pleasant places to go:

Bob's Restaurant: 2901 N. Central Ave.

Organ Stop Pizza: 5330 N. 7th St. Really original decor: and organ from the days of the silent cinema takes up all the room.

The Spaghetti Company: 1418 N. Central Ave. ☎ 257.03.80. If you are not put off by kitsch.

Golden Temple Conscious Cookery: 415 S. Mill Ave, in Tempe; a vegetarian restaurant with a mystic-religious flavour.

Something to be tried:

Food Bazaar: Town and Country Shopping Center: 212 E. Camelback Rd (7 kms north of Downtown). A kind of restaurant supermarket with more than a dozen kitchens serving up specialities from eight different countries. (Open everyday, 8.00–21.00.)

Mexican cooking

Woody's Macayo: 4001 N. Central Ave.

Jordan's Hacienda: 2633 N. Central Ave.

Finally, be sure to visit one of those 'Ice-Cream parlours' where you can try incredible American ice-creams.

things that everyone goes to see and that you shouldn't miss

Papago Park: Desert Botanical Gardens: 10 kms east of Downtown, South of McDowell Rd. (9.00–17.00.) Every kind of desert plant.

Pueblo Grande Ruins and Museum: 4619 E. Washington St. (Free; 9.00–17.00; Sundays, 13.00–17.00.) Perhaps not the most interesting Indian ruins in Arizona but they have the advantage of being easy to get to.

things that everyone doesn't go to see but which are worth seeing

The Heard Museum: 22 E. Monte Vista Rd (Monday to Saturday, 10.00–17.00; Sunday, 13.00–17.00. For those who have a special interest in Indian arts and crafts.

Big Surf: 1500 N. Hayden Rd, Tempe (south of the city). ☎ 947.24.77. Closed on Mondays. Absolutely unique, this is a lake in the middle of the desert on which you can go surf-riding thanks to machinery which makes waves several yards high.

Biltmore Hotel: 24th St/E. Missouri, at the foot of the Camelback Mountains. A little-known work by F. Lloyd Wright who was responsible for the façades and much of the interior detail.

great scenes

Every kind of sport can be played in Phoenix except for ski-ing. Cowboy style horse-riding is great fun in particular:

All Western Stables: 10220 S. Central Ave. ☎ 276.58.62.

Weldon's Riding Stables Inc: 5400 E. Van Buren St. ☎ 267.90.71.

There's one completely mad sport which only the Americans could have invented: **'Tubing'**. This consists of sailing down a river in a tube-shaped receptacle. As the water is ice-cold it's a good way of cooling down in summer. Probably as well to make do with going to watch the experts on the River Verde (take Shea Bld as far as Bee Line Rd, then continue as far as the bridge over the river).

Architecture

Those interested in architecture should go and see **Taliesin West,** Frank Lloyd Wright's school. Catch an eastbound bus on McDowell as far as Scottsdale, and then hitch-hike on Scottsdale Rd. Taliesin is on 108th St north of Shea Bld (15 kms from Downtown). Seventy miles north of Phoenix, in the middle of the desert, Paolo Soleri, with the help of student friends, has built his **'Arcology'** (a community-city of 3,500 inhabitants). To get there, it is best to ask at the Cosanti Foundation whether someone can take you.

Cosanti Foundation: 6433 E. Doubletree Rd, Scottsdale. Follow Scottsdale Rd as far as Double-tree Rd, which is a real desert road; the Foundation is on the left about 3 kms from Scottsdale Rd.

around Phoenix

Grand Canyon (see Chapter on 'National Parks').

Must be seen:

near Holbrook north-east of Phoenix, the **'Painted Desert'**.

Apache Junction, 40 kms east of Phoenix, famous for its film settings, 'Apacheland Movie Ranch'.

Eighty kms south-east of Phoenix, the ruins of **Casa Grande,** 600-year-old Indian buildings.

Tucson

Tucson, 160 kms south-east of Phoenix, is one of the oldest Spanish colonies in the West. Tucson is really worth a visit, much more pleasant than Phoenix.

General information

Tucson Tourist Information Center: Chamber of Commerce, 420 W. Congress St.

Car hire

Budget: 2707 E. Valencia and also at 723 E. 22nd St. ☎ 623.57.43.

Dollar: 6930 S. Tucson Bld. ☎ 294.16.41.

Accommodation

Downtown: *Pueblo Hotel:* 145 S. 6th Ave. ☎ 622.74.01.

Cheap Motels: *Arizona Motel:* 1749 S. 6th Ave. ☎ 624.25.79.

Tucson Inn: 127 W. Drachman. ☎ 624.85.31.

Casa Radin Motel: 2601 N. Miracle Mile. ☎ 624.95.35.

Terrace Motel: 631 W. Miracle Mile. ☎ 624.82.48.

Major Motel: 1635 N. Miracle Mile. ☎ 623.07.59.

Good places to eat

Club 21: 2902 Miracle Mile (closed on Mondays).

Cazadores: 248 E. 22nd St.

Solarium: 6444 E. Tangue Verde.

The Ranch: 5440 E. Speedway.

Phoebe's Pie and Ice-Cream Parlor: 2930 E. Speedway.

Peppy Lou's: 2227 Miracle Mile.

Worth seeing

Old Tucson: Tucson Mountain Park (12 miles to the west of the city, take the Speedway and then Gates Pass Rd). Many 'westerns' have been filmed here since the early 1940s.

La Placita: in the middle of Downtown, a small shopping centre in perfect harmony with its surroundings from an architectural point of view. Very busy.

SAN FRANCISCO

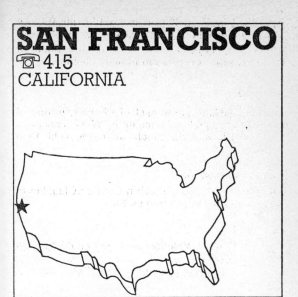

☎ 415
CALIFORNIA

A bay which is absolutely unique, streets like fairground helter-skelters, a bridge unequalled by the finest of sculptures, incredible hillside houses, the 'coolest' people in the States . . . there is no point in continuing, quite simply San Francisco is the most attractive city in the U.S.A. You can go for a ride in a 'cable-car' at sunset, eat crab in the fishing port or listen to such as Jerry Garcia play the guitar in a Haight St club. And don't leave San Francisco without having seen the murals in the 'chicano' quarter: street art isn't an empty phrase in California's second city.
The ever-present threat of an earthquake, furthermore, doesn't detract from San Francisco's fantastic atmosphere!

arriving in San Francisco

Coach
Greyhound: 7th St/Mission St. ☎ 433.15.00.
Continental Trailways: 1st St/Mission St. ☎ 982.64.00.

Plane
From **San Francisco International Airport:** The cheapest is Greyhound.
Airport Bus Stop: Taylor St/Ellis St. near Union Square.

don't panic

Finding your way arouud

There is one main (but uninteresting) shopping
street: Market St; parallel streets run from this
artery towards the port, the two most important
being Powell St and Grant St. The latter goes

through Chinatown. Union Square forms the centre of the town; Berkeley is on the other side of the bay, to the east. Haight Ashbury is near Golden Gate Park.

N.B. For Berkeley, see separate chapter.

Maps: maps of bus-routes are free; you can also get one free from the S.F. Convention and Visitors' Bureau. Rand McNally: Market St/2nd St.

Transport

Very easy when you know how to use the three different kinds of public transport: the famous Cable Car, the Trolley and the BART (Bay Area Rapid Transport) Subway.

Cable Car: There are two Cable Car lines: one goes from Market St to Fisherman's Wharf via Powell St, Washington St and Hyde St; the other leaves from the end of California St (at the Embarcadero) and stops on the same street at Van Ness Ave.

Bus: the buses have numbers, and trolleys capital letters. On each one is shown the name of a main street on the route or the terminus, sometimes both.

BART: very complicated ticket system: they are magnetic and must be produced for inspection at the exit: fares depend on distance travelled and are shown on signboards in the stations; tickets obtainable from automatic distributors. Absolutely essential to get hold of the explanatory pamphlet *All about BART*! Basically, there are four lines which carry you north as far as Richmond (via Berkeley), east as far as Concord, south-east as far as Fremont and south as far as Daly City. The BART stops at midnight and doesn't operate on Saturdays and Sundays.

For information: BART: ☎ 788 BART. A.C. Bus: ☎ 653.35.35 (East Bay).

Bicycle and roller skate hire

Bicycle Rental: 772 Stanyan St. ☎ 221.24.15.

Avenue Cyclery: 750 Stanyan St. ☎ 387.31.55.

Leaving San Francisco

Driveaway: *AAACON*: 1095 Market St. ☎ 431.06.63.

Auto Driveaway Company: 785 Market St. ☎ 777.37.40.

Ride Center: *San Francisco Ride Centre:* 3260 24th St. ☎ 824.83.97.

Car hire

It's not essential in San Francisco to hire a car if you are staying for less than a week, but a good idea if you want to make excursions towards the north (Muir Woods, Bolinas, Marin County). Bear in mind that parking in the city is very expensive. The cheapest companies:

Rent-a-Heap-Cheap: 777 Van Ness Ave. ☎ 776.54.50.

Aero Rent-a-car: 401 O'Farrell St. ☎ 771.66.44. and 301 Ellis St. Near the Hilton on the corner of Taylor. ☎ 474.66.11.

Economy Rent-a-car: 404 O'Farrell St. ☎ 673.75.55. (They have Volkswagens).

Thrifty: 542 Mason St. ☎ 421.82.00.

Airways Rent-a-car: 415 Taylor St. ☎ 673.57.72.

Pacific Car Rental: 332 Mason St. ☎ 771.53.00. (Probably the cheapest.)

Refuge

Y.M.C.A.: 220 Golden Gate Ave. ☎ 885.04.60.

Y.M.C.A.: 166 Embarcadero (mixed). ☎ 392.21.91.

Y.M.C.A.: 855 Sacramento St. ☎ 982.44.12.

Y.M.C.A.: 351 Turk St (mixed). ☎ 673.23.12.

Y.M.C.A.: 4080 Mission Ave ('Chicano' quarter). ☎ 586.69.00.

Y.W.C.A.: 620 Sutter St. ☎ 775.65.00.

S F Youth Hostel: Fort Mason. ☎ 771.46.46.

In Berkeley

Y.M.C.A.: 2001 Allston Way. ☎ 848.68.00.

In Oakland

Y.M.C.A.: 1525 Webster St.

Y.M.C.A.: 2101 Telegraph Ave. ☎ 795.33.55.

keys to San Francisco

General information

San Francisco Convention and Visitor's Bureau: Fox Plaza, Larkin St/Market St. ☎ 626.55.00.

Visitor's Information Center: 360 Post St (☎ 421.65.54) and also **Powell BART** in Market St/Powell St.

International Hospitality Center: 312 Sutter St, 4th floor. The best of the four.

Telephone number for tourist information 24 hours a day: ☎ 391.20.00.

Post Office: G.P.O. 7th St/Mission St (opposite the Greyhound station).

Shows, sporting events. Information and tickets from:

Downtown Box Office: 325 Mason St. ☎ 775.20.21.

Emporium Box Office: 835 Market St. ☎ 982.11.11.

Macy's Box Office: Union Square. ☎ 397.33.33.

Newspapers and magazines

Buy the Sunday edition of the **San Francisco Chronicle** (mornings) and **San Francisco Examiner** (afternoons). All the week's programmes are in the pink pages.

The Berkeley Barb: the best-known of the 'underground' papers is far from being what it was in the sixties, but can still prove useful: rock concerts, films, advertisements.

The Bay Guardian: Excellent political coverage.

Key: free in all the major hotels. Very practical (content and layout).

Where: not as good as *Key*.

If you are staying more than a month, buy the **People's Yellow Pages.**

Colleges and campuses

Berkeley: see later.

The University of San Francisco is at: 2345 Golden Gate Ave. Has much less to offer than Berkeley.

Meeting places

Fisherman's Wharf (Cable Cars run to and from Market St/Powell St). Full of people in the evening, a good place for strumming a guitar. Go and see the two old warehouses which have been converted into a number of small shops (rather expensive but you can meet high society): The Cannery and Ghirardelli Square.

Golden Gate Park: really must be seen, very crowded on Sundays for the concerts (see later for the Park museums). Take trolley number 7 on Market St.

Haight-Ashbury (Haight St/Ashbury St intersection): This almost mythical place has had its ups and downs. Worth investigating, you might be pleasantly surprised.

North Beach: Grant Ave towards the port, and around Telegraph Hill, the 'beatnik' movement began in North Beach and it's perhaps the best place to meet people in Frisco.

City Lights Bookstore: Broadway Ave/Columbus Ave (until midnight). This 'historical' bookshop founded by Ferlinghetti is a good place for meeting people.

Berkeley and Telegraph Avenue: A kind of Mecca for West Coast freaks:

Survival

As far as this is concerned, San Francisco remains unequalled: American counter-culture is more active and better organized here than anywhere else in the U.S.A. Buy the *Berkeley Barb*.

Crashing

Survival House: 758 Haight St. One night only, arrive before 18.00.

Haight Ashbury Switchboard: 1931 Haight St. ☎ 387.70.00.

Harbor Light Salvation Army: 240 4th St.

S.F. Neighborhood Legal Assistance: 1095 Market St. ☎ 626.38.11.

Health

Central Emergency: 50 Ivy St (between Hayes and Grove).

S.F. General Hospital: 22nd St/Portrero (bus 47 on Van Ness Ave).

Transport

S.F. Ride Center: ☎ 824.83.97.

People's Transhare: ☎ (800) 547.09.33 and 655.12.31.

Underground Ride Center: ☎ 864.56.63.

People's Ride: ☎ 282.14.82.

KSAN Radio: ☎ 478.97.00.

Work

Distributing publicity hand-outs: the working day begins at 5.00 in the morning, and the company provides transport by van for students:

Coronet Distributors: 450 8th St. ☎ 626.19.11.

Dale and Advertising: 1016 Howard St. ☎ 864.33.03.

Sala Advertising: 445 Natoma St. ☎ 391.07.20.

Progress (Wednesday and Saturday only): 861 Howard St. ☎ 982.80.22.

American Express: 251 Post St. ☎ 929.34.91 and 295 California St. ☎ 788.43.67.

---

good night

Student accommodation

San Francisco State College: 800 Front St. ☎ 469.10.67. In summer accommodation is arranged at **Verducci Hall,** Lake Merced Bld.

Lone Mountain College: 2800 Turk St. ☎ 752.70.00. Open from June to mid-August, reserve a week in advance.

San Francisco University: 2345 Golden Gate Ave. Apply the day before. ☎ 752.10.00. Ask at the Hospitality Center: ☎ 398.68.06.

Berkeley: see later.

Cheap hotels

Quite a lot of small fairly cheap hotels on Mission St. between 3rd and 6th St and around Powell St and O'Farrell St; also Post St.

Ansonia Residence Club: 711 Post St. ☎ 673.26.70.

Hotel Arlington: 480 Ellis St (corner of Leavenworth). ☎ 673.96.00.

Carlton Hotel: 1075 Sutter St. ☎ 673.02.42.

Cecil Hotel: 545 Post St. ☎ 673.37.33.

Commodore Hotel: 825 Sutter St (near Jones St). ☎ 885.24.64.

Geary: 610 Geary St. ☎ 673.92.21.

Golden State: 114 Powell St. ☎ 397.30.00.

Grand Central: 1412 Market St. ☎ 431.91.91.

Hart Hotel: 93 6th St (Powell St/Market St). ☎ 986.98.36.

Harvard Hotel: 685 Ellis St. ☎ 771.60.60.

New Continental Hotel: 127 Ellis St. ☎ 986.37.72.

Hotel Odeon: 40 7th St (next to the Greyhound Station). ☎ 552.37.00.

Powell Hotel: 17 Powell St (very well situated at Cable Car Terminal). ☎ 421.63.78. Always a room.

Regent Hotel: 562 Sutter St. ☎ 421.58.18.

Ritz Hotel: 216 Eddy St. ☎ 673.72.77.

Riviera Hotel: 420 Jones St. ☎ 441.93.39.

Senator Hotel: 519 Ellis St. ☎ 775.05.06.

Sentinel Hotel: 587 Eddy St. ☎ 885.98.68.

Stratford Hotel: 242 Powell St. ☎ 421.75.25.

Virginia Hotel: 312 Mason St. ☎ 362.93.00.

Hotel Yerba Buena: 55 5th St. ☎ 543.31.30.

N.B. Avoid the Post Residence Club Hotel; no longer cheap or pleasant.

Less cheap hotels

Mark Twain Hotel: 345 Taylor St. ☎ 673.23.32.

Myako Hotel: 1625 Post St. ☎ 922.32.00. In the centre of the Japan Center. Japanese Baths.

Motels
Wide choice on Van Ness Ave.

---

getting fed

San Francisco offers a wider variety of gastronomic pleasures than anywhere else in the U.S.A. Try a Chinese restaurant one evening, a steak house the next, an Italian restaurant the next and after all that there is still Mexican cooking to be discovered (24th St and Mission St).

Restaurants
Jack-in-the-box: Opposite Greyhound Station. Half-price hamburgers.

Magic Pan: 341 Sutter St. Pancake house.

Joe Jung's Restaurant: 891 Market St. Rather ordinary interior (basically an eating factory) but unbeatable prices.

Yenching: 939 Kearny St. An excellent place to eat.

Chinese restaurants
Chinatown: The restaurants aren't always cheap, but if you get away from Grant St, the main street in Chinatown, it's easy to find good cheap places.

Cathay House: 718 California St.

Eight Immortals: 750 Kearny St.

Happiness Cafe: Market St/7th St. Decor a bit flippant but quite good food for the price.

Harbin Manchurian Cuisine: 327 Balboa St.

North China Restaurant: 2315 Van Ness Ave. Closed Sundays.

Sun Ya: 823 Clay St. Cheap and not too many tourists.

Higher class
The Far East: 631 Grant Ave. Closed Wednesdays.

Three 'souperies'
Salmagundi: 442 Geary St.

Salmagundi: 355 Bush St. Closed Sundays.

Salmagundi: No. 2 Embarcadero Center. Closed Sundays.

Steak houses

Most of them are around Union Square and on Powell St at the Cable Car terminus. Excellent steaks for a reasonable price.

Sal's Steakhouse: 1032 Market St/6th St.

Tad's Steakhouse: 120 Powell St, an institution. Victoria Station: Pier 9.

Mexican

Celia's: 5723 Geary Bld.

La Pinata: 1851 Union St. Closed on Mondays.

Mario's Mexican Restaurant: 900 Bush St.

Cuban

Restaurant Cuba: 2886 16th St (near Van Ness Ave). Closed on Wednesdays. Open until 21.30 hrs.

Italian

There are a lot of Italian restaurants at North Beach on Broadway.

The Cove: 4401 Balboa St (corner of 45th Ave).

The New Pisa: 550 Greenwich Ave (near Vallejo).

The Old Colony: Clement St/24th Ave.

The Old Spaghetti Factory: 478 Green St (near Grant St). A real classic.

Gold Spike: 527 Columbus St. Small, dark and often full-up. Family style.

Iron Pot: 639 Montgomery St. Closed Sundays.

Nero's Italian Restaurant: 712 Geary St.

Coffee shops

Cafe Trieste: 601 Vallejo St.

The Network Coffee House: 1036 Bush St.

Enrico's Sidewalk Cafe: 504 Broadway. ☎ 392. 62.20.

The Meat Mark and Coffee House: 4123 24th St.

Other alternatives

Bogart: 661 Clay St. Specializes in crab.

La Bohème: 24th St/Mission St.

Fish and Chips:

Edna's: 311 Columbus Ave.

Old Chelsea: 932 Larkin St (between Post and Geary). Excellent place to eat. See Edinburgh Castle (under 'Pubs').

Sandwiches:

The Dell: 1980 Union St.

The Haven: 178 Geary St (close to Union Square).

Four star:

The Original: Van Ness Ave/Geary St. A bit far from the centre, but worth the detour.

Sam's Original: Market St/Mason St.

Panelli Bros: Vallejo/Stockton. The best 'sandwich shop'.

Full Moon Coffee House: 4416 18th St. Feminist.

Ghirardelli Square Chocolate Manufactory Soda Fountain: You can really stuff yourself with chocolate, it's fantastic – there's always a queue.

Tassajara Bakery: Cole St/Parnassus St. Good cakes and croissants.

things that everyone goes to see and that you shouldn't miss

There are so many things to do and see in San Francisco that you have to make a choice. But be sure not to miss the Golden Gate Bridge (or Fisherman's Wharf).

Golden Gate Bridge: 2 kms walk to cross it and make sure you are warmly dressed! Take a Golden Gate Transit Bus as far as Toll Plaza. By car: free in a south–north direction, but toll to pay in the opposite direction.

Fisherman's Wharf: San Francisco's most famous quarter in the port. Restaurants (expensive), souvenir shops, sailing-boats that you can visit, galleries; but what is most interesting is the street itself, particularly in the evening. If you have a guitar with you and want to make a few dollars, this is the place to play. To get to the Wharf: take the Cable Car on Powell St and Market or else on Powell St and Jackson as far as the terminus.

Golden Gate Park: to get there from Downtown take McAllister bus No. 5 on Market St or else trolley No. 7. Considering the size of the park it's useful to hire a bicycle on Stanyan St (see 'Transport'). Things to see – apart from the park itself where you can while away a very pleasant day: the Japanese tea garden, the M. H. De Young Memorial Museum with, in particular, Mr Avery Brundage's (of Olympic Games fame) exceptional collection of Chinese antiques: entrance free. Everyday, 10.00–17.00 hrs.

Civic Center: Scene of demonstrations and meetings. Made up of nine buildings.

Pier 39: San Francisco's new harbour. Lots of restaurants and shops – but everything is rather expensive.

Ocean Beach: Beyond Golden Gate Park – surfing.

Ghirardelli Square: Originally the buildings which housed the Ghirardelli chocolate factory. Interesting architecture – also shops, restaurants etc.

Chinatown: The biggest Chinese community outside China. Grant Ave is at the heart of the area. Easy to reach by cable car or by foot from downtown.

Also worth seeing: the **Steinhart Aquarium** (opposite the De Young Museum, in the California Academy of Sciences Museum). 10.00–17.00 (10.00–21.00 in summer).

The **Planetarium** sometimes puts on a laser show. For information: Laserium, ☎ 752.42.64.

San Francisco seen from the Bay: the city is most impressive when seen from a boat.
Red and White Fleet: Pier 43½ at Fisherman's Wharf; a 1¼-hour trip in the Bay, taking in Golden Gate Bridge and Bay Bridge, a close-up view of Alcatraz etc. Sailings from 10.00 hrs.
Gold Coast Cruises: Pier 45. Takes two hours ... which is a bit too long; also expensive.
Ferry to Sausalito: Ferry Building at the Embarcadero. Enables you to visit Sausalito and return by bus, which is the best way if you are not staying long in San Francisco.

San Francisco seen from the Sky: *Commodore Helicopters:* on Pier 43.
Panoramic views: (see later for less popular viewing points).

Coit Tower; Telegraph Hill: Lombard St/Kearny St.
Nob Hill: Powell St/California St. Go to the top of the Fairmont Hotel.
Take the outside lift which goes to Fairmont Crown. It's also possible to go to the top of the Transamerica Building, the Pyramid which gives a fine view over Telegraph Hill and Nob Hill.

North Beach: Columbus St/Broadway. A quarter which comes alive at nightfall; there remain a few good places to go, see later.

---

things that everyone doesn't go to see and which are worth seeing

---

Cable Car Barn and Museum: Washington St/Mason St. 10.00–18.00. Entrance free. The Cable Cars are controlled from here. The museum traces the history of this means of locomotion.

Levi Strauss History Room: 2nd level and Embarcadero. Monday to Friday, 10.00–16.00. History of jeans.

California Palace of the Legion of Honor: Lincoln Park. 10.00–17.00. Entrance free. Take bus No. 2 from Sutter St and Market, or else on Sutter St. Amongst other artists: Corot, Degas, Manet, Monet and many works by Rodin. A very pleasant setting.

Exploratorium: Palace of Fine Arts: 3601 Lyon St. ☎ 563.73.37. Wednesday to Sunday 13.00–17.00; Wednesday evening 19.00–21.30. Entrance free. A museum where you're not allowed not to touch! The Tactile Gallery is really something.

Wine Museum: 633 Beach St. Opposite The Cannery. Tuesday to Saturday, 11.00–17.00; Sunday, 12.00–17.00. Wine-tasting (except Sundays). Beautiful glass collection.

Lyle Tuttle's Tattoo Museum: 30 7th St (near the Greyhound station). Everyday, 12.00–16.00. If you want to be tattooed after your visit Lyle Tuttle will do it for you for a reasonable price.

Japan Center: Post St/Buchanan. Take bus No. 38 on Geary St and get off at Laguna St.

The best points of view over San Francisco

A good trip: Take the Golden Gate Transit to corner of Market St and 7th St. Go down to Bridge Toll Plaza, i.e. to the foot of the Golden Gate Bridge. Cross on foot (2.5 kms), then take the road to Sausalito. From there catch the ferry back.

Baker Beach: on the south-west flank of the Presidio, beyond Lincoln Bld.

Cliff House: Great Highway/Point Lobos Ave.

Cornelian Room: 52nd Floor of the Bank of America.

Top of the Mark: top of the Mark Hopkins hotel.

Victor's: restaurant at the top of the St Francis Hotel.

Land's End: Point Lobos Ave and El Camino Del Mar Ave.

Mount Davidson: take Portola Drive and Rex Ave.

Water Tower at John McLaren Park: take Highway 101 southwards as far as Mansell St, take Mansell St, and turn right on to Shelley Drive.

Sutro Heights Park: 48th Ave/Point Lobos Ave. View of the cliffs and Cliff House.

Angel Island Park: Right in the Bay, marvellous views. Nice for walking, cycling or just sunbathing.

things that everyone goes to see and that can be given a miss

Alcatraz: Harbor Tours Pier 43. Reservation obligatory. ☎ 546.28.05. Or Pier 41. Al Capone is buried in this famous island-prison.

Lombard St: the most twisting and winding street in existence: a scene from *Bullitt* was filmed here.

Mission Dolores: Dolores St/16th St. 9.00–17.00. The oldest mission-house in San Francisco: 1776, and also the best known. Very well preserved.

Old Mint: 5th St/Messia St. Everyday except Monday, 10.00–16.00. Currency museum: don't miss the pyramid of gold ingots.

San Francisco Museum of Modern Art: War Memorial Veterans Building: Van Ness Ave/McAllister St (at the Civic Center). Tuesday to Friday, 10.00–18.00; weekends 10.00–17.00; free. No more than acceptable museum of contemporary art. Occasionally there are some interesting temporary exhibitions ('Chicano' painting for example).

San Francisco National Maritime Museum: Aquatic Park, at the bottom of Polk St. Everyday, 10.00–17.00; free.

Wells Fargo Bank: 420 Montgomery St on California St. Everyday, 10.00–15.00; free. For stagecoach fans, this bank has some fine specimens on exhibition. It's surprising to see that the bank still uses the stagecoach as a symbol in its advertising.

National Historic Ships Park: at Fisherman's Wharf on Hyde Street Pier. 10.00–20.00 hrs in summer, 10.00–18.00 hrs the rest of the year. You can visit four boats including a paddle-steamer.

Museums of the Strange: everything to do with magic and the esoteric is all the rage in the U.S.A. and gives rise to such pitiable commercial enterprises as the two museums on Fisherman's Wharf. *World of the Unexplained:* 235 Jefferson St. 9.00–24.00. Not very convincing.
Ripley's 'Believe it or not' Museum: 175 Jefferson St. Even less amusing.

Wax Museums:

Chinatown Wax Museum: Grant Ave/California St. Summer, 9.00–24.00, otherwise 10.00–23.00.
Wax Museum: Fisherman's Wharf. 145 Jefferson St.

great scenes

Music

Lots of great places on Clement St for music.

The Last Day Saloon: 406 Clement St (5th/6th).

The Boarding House: 960 Bush St. ☎ 441.43.33.

Planshares Coffee House: Fort Mason Building, 312 Laguna and Maria Bld. ☎ 441.89.10. Folk on Sundays.

Jazz

Keystone Korner: 750 Vallejo. ☎ 781.06.97. All the big names appear here.

Great American Music Hall: Polk St/O'Farrell St. ☎ 385.07.50.

Old Waldorf: 444 Bottery St. ☎ 835.43.42.

The San Francisco of the Poets, the 'Radicals', and the Musicians

For the tourist in a hurry, North Beach is the quarter of striptease clubs, massage-parlours and such like, but there is still a café life where you can listen to folk-music whilst putting the world to rights. As in New York, everything begins late at night (midnight, 1 a.m.). Here is a selection of the liveliest places in San Francisco from a musical, political and poetical point of view:

North Beach: City Lights Bookstore on Columbus/Broadway is a centre of attraction in the quarter for the emulators of Kerouac and Company.

Gulliver's: 508 Sutter St. Very cool, musicians, good atmosphere.

Specs: in the cul-de-sac opposite City Lights Bookstore on Columbus Ave. More sophisticated than Gulliver's.

Paradise Café: Broadway/Montgomery St. Billiards and a juke-box. Excellent brunch on Sunday mornings.

Vesuvio: on Columbus next to City Lights. Very literary atmosphere, the poets' café.

Coffee Gallery: 1353 Grant St. Janis Joplin began singing in this cradle of West Coast poetry. Ginsberg and Ferlinghetti are regulars.

Washington Square Bar and Grill: in Washington Square, 200 metres from Broadway/Columbus, 1707 Powell St. The 'Radicals' ' café, particularly the rich ones.

Gin and Carlos: on Green near Grant Ave and Washington Square.

The Gorilla Grotto: 775 Frederick St (bookstore and café).

At Haight

Other Café: Cole St/Carl St. Meeting place for the last of the hippies.

Sacred Grounds Coffee Shop: Cole St/Hayes. Music, poetry, sandwiches.

The 'Gay' bars

where the best music for dancing is played

Buzby's: Polk St. Ultra sophisticated disco.

The Palms: Polk St. Music: 'distinguished' atmosphere.

Eagle Creek Saloon: Market St/15th St (under the Viking Hotel). Full of Punks.

Mineshaft: on Market St (between 14th and 15th St).

The Stud: 12th St/Folsom St.

Cissy's Saloon: 12th St/Folsom St.

Hamburger Mary's: 12th St/Folsom St.

Rainbow Cattle Company: Valencia St/Duboce St.

Cinema for film buffs

The Strand: 1127 Market St (between 7th and 8th St). ☏ 552.59.90.

Le Castro: 429 Castro St. ☏ 621.61.20.

Canyon Cinematheque, S.F. Art Institute: 800 Chestnut St. ☏ 332.15.14.

Cento Cedar: 38 Cedar Alley (near Larkin St). ☏ 776.83.00. Excellent programmes.

Avenue Photoplay: 2650 San Bruno Ave. ☏ 468.26.36.

Lumière: 1572 California St. ☏ 885.32.00.

Gateway: 215 Jackson St. ☏ 421.33.53.
See also under Berkeley.

Architecture

San Francisco is a gold-mine for the student of architecture or quite simply for the lover of beautiful buildings. Here is a minimal list of things to see:

The famous **shop of Frank Lloyd Wright** at 140 Maiden Lane (very close to Union Square). Originally for a washing-soda manufacturer.

Hyatt Regency Hotel: 5 Embarcadero Center. The architecture inside is completely mad! Indescribable, so go and see it. Take the side lift to the restaurant to cross the roof. Don't eat here – it's very expensive.

Vedanta Society Building: Filbert St/Webster St. This house built in 1905 manages to combine a very Eastern style with basic Victoriana (verandah windows). Remarkable.

A row of small houses: 2637 to 2673 Clay St. Magnificent example of well-preserved architecture.

The School of Plastic Arts: on Francisco and Jones St. An example of good contemporary building in concrete.

Hallidie Building: 130 Sutter St. A really prodigious glass building dating from 1917.

Murals

There are dozens of murals in San Francisco. Here are some of the best ones:

in Chinatown: Grant St/Vallejo St.
In the housing-block on Valencia/14th St.
From Mission walk along 24th St.
23rd St/Folsom: Mural on a free clinic.
Alamo Square: Fulton St/McAllister St.

Cheap clothes

Fashion Joint: 4170 Piedmont Ave.

The Liquidation: 4042 24th St.

Pubs

Buena Vista: 2765 Hyde St. Irish coffee.

The Flagship: 827 Sutter St. Darts.

Lord Nelson: 970 Sutter St.

The Abbey Tavern: 4100 Geary St. So out-of-the-way that there are few tourists.

The Edinburgh Castle: 950 Geary St. Buy fish and chips at the *Old Chelsea* on Larkin and have a Guinness in this old pub.

House of Shields: 39 New Montgomery St.

Mooney's Irish Pub: 1525 Grant St.

The Plough and the Stars: 116 Clement St. See an authentic Irish bar.

Cafés

Pier 23 Café: Jazz at weekends.

The Tosca Café: 242 Columbus St. Excellent capuccinos in an authentic setting. Full of atmosphere.

Enrico's Sidewalk Café: 504 Broadway. An institution.

Café Trieste: 601 Vallejo St.

Earthquake McGoon's: 128 Embarcadero. Quite expensive. Open on Thursday, Friday and Saturday. Jazz.

Etcetera

Cost Plus: Taylor St/North Point St. Near Fisherman's Wharf. You can easily spend an afternoon exploring this collection of shops which specialize in imported furniture, etc.

Scenic Drive: recommended for red-blooded motorists! Start at the corner of Powell St and Market St and follow the 'Scenic Drive' signs for 49 miles round San Francisco.

The Magazine: 839 Larkin St. Astonishing collection of old magazines.

Billiards Palace: 949 Market St (between 6th and 5th St). Worth seeing even if you have never played billiards: fringe characters in a decadent atmosphere.

The Antique-dealers' quarter: go for a walk around Montgomery/Jackson intersection, in Jackson Square and Pacific St. The antique-dealers' shops are in very fine brick-built houses.

Kite Festival: every evening in June in Golden Gate Park.

Grace Cathedral: Nob Hill, behind Fairmont Hotel. A poor imitation of Paris's Notre-Dame.

Bach Festival: Every June there is a Bach Festival held in different churches in the town.

Midsummer Music Festival: free open-air concerts at Sigmund Stern Grove 19th Ave/Sloat Bld. Classical music and a lot of jazz.

Sport: Football and baseball matches take place in Candlestick Park. Oakland has one of the best football teams in the States.

Bicycle outings: ask at the Sierra Club, 530 Bush St (☎ 981.86.34) for their programme of outings.

Alameda Flea Market, Oakland. Saturdays and Sundays only. Things in **Golden Gate Park** off the beaten track:
Bison: go to Buffalo Paddock, in the western part of the park.
Merry-go-round: Be sure to see the magnificent merry-go-round, which has few equivalents in the U.S.A., in the Children's Playground (southern side near the entrance).
Pétanque: On a fine weekend you can see Frenchmen playing this game behind the Buffalo Paddock. To get to Golden Gate Park take bus No. 21 on Market St or Hayes St.

around San Francisco

The region around San Francisco has such a wide variety of landscapes to offer that even a month would be too short to explore all their riches.

To the north

On the other side of Golden Gate Bridge begins *Marin County* a district made up of small villages of which the most famous (and therefore the least interesting) is *Sausalito*. None the less, it's worth worth stopping there, if only for the fantastic view over the Bay and San Francisco (particularly when the tops of the skyscrapers and towers are enveloped in mist). See also the floating village known as *Marin City*, north of Sausalito. There are a few pubs on Bridgeway Ave. To get to Sausalito if you haven't got a car, take one of the numerous ferries which leave from the Ferry Building or else a Golden Gate Transit Bus. In summer, avoid going on a Sunday.

N.B. Worth seeing: the model of San Francisco Bay by the American Army at 2001 Bridgeway Ave (Wednesday to Friday and the 1st and 3rd Saturdays of every month, 9.00–16.00). A little marvel.

Less popular but just as attractive as Sausalito: *Tiburon,* a village of fine houses belonging to well-off artists situated on the Belvedere Peninsula. You can catch the ferry back to San Francisco.

Golden Gate National Recreation Area: from Fisherman's Wharf to Point Reyes National Seashore. Interesting minibus tours, For information ☎ 556. 05.60.

Mount Tamalpais: a winding road takes you to the top, from where you have an exceptional view over the whole of the Bay. Often you can see the Golden Gate Bridge emerging from a sea of clouds; superb!

Muir Woods: a forest of sequoias which make you feel giddy just to look at them (the 'sequoia sempervivens' of Muir Woods are the tallest trees in the world, and not to be confused with the 'sequoia gigantea' which are not so tall but much wider – 12 metres in diameter – and which can be found in the Sequoia National Park, 90 kms east of Fresno. You can hitch-hike from Mill Valley onwards.

Marin County Civic Center: above Highway 101 after San Rafael this enormous building was designed by Frank Lloyd Wright shortly before his death. You can get a good but cheap 'brunch' in the Civic Center Restaurant.

The Pacific Coast: take the road which goes to Stinson Beach and Bolinas. The whole of the coast is magnificent with very beautiful classically-shaped greywood houses dotted here and there on the hills.

Bolinas is a small village which time has to some extent forgotten. Not yet having been discovered by the Gray Lines tourist, it has kept its Californian bohemian atmosphere. There are some dome-shaped houses on the plateau. The further north you go the more nature is protected and there are some absolutely fantastic places.

250 kms east of San Francisco is the *Yosemite National Park* (see section on National Parks). The whole of the southern side of the city is reputed for its scenery. Big Sur, Carmel, Monterey which were gathering-places at the time of the hippies have now been sold up at huge prices as retreats for millionaires, artists or otherwise. Most of the communities and religious temples such as the Zen monastery at *Tassajara* are situated further inland.

Two of the University of California's campuses are sited south of San Francisco: the very famous and private *Stanford* at Menlo Park, and *Santa Cruz* which is an hour's drive away.

The Santa Cruz campus is a semi-paradise with its site overlooking the Pacific. An ideal stopping-place on the road from San Francisco to Los Angeles.

Meditation in the open air: a Zen community, near Carmel Valley in *Tassajara Springs* takes in visitors from May 1 to the end of August for stays of up to six weeks' duration. The conditions are the following: a fixed price per day for board and lodging, four obligatory sessions of zazen per day and above all the main condition, you must have spent a whole week in the Zen centre at San Francisco (City Center, 300 Page St, ☎ 863.31.36) or Sausalito (Green Gulch Farm Star route, ☎ 383.31.34).

Where to go for 25c

Some places to see and how to get to them.

Exploratorium: Bus No. 30 at Stockton St/Sutter St. Get out at Broderick St/Beach St.

Golden Gate Park: Bus No. 38 on Geary St. Go west to 10th Ave. Take a transfer for the No. 10 bus to Monterey and get out at the Museum Complex.

Golden Gate Bridge: Take the Golden Gate Transit at the corner of Market St and 7th St opposite the Shaw Hotel. Get out at Bridge Toll Plaza.

Fisherman's Wharf: Take the cable car Powell/Mason on Powell St, heading north. Get out at the terminus and walk.

Ghirardelli Square: Take the cable car Powell/Hyde on Powell St. Get out at the terminus.

Maritime Historic Park: The same as for Ghirardelli Square, then head north on foot.

Seal Rocks, Ocean Beach, Cliff House: Take bus No. 38 Geary or No. 38L at the corner of Powell St and Geary St. Get out at Lobos Point and 48th St.

BERKELEY

☎ 415
CALIFORNIA

On the other side of the Bay, Berkeley is one of the most important University centres in the U.S.A. The town has much charm (the campus is very attractive) and is always very busy. At weekends the campus surrounds become one big good-humoured bazaar where long-haired but gentle characters come to sell a bit of everything: leather belts, pottery, religion, cloth, drugs, books, candles, politics, music ... Others are there to beg from the tourists.

How to get there

BART: take the BART Concord at San Francisco, change at MacArthur (direction Richmond), and get off at Berkeley Station. Bus: take bus F at the Transbay Transit Terminal, Mission St/Fremont St.

Car: by the San Francisco–Oakland Bay Bridge (toll to pay on the way back), then Freeway 80 as far as the exit Berkeley University.

Hitch-hiking: stand at the beginning of the motorway link-road with a board showing 'Berkeley' (Oak St/Fell St).

Greyhound: if you have Ameripass vouchers, make full use of them: you can go as far as Oakland and take bus No. 40 on Telegraph Ave.

keys to Berkeley

General information
Chamber of Commerce: 1834 University Ave.

Newspapers and magazines
The Berkeley Barb is not what it was, but is still useful for rock concert, folk club etc. programmes.

The Berkeley Daily Gazette: a classic.

The San Francisco Bay Guardian: also useful for Berkeley.

University Art Museum, Berkeley: free, gives the campus cultural programmes.

Survival
Switchboard
Berkeley Switchboard: 1901 8th St. ☎ 848.08.00.
University Lutheran Church: 3102 Telegraph Ave. ☎ 843.62.30.

Transport
Carpool Transit Systems: 2720 Grove St. ☎ 845.17.69

U.C. Campus Information: ☎ 642.60.00.

Second-hand cars: *Auto Data:* 1525 Shattuck Ave.

BART: you can take your bicycle except during rush hours. Avoid the San Francisco–Berkeley ferry because of congestion.

Health
Berkeley Community Health Project (free clinic): 2339 Durant Ave. ☎ 548.25.70.

Berkeley Women's Health Collective: 2908 Ellsworth. ☎ 843.61.94.

West Berkeley Health Center: 830 University Ave. ☎ 644.69.39.

Food
Berkeley Emergency Food Project: 2425 College Ave. ☎ 843.62.30.

A Creative Community Project: 2269 Washington St. Evening meal at 18.00. ☎ 567.74.88.

Legal Aid
Berkeley Own Recognizance: 2400 Bancroft Way. ☎ 548.24.38.

Meeting places

Telegraph Ave.

South American Cultural Center: La Peña. 3105 Shattuck Ave. ☎ 849.25.68. Very busy.

good night

Student accommodation

International House: Piedmont Ave/Bancroft Way (above the campus).

Y.M.C.A.: 2001 Allston Way. ☎ 848.68.00.

Student Union: ask for the addresses of the University Halls.

Spen Black Hall: 2400 Durant St. ☎ 849.14.02.

Ida Sproul Hall: 2400 Durant St. ☎ 642.59.25.

Newman Hall: 2700 Dwight Way. ☎ 848.78.12.

Berkeley Youth Hostel: 711 Harrison. ☎ 526.99.63.

Cheap hotels

Berkeley Inn: 2501 Haste St. ☎ 845.63.70.

Hotel Carlton: 2338 Telegraph Ave (between Durant and Bancroft).

University Hotel: 2057 University Ave. ☎ 848.94.33. Not as well placed as the two previous hotels.

Nash Hotel: 2045 University Ave. ☎ 841.11.63.

Berkeley Motel: 2001 Bancroft Way.

getting fed

There are lots of small restaurants on Telegraph Ave near the campus. Don't forget the cafeterias on the campus itself (closed on Sunday) where you can eat well and cheaply.

One World Family: Telegraph Ave/Haste St. Health food.

On the other side of the campus on Euclid St:

Sandwich Shop: 1829 Euclid St.

To the south of the campus:

Oleg's Restaurant: 1974 Shattuck Ave (near University Ave). Ultra-sophisticated decor.

Smokey Joe's Cafe: 1620 Shattuck Ave. Simple and cheap.

The Upper Level Expresso: Walnut Square. Walnut/Vine St. Marvellous view over S.F. from the small terrace.

The Egg Shop and Apple Press: 2327 Shattuck Ave. Natural food. There are three other restaurants with the same name in Berkeley.

The Haven: 2399 Shattuck Ave. Sandwiches.

Machu Pichu: 2400 San Pablo Ave (every day except Monday). Peruvian cooking.

Soup 'n Such: on Telegraph Ave near Durant on the corner. A wide choice of hot and inexpensive soups to take away or eat on the spot.

Chez Panisse: 1517 Shattuck Ave. 'The' French restaurant, excellent if you are inviting somebody out, or rather if somebody is inviting you out, as it's rather expensive.

Taiwan: University Ave near Shattuck Ave. Chinese.

Spenger's Fish Grotto: Berkeley Marina. Nice decor.

Wines and Liquors: College Ave/Alcatraz St. Good sandwiches made for you. Reasonably priced.

---

things that (nearly) everyone goes to see and that you shouldn't miss

---

The U.C.B. campus: A magnificent campus in a park on a slight hillside, view over the Bay from the top of Sather Tower (10.00–17.00).

University Art Museum: Bancroft Way, opposite the campus. Very fine contemporary architecture, an interesting collection, good cafeteria in the basement, entrance free (only the museum!) 11.00–17.00 except Monday and Tuesday.

Berkeley Marina Yacht Harbor: Good place for walks.

---

things that everyone doesn't go to see and which are worth seeing

---

Cramont Park: a little park on Student Ave with a beautiful view of the Bay.

Hearst Mining Building: on the north side of the campus, built by John Howard in 1907, this building is remarkable for its interior dimensions and transparent domes.

great scenes

Theatre

On the campus:

Wheeler Auditorium, Zellerbach Playhouse. Information ☎ 642.25.61.

Starry Plough Irish Pub: 3101 Shattuck Ave. ☎ 848.95.60. Very active theatre-pub.

Popular Theater: 5636 College Ave. ☎ 548.20.61.

Keystone Berkeley: 2119 University Ave. Often very good concerts.

The Freight and Salvage Coffee House: 1827 San Pablo Ave. ☎ 548.20.60. Beer and wine. Folk music.

Cinema for film buffs

Rialto 4: 841 Gilman St. ☎ 526.66.69.

The Sunset: 2411 Telegraph Ave. ☎ 848.20.60.

Telegraph Repertory Cinema: 2519 Telegraph Ave. ☎ 548.25.19.

And of course have a look at the programmes of:

Pacific Film Archive: Art Museum, 2625 Durant.

Shopping

Cody's Book: 2454 Haste St. Good bookshop.

Yasai: College Ave/Alcatraz St. Cheaper than a supermarket and their fruit and vegetables are much better.

There are two shops in Berkeley which are guaranteed to please certain fans: **Rather Ripped Records:** 1878 Euclid Ave. Has one of the largest selections of 'bootleg' records on the West Coast, if not in the whole of the United States.

Berkeley Comic Art Shop: 2512 Telegraph Ave. The whole of American Comic art on sale, back numbers included.

The Co-op: 3000 Telegraph Ave, 1581 University Ave, 1414 University Ave, and 1500 Shattuck Ave. This chain of consumers' co-operative supermarkets is the only one of its kind: all the products are tested and warnings put in front of those which are not natural or 'ecological' enough. But the most important thing is that each shop has a large bulletin board which supplies useful information on: travelling, accommodation, buying and selling etc.

Etcetera

Grizzly Peak Bld: a beautiful road up in the hills round Berkeley, with a view over the whole of the

Bay. Note the number of fruit and other trees there
are in Berkeley – about 32,000 – lining every road.

University of Washington, Floating Bridge

Seattle
Downtown

| 0 | 0,1 | 0,2 | 0,3 mi |

| 0 | 100 | 200 | 300 | 400 | 500 m |

1 Rainier Bank Bldg.
2 Olympic Hotel
3 First National Bank
4 Public Library
5 Federal Court
6 Federal Office Building
7 Chamber of Commerce
8 Public Safety Building
9 City Hall
10 Smith Tower
11 King County Court House
12 Seattle Convention &
   Visitors Bureau
Pier 51 Ye Olde Curiosity Shop
      Polynesia Restaurant
Pier 59 Marine Aquarium

Olympic N.P., Tacoma (Airport)   Kart. Inst. G. Schiffner, Lahr/Sc

SEATTLE
📞 206
WASHINGTON

In the far north-west corner of the United States is the mythical land of the Indian, the gold-digger and the lumberjack. There Seattle, with its one million inhabitants, prospers, built on its hills and surrounded by an exceptional natural landscape. High mountains (Mount Rainier) overlook the wild Pacific shoreline. The weather, warm in summer and not too harsh in winter, makes for a wide range of leisure and sporting activities. Seattle is famous for its Boeing factories but also for its many places and features of interest to fire the imagination of even the most travel-weary of visitors.

arriving in Seattle

Coach
Greyhound: 8th and Stewart St. 📞 624.34.56.
Continental Trailways: 1936 Westlake Ave. 📞 624.59.55.

Plane
Sea-Tac Airport (between Seattle and Tacoma) 📞 433.53.88. Take the Interstate 5 or the Hustlebus to the centre of town.

Train
Amtrak: 3rd at Jackson. 📞 421.83.20.

don't panic

Finding your way around

All the avenues run from north to south and are numbered from west to east. For fast traffic, the Alaskan Way Viaduct runs just above the Alaskan Way, along the harbour to the west of the town. The streets have names (Market, Pine etc) and run from west to east.

Transport

The Metro Transit System runs the city's bus network and fares are calculated in zones of travel. A 'horizontal monorail elevator' links the Seattle Center with the centre of town, in 90 seconds!

Taxis

Yellow Cabs: ☎ 622.65.00 or 622.73.95.
Grey Top Cabs: ☎ 622.49.49.
Far West Taxi Cabs: ☎ 622.17.17.

Car hire

Budget: Westlake and Virginia Street, ☎ 622.19.62.
Compacts Only: Denny Street and 7th Ave, ☎ 623.04.73.
American International Rent-a-car: 4th Ave and Columbia Street, ☎ 682.89.89.

Refuge

A.Y.H.: Pike Street and Minor Ave (Membership card needed)
Y.M.C.A.: 909 4th Ave, ☎ 447.45.11 and 1118 5th Ave, ☎ 447.48.88.

keys to Seattle

General information

Doctor (24 hours): ☎ 622.69.00.
Emergency (Police, Ambulance, Fire): ☎ 911.
Weather: ☎ 662.11.11. Post Office: 3rd Avenue.
Seattle King County Convention and Visitors' Bureau: 1815 7th Ave, ☎ 447.72.73.
Traveller's Aid Society: 117 2nd Ave, ☎ 447.38.38.

Newspapers

Seattle Post-Intelligencer; Seattle Times, very popular.

Weeklies: **The Argus** and **The Weekly.**
You can also pick up a free copy of the **Seattle Guide** in many public places.

Colleges and campuses

Washington University: North-East of town and North of Lake Union, near Portage Bay. Very pleasant area, lively and with shops and restaurants.

Meeting places

Seattle Center: at the foot of the Space Needle, built in 1962 for the international fair which put Seattle on the map of world trade.

Pike Place Market with its little craft workshops, all under one roof, on Elliot Bay.

University Village, at Washington University, for campus life.

Pioneer Square, the heart of the old town, well renovated, with antique shops, galleries, restaurants and lots of shops. Starts at 5th Avenue and James Street, and is where visitors and nightowls congregate.

Survival

Legal Assistance: ☎ 625.92.90.

---

good night

Cheap hotels

Milner Hotel: 317 Marion St. ☎ 622.39.85.
Savoy Hotel: 1214 2nd Ave. ☎ 682.27.33.
St. Regis Hotel: 2nd and Stewart. ☎ 622.63.66.
Gatewood Hotel: 1st and Pine. ☎ 624.41.44.

More expensive hotels

Vance Downtown Motor Hotel: 620 Stewart. ☎ 623.27.00.
Motor Inn Motel (long way from centre): 1629 N. Aurora. ☎ 285.97.13.
Mayflower Park Hotel: 4th and Olive. ☎ 623.87.00.
Claremont Hotel: 2004 4th Ave. ☎ 622.86.00.
Windsor Hotel: 1405 6th Ave. ☎ 623.52.30.

getting fed

Snacks

Soup and salad in the Pike Market and **Fish and chips** anywhere along the Alaskan Way.

Sandwiches, Coffee houses

Cafe Kaleenka: 1933 1st Ave.

Block's: N. Queen Anne and Thomas St. W.

Restaurants for good value

Bavarian House: 315 Seneca St. German beers.

Casa Espinoza: 521 Pike St. Se habla español! Mexican food.

Charlie's: 217 Broadway E. Old-world decor.

The Dog House: 2230 7th Ave. Open 24 hours a day.

Jade Pagoda: 606 Broadway E. Cantonese food.

Lebanon Restaurant: 112 5th Ave N. Musical atmosphere.

The Lime Green Grocer: 1118 5th Ave.

The Linyen Restaurant and Cocktail Lounge: 424 7th Ave.

In Seattle's Chinatown

Red Robin Burger: Eastlake and Northgate. 28 varieties.

Steaks and Eggs: 1919 Queen Anne Ave.

Stuart Anderson's Black Angus: 208 Elliot Ave. Dancing on a metal floor.

Pigalle Creperie: 1104 N.E. 47th Ave. Quite a long way, but worth it for the Parisian atmosphere.

things that everyone goes to see and that you shouldn't miss

Pacific Science Center: Denny Way and 2nd Avenue. In the Seattle Center complex, interesting and entertaining, impressive architecture. Weekdays 9.00–19.00, weekends 10.00–19.00.

Chinatown: Very big area in proportion to the size of the city. Due south from the centre of town, interesting murals and market.

Pike Place Market: 72 years old, this, for the most part covered, market houses not only a myriad of little craft workshops, but also fishmongers' stalls, fruit and veg, flowers etc. Open 9.00 to 18.00 except Sunday.

Seattle Art Museum: Volunteer Park. ☎ 447.46.70.

Seattle Art Museum Modern Art Pavilion at the Seattle Center. ☎ 447.47.95. Daily 10.00–17.00, Sunday 12.00–17.00.

Space Needle: For a bird's eye view, go up to the Observatory and have a drink in the revolving restaurant (one revolution per hour). Eating there is expensive. ☎ 682.56.56.

The Fun Forest: A fun fair right next to the Space Needle all summer long.

The Seattle Center Fountain: A musical fountain whose height and water play depends on the choice of music.

Rainier Square Retail: A fascinating building in Rainier Square: the base is narrower than the rest of it!

Seattle Underground: A tour of the old streets of Seattle which are now literally underground. The new town was built on the site of the old after the great fire which ravaged Seattle at the end of the 19th century. The entrance is at the corner of Cherry Street and 1st Avenue. ☎ 682.46.46.

things that everyone doesn't go to see and which deserve to be seen

The Locks: 15th Ave. W. and the continuation of Elliot Ave. They link Puget Sound with the two sweet-water lakes, Lake Union and Lake Washington. The surrounding greenery is a great attraction.

The Floating Bridge: An enormous, unsupported road bridge over Lake Washington.

The Gas Work Park: On the north shore of Lake Union, a rusting wreck of a factory reclaimed as an adventure playground for kids. Repainted in bright colours and designs, it's a work of art in itself.

The Floating Houses: A little island on the west shore of Lake Washington. Very strange!

things that everyone goes to see and that can be given a miss

King Dome: Occidental Ave and King St. Huge covered stadium.

The Aquarium: Pier 59 and Waterfront Park. To take a look at the layout rather than the residents!

Burke Memorial Washington State Museum: 17th N.E. St and 45th St. Indian history retrospective. Daily 10.00–16.30, Sunday 13.00–16.30. Closed Monday.

Fry Art Museum: 704 Terry Ave. Collection of 19th and 20th century paintings. Varied and interesting exhibitions (about every 3 weeks).

Henry Art Museum: On the campus of Washington University. Local museum housing the works of North-West American artists. Open daily 10.00–17.00 (Thursday till 22.00), Sunday 13.00–17.00. Closed Monday.

great scenes

Music

Jazz

Parnell's: Pioneer Square.
Jazz Alley: 42nd and University Way N.E. Jazz and blues.

Blues

Hibble & Hydes: Pioneer Square.

Rock 'n' Roll

Aquarius Tavern: 17001 Aurora Ave N.

The Edmond's Theater: 415 Main St. Films and local groups at weekends only.

Goldies on Broadway: Broadway and Pike. Rock and blues.

The Place: 152nd and Pacific Highway S. Rock, pop, soul and country. Restaurant and bar.

The Rainbow Tavern: 45th N.E., near the University. Rock/and folk.
N.B. Most of the above will not admit under-21s.

Cinemas for film buffs

There are an enormous number of cinema-theatres in Seattle. Check in '*The Weekly*' or the '*Argus*' for programmes and special seasons.

Shopping

Great Winds Kite Shop: 166 S. Jackson St. Kites, kites, kites ...

Pier 70: lots of little craft shops.

Baby & Co.: 1st Ave. and Virgina St. Full of lovely togs for babies and toddlers.

Musicland: 215 Pike St. Very good selection of records.

Man in the Moon: 5th Ave. Second-hand '40s clothes.

Impossible to list all the good shops in the Pike Place Market, but one in particular that's worth a visit is **Left Bank Books:** a 'Berkeley' type bookshop.

Etcetera

Murals

There are some in Chinatown and at the corner of Spring Street and 1st Avenue.

around Seattle

Mount Rainier National Park:
Two hours from Seattle, Mount Rainier rises to 4392 metres. If your stay in Seattle is long enough to include a few days at Mount Rainier, buy yourself the guide book which describes the many scenic walks. It is on sale at the Visitors' Bureau in Paradise, the highest town on the mountain.

Bellevue:
To the east of Lake Washington, a little town next door to the big one, with shops and restaurants of interest.

Water Tours:
Boat trips out to sea. Run from May to end September from Pier 56. Information: ☎ 624.58.15.

Tillicum Village:
An hour from Seattle, on Blake Island. Along the lines of the Indian reservations with the added attraction of being able to eat 'Indian' salmon. Departures from Pier 56. Information: ☎ 329.57.00.

Olympic National Park:
To the west of Seattle, bounded by the ocean on three sides, an earthly paradise within easy reach. You'll find huge glaciers, forests of giant sequoias, lakes, streams and miles and miles of wild and almost deserted beaches. If you haven't got a car, hire one and make a bee-line for it!

WASHINGTON

☎ 202

DISTRICT OF COLUMBIA

Washington is the United States' city of museums.
You can walk for miles through its columned buildings which look like great white cakes. The capital of
the States is full of civil servants in collar and tie.
Fortunately there is a gayer quarter: Georgetown, to
the north-west. A good place to go and relax after a
day's sightseeing, in an old inn or a typically English
pub. But make sure you have a good look round the
museums first: they are in the same part of the city
and are nearly all free.

arriving in Washington

Coach

Greyhound and Continental Trailways: New
York Ave/12th St. ☎ 289.51.00. (Greyhound); 737.
58.00. (Trailways). A few minutes on foot from the
White House.

Plane

The bus is the cheapest and most practical way of
getting into the city from the airports, **Baltimore-
Washington International, Dulles** and **National.**

Train

Amtrak and **Southern Railways:** Union Station,
Massachusetts Ave/North Capitol St. ☎ 523.57.20.

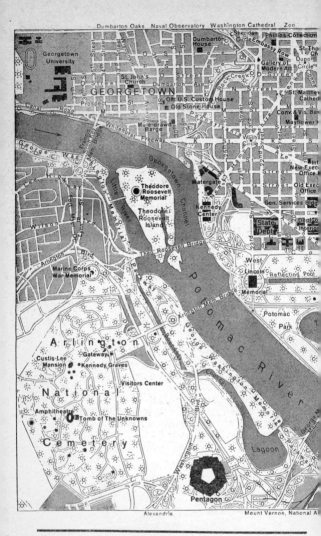

don't panic

Finding your way around

A simple layout but a rather complicated street-
system: Washington is divided into four quarters
(the centre being the Capitol). North-East (N.E.),
North-West (N.W.), South-East (S.E.) and South-
West (S.W.). Each address is followed by its quarter.
North–south streets are indicated by numbers, and
east–west streets by letters, in alphabetical order.
The avenues have proper names. Get hold of the

Washington
(District of Columbia)

0   500   1000   1500 m   1 mi

Jewish S Center
Nat Wildlife Federation
Scott Circle
Luther Church
Thomas Circle
Logan Circle
Central Public Library
St John's On
Contin. Trailways
Greyhound
Treasury Dept.
St Patrick's Church
Art. Mus.
White House
Pet Hall
Ford's Th
Judiciary Square
FEDERAL TRIANGLE
Municipal Center
U.S Court House
Taft Memorial D
Senate Office Buildings
Supreme Court
Washington Monument
Museum
Museum
Nat Gall.
THE MALL
Drive
Madison Drive
Capitol
Congress
Washington Adams Jefferson
Smithsonian Drive
Institution
Independence
Transp NASA
Independence Ave.
Agriculture
Forrester
HEW NASA
House Office Buildings
Engraving & Printing
Dept of Housing & Urb. Dev.
Food & Drug Admin.
Southwest Street
Jefferson Memorial
Freeway
East Potomac Park
Wilson Line
Arena Stage
Friendship Airport
Union Station
Mem bridge
Washington Channel
Anacostia River
Potomac River

cutive House Hotel
ional Rifle Association
ai B'rith Building
ional Geographic Society
nger Hay-Adams Hotel
wick Gallery
coran Art Gallery

⑧ American Red Cross
⑨ Pan American Union
⑩ Bureau of Indian Affairs
⑪ Federal Reserve System
⑫ National Academies of Science & Engineering

⑬ Department of Health, Education & Welfare
⑭ Botanic Garden
⑮ Folger Shakespeare Library
⑯ Museum of African Art

free EXXON map, which is very clear, and you will be able to find your way around.

Exxon Touring Service Office: 1023 Connecticut Ave N.W.

Transport

Bus: rather expensive and not many routes. Rush hour 6.00–9.30 and 15.00–18.30. There is a private company called D.C. Transit, information at 1422 New York Ave N.W. (☎ 637.24.37). Transfer tickets are free. Tickets are bought on board the bus.

Tourmobile: ☎ 638.53.71. A bus service with eleven stops which tours the Mall and Arlington National

203

Cemetery. One fare for the whole day; an excellent way of visiting Washington if you haven't got much time.

Subway: Monday-Friday, 6 a.m. to midnight. Weekends 8 a.m. to midnight. As it's only recently built, the Washington Subway doesn't have many stations. Information: ☎ 637.24.37.

Taxi: for once not exorbitant. Three companies and a zone system. Note however that fares are increased between 16.00 and 18.30 (rush hour). The only town in the U.S.A. where you can share the fare. You share the cost and contribute conversation.

Yellow Cab: ☎ 544.12.12. Taxis are more expensive when you telephone for one than when you hail one in the road.

Car-hire
Budget: 12th/K St N.W. ☎ 628.27.50.
Econo: 1137 19th N.W. ☎ 333.32.50.

Bike hire:
Big Wheel Bikes: 103 L St/33rd St. ☎ 337.02.54.

Refuge

Y.M.C.A.: 17th St/Rhode Island Ave. ☎ 862.96.22. Mixed. Must stay minimum of a month.

Y.W.C.A.: 901 Rhode Island Ave. ☎ 667.91.00. Girls only.

A.Y.H.: 1332 I St. N.W. ☎ 387.31.69.

Catholic University Dormitory: ☎ 635.56.15. Summer only.

keys to Washington

General information

International kiosk: On the Mall near the Museum of History and Technology.

Washington Convention and Visitors' Bureau: 1129 20th St N.W. ☎ 737.88.66 and 659.64.23 (9.00–17.30 during the week). Tourist information.

Foreign Student Service Council: 1860 19th St N.W.

National Visitors' Center: in Union Station, Massachusetts/Delaware Ave. ☎ 523.50.33 (8.00–22.00).

International Visitors' Service Council: 801 19th St N.W. ☎ 872.87.47.

Traveller's Aid Society: 1015 12th St N.W. ☎ 347.01.01.

The day's cultural events by phone: ☎ 737.88.66.

For what's on in the **Smithsonian museums:**
☎ 737.88.11.

Visitor Information: ☎ 381.62.64.

Free Information: ☎ (800) 555.12.12.

For the weather forecast: ☎ 936.12.12.

For the time: ☎ 844.25.25.

Newspapers and magazines

The First Folio: a small newspaper with all the film, theatre and rock concert programmes.

The daily **Washington Post,** particularly on Friday when it includes a complete list of the following week's events.

The monthly review **Washington.**

You can find (free) **This Week** in hotel foyers.

Colleges and campuses

A University near to the town centre:

George Washington University: 20th St/G St N.W.

A University situated in the quarter of Georgetown

Georgetown University: 37th St/O St N.W.

A very big campus, 10 kms north-east of the centre.

University of Maryland in College Park. If you have a car take Rhode Island Ave right to the end, and then Baltimore Ave.

Meeting places

Georgetown is a delightful little quarter, composed of small brick houses, only a few moments by car from the centre, where Washington's students tend to meet. The main streets are Wisconsin Ave and M St N.W. To get there, take a bus on Pennsylvania Ave.

Dupont Circle: 19th St/P St N.W. One of the main meeting-places: situated at the junction of several of the city's main thoroughfares.

The Museums: particularly at the weekend, are obviously places where it's easy to meet people. You can choose between the crowded atmosphere of the big museums on the Mall or the cosier atmosphere of, for example, the Phillips Collection (1600 21st St N.W.).

Survival

George Washington and Georgetown are the best Universities to try. There are quite a lot of students on the Georgetown campus during the summer.
Dupont Circle is a good place to find a kindly soul.
Auto Driveaway: 1341 G St N.W. ☎ 347.34.44.

good night

Student accommodation

Bear in mind that it's always hard to find accommodation in Washington over the summer; try and reserve, otherwise the Y.M.C.A. is the cheapest alternative.

International Guest House: 1441 Kennedy St N.W. ☎ 726.58.08. Must stay more than a week.

Catholic University Dormitory: ☎ 635.56.15. Open in summer only.

For Georgetown University apply at **Summer Housing,** 101 Old North, Georgetown University. ☎ 625.01.00.

If you are staying for more than a week:

Harnett Hall: 1426 21st St N.W. ☎ 293.11.11 (two separate buildings for girls and boys). Two blocks from Dupont Circle.

The cheapest hotels

Harrington Hotel: 11th St/E St N.W. ☎ 628.81.40.

Hotel Ebbitt: 1000 H St N.W. ☎ 628.50.34.

Allen Lee Hotel: 2224 F St N.W. ☎ 331.12.24.

John Kilpen Hotel: 2005 Columbia Rd N.W. ☎ 265.40.06.

Less cheap hotels

Ambassador Hotel: 1412 K St N.W. ☎ 628.85.10 (near 14th St).

Hilton Hotel: 2134 J St N.W. ☎ 338.78.10.

Presidential Hotel: 900 19th St N.W. ☎ 331.90.20.

Capital Hotel: 1016 I St N.W. ☎ 347.06.12.

Connecticut-Woodley Tourist Home: 2647 Woodley Rd N.W. ☎ 667.02.18.

Relatively expensive hotels

Executive House: 1515 Rhode Island Ave. ☎ 232.70.00.

Holiday Inn – Central: 1501 Rhode Island Ave. ☎ 483.20.00.

If you are in a car:

Allstate Hotel: 11936 Lee Highway, Fairfax. ☎ 631.14.14.

Bragg Towers: 99 S. Bragg St. ☎ 354.63.00.

Keystone Motel: 8588 Richmond Highway, Alexandria. ☎ 780.52.10.

getting fed

You will find more or less everywhere, of course, the eternal MacDonald's and other more local restaurant chains such as '*Gino's*' or '*The Little Tavern Shops*', but if you are short of money why not picnic on one of the lawns of the 'greenest' city in the world? The Mall, the banks of the Potomac and Rock Creek Park are some of the most pleasant spots.

Different kinds of cafeterias

Even if you are not mad about museums, you can still take advantage of their cafeterias:

National Gallery: Constitution/6th St N.W. (everyday 11.00–16.00; Sundays 13.00–19.00). Situated in the east wing on the ground floor.

Smithsonian History and Technique Museum: Constitution/12th St (everyday, 11.00–16.00), on the west side.

Library of Congress: 1st St/Independence (Monday to Friday, 7.00–16.30).

Also: the **Air and Space Museum,** the **Museum of National History and Technology,** the **Fine Arts and Portrait Gallery Building** and the **Hirshhorn Museum.**

When Congress is in session (shown by the American flag flying on the respective wings of the Capitol: north wing for the Senate, south wing for the House of Representatives), one can make use of the following cafeterias:

Capitol: the Senate restaurant (Monday to Friday, 8.00–16.00).

Dirkson – New Senate Office Building: 1st St/C St (Monday to Friday).

Supreme Court: 1st St/E. Capitol St N.E. (11.00–14.00 during the week).

Other cafeterias in the centre of Washington:

Rayburn: Independence/1st St S.W. (8.00–10.45; 13.15–14.30 during the week). The House of Representatives cafeteria.

The Promenade: J. F. Kennedy Center, 2700 F St. Everyday 11.30–20.00 or 15.00 if there's no show in the evening.

All States Cafeteria: 1750 Pennsylvania Ave N.W. (one block west of the White House).

Chamberlin Cafeteria: 819 15th St N.W. (open during the week).

Harrington Kitcheteria: 11th/E St N.W. In Harrington Hotel, 2 blocks north of the Natural History Museum. 7.00–midnight.

Holloway House Cafeteria: 771 14th St N.W.

Sholl's Colonial Cafeteria: 1032 Connecticut Ave N.W.

Sholl's New Cafeteria: 1433 K St (corner of Vermont Ave).

White Tower: 741 13th St (corner of K St).

Coffee-shops and sandwiches

Beefe 'N Rolle: 11th St/E St N.W.

Blue Chip: 1641 L St N.W.

Eddie Leonard's Sandwich Shops: 1121 14th St and 3335 Connecticut Ave N.W.

Park Coffee House: 15th St/Pennsylvania Ave. In the Washington Hotel.

World Buttery: 714 18th St N.W. Weekdays, 7.00–24.00; weekends, 7.00–16.00.

Woodward and Lothrop: 11th St/F St N.W. On the seventh floor of this departmental store there are a Tea Room, Buffet Corner and English pub open every day.

Reasonably priced restaurants

The Astor: 1813 M St. A well-known Greek restaurant.

Food for Thought: 1783 Connecticut Ave.

Golden Temple: 1521 Connecticut Ave. Vegetarian.

Luigi's: 1132 19th St N.W. The best pizzas in the quarter.

Emerson's: 1511 K St.

Blackie's Junior: 709 18th St (two blocks west of the White House). Steaks and hors d'oeuvres. Inexpensive.

Beeffeeders: 518 10th St N.W. (between E and F St). Closed on Sundays.

Hammel's: 416 10th St N.W. (between E St and Pennsylvania Ave). ☎ 783.93.00. Closed on Sundays.

Old Ebbitt Grill: 1427 F St. Omelette specialities.

Rustler Steak House: 10th St N.W./E St. Opposite the F.B.I. Excellent steaks and good chicken and fish. Not too expensive.

Cafe Rondo in D.C.: 1900 Q St N.W. Good place for beer and atmosphere. Not so good for food.

Omega Restaurant: in Adams Morgan, on Columbia Ave.

Columbia Station: Columbia Ave. Often good concerts.

Roma: 3419 Connecticut Ave N.W. Impressive decor (proprietor used to be a big-game hunter).

The Broker: 713 8th St S.E. Good salads, pleasant atmosphere.

La Sorbonne: 2507 Penn Ave. Good pastries.

Far and away the best quarter for cheap restaurants is Georgetown. They are concentrated on M St and Wisconsin Ave; relaxed atmosphere.

Casa Yelice: 3214 N St. South-American restaurant. Music on Fridays and Saturdays (closed on Tuesdays).

Gate Soup Kitchen: 3336 M St. Vegetarian.

Little Tavern: 1301 Wisconsin Ave.

Maison des crêpes: 1305 Wisconsin Ave. Excellent atmosphere. There is another one much further north at No. 7756.

Martin's Tavern: 1264 Wisconsin Ave.

Mr Smith's: 3104 M St.

Yes! Soup Kitchen: 1039 31st St N. . Vegetarian.

More expensive restaurants

Blackie's House of Beef: 22nd/N St.

Black Circus: 1 Dupont Circle N.W.

Cherry Tree: 1515 Rhode Island Ave N.W.

Circle One Restaurant: 7 Washington Circle N.W.

Habitat Restaurant: 421 11th St N.W.

Harvey's: 1001 18th St (corner of K St), known as the restaurant of the Presidents of the United States since 1858. Crab specialities. Reserve your table. ☎ 833.18.58.

Marigold's: 814 18th St N.W.

Billy Martin's Carriage House: 1238 Wisconsin Ave N.W.

The Palm Restaurant: 1225 19th St N.W. Crayfish.

Paramount Steak House: 1519 17th St N.W. and also 1227 Wisconsin Ave N.W.

Publick House: 3218 M St (in Georgetown). A classic.

Sagittarius Restaurant: Connecticut Ave/R St N.W.

Californian Steak House: 831 14th St.

Sea Food restaurants

Less than an hour's drive from Washington, on Highway 50, the little port of **Annapolis** has half a dozen excellent sea-food restaurants. There is also a covered market near the waterfront. The setting is very attractive and really worth the journey. You can also find excellent sea-food restaurants in the capital, but they are much more expensive than on the Atlantic:

Flagship: 900 Water St S.W.

Hogate's Spectacular Seafood Restaurant: 9th St/Maine Ave S.W.

Marker Inn: 200 E St S.W.

O'Donnell's Sea Grills: 1221 E St N.W. and also 8301 Wisconsin Ave.

---

things that everyone goes to see and that you shouldn't miss

Museums

The Smithsonian Institution has no fewer than five museums situated around the Mall between the Capitol and the Washington Monument. (Open every day from 10.00–21.00.)

Museum of History and Technology: Constitution Ave/12th St–14th St. Really huge: reckon on at least two and a half hours to go round it. Don't miss the enormous locomotive which is so beautiful it will take your breath away. If you don't want to spend money on newspapers go and read the news as it comes in on the teleprinters (1st floor, Communications Dept).

National Air and Space Museum: Independence Ave, between 5th and 7th St. This museum is the latest in the series of Smithsonian museums, and is also the most spectacular. It contains full-scale models of all the spacecraft, including Skylab and the Soviet Soyuz. The films shown in the museum are remarkable. You can also touch a rock from the moon on show on the ground floor between two guards.

Freer Art Gallery: 12th St/Independence Ave (open until 17.30 in summer). Free. Contains marvellous Japanese, Chinese and Indian paintings. Also worth seeing: the works of the American painter James Whistler (1834–1903) and particularly the room which he decorated in its entirety ('Whistler Peacock Room').

National Art Gallery: Constitution Ave/16th St (April to early September, 10.00–21.00; Sundays 12.00–21.00; winter 10.00–16.00). A small brochure with plans of the museum is given away free. One of the finest museums in the world. Some superb Grecos, three key works by Vermeer, and some first-class Monets and Cézannes are among the marvels that you can find here.

Natural History Museum: Constitution Ave/ 10th St N.W. The lifesize, glassfibre whale is worth having a look at. Everything is beautifully presented.

Arts and Industries Building: 900 Jefferson Drive/ 9th St S.W. Houses some very interesting exhibitions.

National Collection of Fine Arts: 8th St/G St. Open every day 10.00–17.30.

National Portrait Gallery: 8th St/G St. Open every day 10.00–17.30 This version of neo-classical architecture, more successful than other Greek imitations in Washington, houses two collections, one of which is devoted to American art and the other to photographic portraits of famous American citizens.

Corcoran Art Gallery: New York Ave/17th St N.W. (every day (except Monday) 11.00–17.00). An imposing collection of American paintings plus a small number of European works (Corot, Daumier, Degas).

F.B.I. Department of Justice: 9th St/10th St and Pennsylvania Ave/Constitution Ave (9.15–16.15 during the week). Incredible but true: it's really exciting to visit the F.B.I.! See in particular the department devoted to the 'fight against Communism' (*sic*).

things that everyone goes to see and that can be given a miss

The White House: 1600 Pennsylvania Ave N.W. (10.00–13.00, Tuesday to Friday; 10.00–14.00 on Saturdays). When you visit the White House, think with every step you take that one of the mightiest powers in the world operates from here. It is advisable to get there at 8 a.m. and buy a ticket for 10.00. Otherwise you have to sit around for a couple of hours. As a consolation there is an orchestra and dancers!? ...

The Capitol: (Every day 9.00–16.30, free; 9.00–15.45 guided tours). See the *Washington Post* for times of sessions in the Senate and the House of Representatives.

Washington Monument: a huge obelisk right in the centre of Washington (8.00–midnight in summer; 8.00–17.00 the rest of the year). The best view of the city from the top; inexpensive, but often a long queue.

Jefferson Memorial: South of the 'Tidal Basin'. From an architectural point of view, the most interesting monument in Washington. Like the

211

Capitol, at its most impressive when lit up at night.

Lincoln Memorial: at the west end of the Mall. The famous Statue of Lincoln. N.B. both Memorials are open from 8.00 to midnight.

Hirshhorn Museum: 8th St/Independence Ave S.W. Not many outstanding works in this architecturally mediocre museum.

Arlington National Cemetery: on the other side of the Potomac. (Every day 8.00–16.00 hrs, free.)

National Zoo: 3000 Connecticut Ave N.W. If it doesn't distress you too much to see all those caged animals, go and look round. It's just as good as any other. (Open 9.30–18.30, April to September; closes 16.30 the rest of the year.)

things that everyone doesn't go to see and which are worth seeing

The Congress Library: Independence Ave/1st St. Behind the Capitol (8.30–21.00 Monday to Friday; 8.30–17.00 Saturdays; 13.00–17.00 Sundays). Impressive. Free guided visits every hour. You can listen to folk-music records and even recordings of Indian chants dating from the beginning of the century: in fact an embarrassment of riches!

Bureau of Engraving and Printing: 14th St/C St S.W. South of the Monument. (8.00–14.30, closed at weekends.) This is where His Highness the Dollar is printed. Unfortunately very difficult to get your hands on some!

Phillips Collection: 1612 21st St N.W. near Dupont Circle (10.00–17.00, Tuesday to Saturday; 14.00–19.00 Sundays). Remarkable collection of Impressionist paintings, also some excellent works by Klee and Nicolas de Staël. Classical concerts every Sunday at 17.00 hrs.

Textile Museum: 2320 S St N.W. (Tuesday to Saturday, 10.00–17.00). Everything from Middle-Eastern tapestries to Peruvian embroidery and Indonesian batiks.

National Historical Doll and Toy Museum: 411 King St in Alexandria (6 miles south of the capital on the George Washington Parkway). Every day, 10.00–18.00. ☎ 836.81.31.

Museum of African Art: 316 A St N.E. (Weekdays 11.00–17.00; weekends 12.00–17.00.) African sculptures, musical instruments, jewels and handicraft. With Philadelphia's, the second museum in the United States devoted entirely to Africa.

The sixth largest **Gothic cathedral** in the world. Begun in 1907 it will be finished in 1980 or 1981.

Situated on St Alban's Mount, it is worth seeing if only to admire the quality of the reproduction.

great scenes

Some good clubs

The Bayou: 3135 K St N.W. Mainly hard rock. Free entry.

Crazy Horse: 3259 M St (corner of M St and Wisconsin Ave).

French Underground: 1401 20th St N.W.

Pall Mall: 3235 M St ☎ 965.53.53. 'Live' groups. No shabby jeans!

Etcetera

Blues Alley: 1073 Wisconsin Ave. ☎ 337.41.41. Dixieland jazz. You can eat here – dress up a bit.

Hardd's Rogue and Jar: 1814 N St. Free jazz on Monday evenings.

Top O'Foolery: 2131 Pennsylvania Ave. ☎ 333. 77.84.

The Corsican: 1716 Eye St.

Bogie's: 1214 Connecticut Ave. Pleasant atmosphere.

The Childe Harold: 1620 20th St. ☎ 483.67.02. Blues, rock, country and blue grass. Closed Mondays.

Rocky Raccoon's: 1243 20th St. Mexican specialities.

Free swimming pools

Georgetown Swimming Pool: 34th St/Volta Place.

Francis Swi-Pool: 25th St/N St. Everyday 11.00–19.00.

Student bars

Clyde's Bar: 3236 M St (in Georgetown). A real institution (at weekends you have to wear a jacket and tie to get in!).

The Tombs: 1226 36th St N.W. Excellent.

The Cellar Door: 34th/M St. Situated in the heart of Georgetown, this is one of the capital's best-known cellar clubs.

Cinema for film buffs

Circle Theatre: 21st St/Pennsylvania Ave. Old films from all over the world.

The Biograph: 32nd St/M St.
Films and Festivals: ☏ 337.13.11.

Free open-air concerts

Every summer, concerts are organized in front of different places such as: the Jefferson Memorial, the Lincoln Memorial, and the steps of the Capitol. Details in the newspapers.

Shopping

Most of the big shops are between F and G streets N.W. and on 7th St and 15th St.

Brentano's: 1326 F St. Books and more books.

Globe Books: 1700 Pennsylvania/17th St. Still more books.

New & Used Books: 808 9th St/H St. Books plus old numbers of the *National Geographic.*

Hecht's: 7th St/F St. ☏ 628.51.00. Open Sundays, 12.00–17.00. Monday and Thursday 10.00–18.00. Other days 10.00–20.00. Seven storeys of just about everything at moderate prices.

When walking round Georgetown, drop into Second Story Books. A charming little bookshop on P St near Wisconsin Ave. Savour the rare smell of old books as you enter.

around Washington

Mount Vernon: George Washington's house. 10 miles from the capital. Take a number 11A bus on 10th St/Constitution Ave (buses every hour) or take a Wilson Boat (6th St/Water St S.W. 9.30–10.00–14.00 –14.30). Visits 9.00–17.00, March to October; 9.00–16.00, the rest of the year.

Shenandoah National Park (see section on National Parks).

Part III
The National Parks

The American National Parks deserve their reputation; if you are looking for beautiful scenery, you will be well and truly satisfied. When the frenzied pace of the cities begins to get you down, it really does you good to go and relax in the wide open spaces where every slightest sign of life is preserved.

Some general remarks

There is an entrance fee. Keep your ticket because it will be collected when you leave. If you buy a Golden Eagle pass, you can visit all the parks free of (further!) charge. The pass is on sale at all the parks, or it can be sent by post if you write to: **National Parks Service,** Bureau 1013, Washington D.C. 20240.

The parks provide a large number of services: camping sites, hotels, motels, restaurants, food shops, bicycle hire, riding ... The hotels are always expensive and sometimes you need to book weeks in advance.

Buy your food before going into the park because it is always more expensive inside. The same goes for car-hire: it is better to make your arrangements outside. It is always better to share the hire of a car with several other people than to use the bus service.

Find out, at the Visitors' Center, about all the activities catered for and ask for a plan of the trails. Rely on the trails rather than on your own sense of direction.

Do take adequate clothing. At the end of the summer it is never very warm, for example, in the Grand Canyon or in Yellowstone Park.

Great Smoky Mountains National Park

Situation: In North Carolina and Tennessee (80 kms from Ashville, North Carolina). Open all year. Don't forget a raincoat, even in summer.
The best way to see it is to follow the tracks of the *'Appalachian Trail'*, all of which are well provided with camping sites and shelters where you can stay for a night.
Don't miss the open-air museum of Indian life and customs, at *Cherokee Indian Museum* and *Oconaluftee Indian Village*.

Everglade National Park

Situation: in Florida, 60 kms south-west of Miami. Open all year. Camping at Flamingo and at Lone Pine Key. Very well marked trails.
Everglade Park is a huge, tropical swamp, with everything that implies by way of luxuriant and colourful vegetation. Watch out for the crocodiles and alligators!
You can take a trip around the park by boat. Boats can be hired at the north end of the Park, along the Tamiami Trail, between Miami and Naples.

Grand Canyon National Park

If you can only see one park, it must be this one. You will not be disappointed. It is a unique sight and no photograph can ever do it justice. The sheer size of the canyon will astound you and its beauty will really make you think . . . It is an absolutely fantastic place.
Situation: in Arizona, 2 hours by road from Flagstaff (north of Phoenix). The Greyhound 'rover' ticket entitles you to a reduction on a return trip Flagstaff–Canyon on the Nava-Hopi coaches. There are only three shuttles a day: leaving at 7.30, 9.00, 17.45 and returning at 9.45, 17.00 and 18.00.

The South Rim is open all year and more interesting than the North Rim which is only open in summer. Accommodation: Naturally such a popular place is outrageously commercialized. Rooms in bungalows are very expensive. The three cheapest places to stay are: Yavapai Lodge, the Motor Lodge, and as long as there are several of you to share the same room, the Bright Angel Lodge. The latter is closed from January until March: Otherwise, there are three other groups of bungalows or hotels: The Thunderbird Lodge, Kachina Lodge and El Tovar Hotel. It is more than advisable to phone two or three days in advance for a booking in the height of the season (mid-July to mid-August); there is one phone number for all the places to stay: 638.26.31. If you want to send for the prices for the year, write to Fred Harvey, Grand Canyon, AZ86023.

There are very well equipped camping grounds at Grand Canyon Village (open all year) and at Desert View (open May 1–October 15). You can't stay longer than a week and it's not possible to book.

There is quite a choice of ways to see the Canyon: a plane-trip over it, going down into it on a mule or on foot, or a coach trip around the rim. In fact it is impossible, in summer to get a mule, unless you have booked one at least four months in advance . . . such is the success of this means of transport. The helicopter trip costs thirty-odd dollars, but you can be sure that you will never regret it. Only a helicopter can give you an idea of the scale of the place. It is as well to check the visibility before going to the heliport. 9.00 is usually the best time; there is still some shadow to bring out the contrasts and the sky is clearer than in the afternoon. The *Grand Canyon Helicopter Company* will come and pick you up, in a mini-bus, to take you to the heliport, which is five kms from the rim. Ask for details at the Tourist Center.

The trails are for walkers. If you only have a day, do the one which skirts the side of the Canyon – you will get wonderful, and changing, views. If you are staying longer, try the complete descent. It takes from three to five hours to get down to *Phantom Ranch* (free camping, food) and from five to seven hours to get back up: follow the *Kaibab trail*, then *Angel River Falls*. You should be well equipped, with water, food, a sleeping-bag and a hat. If you want a day excursion, go as far as the plateau which overhangs the Colorado, and make one stop on your way back, at the *Indian Gardens*. There are some interesting things to see in the *Yavapai Museum*, open in summer only.

A few words of advice: Grand Canyon Village is at an altitude of 2000 metres. It is often cool, even in the middle of August. By contrast, at the bottom of the Canyon it is terribly hot, 45°C and more.

On the subject of photography: the Grand Canyon is quite tricky. You snap away because it is all so beautiful, then you have a great disappointment when you get back–all the photos look alike and none is really good. You might as well buy the professionals' pictures – it's less expensive in the end and there are some fabulous ones.

When you do the Grand Canyon, you should also go and see *Monument Valley Navajo Tribal Park* which is about 200 km north, on route 160, north of Kayenka. It is the splendid desert where hundreds of Westerns have been filmed. Fantastic scenery with great pillars of red sandstone.

Monument Valley National Park

Much less crowded than the Grand Canyon, Monument Valley is perhaps even more spectacular in the sense that the size does not just overwhelm you but enables you to take it all in at one glance. The great problem, however, is the journey: without a car the only alternative is an organised excursion in a Land Rover. In summer there are frequent storms which make a long stretch of the road impassable for several hours. The colours, after a storm, are exceptional.

Accommodation: there are only three motels in the vicinity, including a Holiday Inn at Kayenta. Camping is possible near the Visitors' Bureau.

Mesa Verde National Park

Situation: at the extreme south of Colorado, about 50 kms from Durango and about the same from Four Corners Point (the point where the States of Colorado, Utah, Arizona and New Mexico meet).

This impressive rocky plateau used to be inhabited by Indian tribes and there are very well preserved troglodyte dwellings to be seen. You have to take quite a steep route to get up to the level of the plateau. The view is very good from Far View Visitors' Center, but that's all. You really have to go further before it gets interesting, with the ruins of *Spice Tree* and of *Cliff Palace,* the village suspended on the side of the cliff.

Accommodation: the best bet is to go down to a motel in Cortez, 15 kms away. You really have to have a car to do Mesa Verde.

Mount Rainier National Park

The name of the park comes from the peak which dominates it: Mount Rainier (4392 metres), a dormant volcano.

Situation: 170 kms south-west of Seattle (Washington State), you can see the mount from certain, high parts of the town on a clear day.

Accommodation: you can get a good look around the park in a day, but if you want to stay longer, try either Paradise Inn or National Park Inn, open mid July to beginning September. The Park has seven camping grounds, including Sunshine Point, open all the year, and Sunrise, which you can only get to on foot. Stays are strictly limited to two weeks maximum. You need special authorization to camp outside the recognized camping grounds.

For information, go the reception desk at Paradise Inn or, if you want details before going to the Park, write to the Superintendent, Mount Rainier National Park, Longmire, Wa 98397.

You really can't go across the north-west without going there to stretch your legs, and your lungs.

Olympic National Park

Situation: on the Pacific Coast in Washington State. Considered by many to be one of the most beautiful Parks in the U.S.A. The area is mountainous and very wild. There are three *Indian reserves* in the Park. In the north there is a village where young people study Indian life. The atmosphere there is very cool.

Access: by the coast road No. 101 (coming from the south of Seattle). The nearest town is Port Angeles. The park is open all the year, mid-May to mid-October being the best period. Entrance is free.

There is plenty to do there: 957 kms of walks, climbing, swimming etc. There are facilities for camping.

For information: Olympic National Park, 600 east Park Avenue, Port Angeles, Washington 98362.

Shenandoah National Park

Situation: near Front Royal in Virginia, 140 kms from Washington.

Access: by route 211 from the capital. Open all year,

but most of the tourist activities and facilities are closed in winter.

Accommodation: Camping. Book in advance: ARA Virginia Skyline, Box 727, Luray, Va 22835.

Activities: panoramic routes; walks around the Park (the *Appalachian Trail* cuts right across the Park). For information, maps etc: Visitors' Center at Dicky Bridge and at Big Meadows (open May–October).

Yosemite National Park

Waterfalls of more than 700 metres, huge granite rocks, lakes ... a magnificent park, too much, even, because it has to suffer over a million visitors each year.

Situation: 240 kms east of San Francisco. Open all year. There are four entrances: two are open all year: Arch Rock, 110 kms from Merced (route 140), and the south entrance, 95 kms from Fresno (route 41). The north entrance, Big Oak Flat Road, 115 kms from Oakdale, is open from May to October. Tioga Pass Road from June 15 to October 1.

Accommodation: apart from camping (official or wild) there is one hotel which is less expensive than the others: Big Trees Lodge.

Food is amply provided for with restaurants, cafeteria and shops. It is cheaper to buy food before getting into the park. Activities: Ask for the programmes of camp fires and guided tours from the Yosemite Valley Visitors' Center. There is a two-hour trip, by tram, in the Yosemite Valley (departure at 8.00, 9.00, 10.00, 13.00, 14.00 and 15.00 from Awahnee Hotel, where you should book.

From the place called 'Indian Circle', a naturalist, every morning in summer, shows how the Indians lived.

Yellowstone National Park

The biggest of the national parks (9000 square kilometres), famous for its thousands of geysers and thermal springs; it provides a refuge for bears, elks, deer, bisons ... in an absolutely fairy-tale setting. That being said, it isn't always guaranteed that your car will be held up by bear or bison crossing. In the height of summer, when the commonest animal in the park is the foreign tourist, you can't expect a miracle.

Situation: in the north-west of Wyoming (with some parts in Idaho and Montana), about 850 kms north of

220

Salt Lake City (highway 191). Open practically all year, but the season runs from May to October. If you arrive by Greyhound (coming from Salt Lake City), you can, at the village where you enter, rent a car to be shared amongst several people ... quite reasonable.

Accommodation: no problem. Riefsteck Cabins at Gardiner and bungalows (most economical).

Economy cabin: Fishing Bridge Camph's Cabin. Excellent if you are in a party.

Activities: you can't really miss out on the famous geyser *Old Faithful* which, every 90 minutes rises 45 metres. ... give or take a few! Certainly the endless cameras all around are quite impressive. Also, hundreds of kilometres of walks, and *Mount Washburn* to be climbed. The *Mammoth Hot Springs* are very interesting. The waterfalls (*Tower Falls*) are the finest sight in the park. You must also see the interior of the *Old Faithful Inn* where a huge wooden scaffolding creates an enormous amount of space under a single roof.

Notes